THE MIND ECONOMY

THE MIND ECONOMY

MEMORY, COGNITION, AND PSYCHOLOGICAL TRANSFORMATION

OLIVER HOFFMANN

ANTHEM PRESS

Anthem Press
An imprint of Wimbledon Publishing Company
www.anthempress.com

This edition first published in UK and USA 2026
by ANTHEM PRESS
75–76 Blackfriars Road, London SE1 8HA, UK
or PO Box 9779, London SW19 7ZG, UK
and
244 Madison Ave #116, New York, NY 10016, USA

© 2026 Oliver Hoffmann

The author asserts the moral right to be identified as the author of this work.

All rights reserved. Without limiting the rights under copyright reserved above, no part of this publication may be reproduced, stored or introduced into a retrieval system, or transmitted, in any form or by any means (electronic, mechanical, photocopying, recording or otherwise), without the prior written permission of both the copyright owner and the above publisher of this book.

British Library Cataloguing-in-Publication Data
A catalogue record for this book is available from the British Library.

Library of Congress Cataloging-in-Publication Data: 2025938195
A catalog record for this book has been requested.

ISBN-13: 978-1-83999-657-3 (Hbk)
ISBN-10: 1-83999-657-9 (Hbk)

Credit: Kommerzielle Bilder iStock

This title is also available as an eBook.

TABLE OF CONTENTS

List of Illustrations		vii
List of Tables		ix
Prologue I—Thoughts on the "Economy of Memory"		xi
Prologue II—Introduction and Overview		xix

CHAPTER 1	**The World Within—Identity, Culture, and Memory**	1
CHAPTER 2	**The Core of Being—Change, Fluidity of the Ego, Narration, and Cognition**	17
CHAPTER 3	**Working with the Spirit System—Transformative Processes**	69
CHAPTER 4	**Methods and Techniques of Economic Cognitive Therapy**	95
CHAPTER 5	**The Support Systems—Yoga, Meditation, Culture, and Esthetics**	149
CHAPTER 6	**Remembering Is the Value of Life—Or Capitalism in Ourselves**	177

Epilogue I—What Remains of Life	195
Epilogue II—What Goes Beyond That	201
Glossary	207
Further Reading	217
Bibliography	221
Index	243

LIST OF ILLUSTRATIONS

1	Economization of the spirit system	22
2	Schematic representation of the psychic mind system	25
3	Schematic representation of the economic mind system	26
4	The inner structure of memory	29
5	The memory cascade of the spirit system.	33
6	Equilibrium of the fluid ego	41
7	The connection between different levels of consciousness	62
8	Overall visualization of the spirit system	66
9	Basic motives of economic narratives	73
10	The integrated process of transcendental narration (self-recognition and self-acceptance)	80
11	Overview of the economic spirit system	84
12	Overview of the specific methods and techniques of economic cognitive therapy	110
13	Overview of auxiliary systems	150
14	The two strands of the cognitive process	182

LIST OF TABLES

1	The three economic exchange processes	30
2	Resilience as an economically active resource	40
3	The five basic types of intrapsychic narrative and imagination techniques	43

PROLOGUE I—THOUGHTS ON THE "ECONOMY OF MEMORY"

> There are no two moments in a living being that are identical. Take the simplest feeling and assume that it is constant and absorbs the whole personality: the consciousness that accompanies this feeling that accompanies this feeling cannot remain identical throughout two successive moments since the following moment always contains the memory of the previous one. Memory that the previous one left behind.[1]

Cognition is the decisive cornerstone of human existence—whether it is directed outward (which it usually is in liberalist-capitalist modernity) or inward. Practically, every philosophical, scientific, or spiritual school of thought is fueled by knowledge; knowledge is the way outward into the world.

It would be absurd to dismiss all this as nice calendar sayings or unrealistic theorems precisely because modern psychology and neuroscience also boil down to the fact that all knowledge is from the self in order to be effective.[2] The really big challenge in life is the exploration of the self and the attainment of knowledge about one's inner world (simply because of the sheer size of the inner world). Here lies both the root and the solution to all the problems that befall us in life—there are few things that the mind cannot solve for itself.[3] The concept presented in this book revolves around this simple fact.

The title of this book may be confusing at first. This is because most people initially find it difficult to transfer the principles of economics, which are so

---

1 Bergson (1948), p. 186.
2 Cf. Freire (2022), p. 365f.
3 See Roth (2010), pp. 5–18.

unchallenged and unquestioned in the external world,[4] to what they refer to as the "inner world"—the vague, usually diffuse area of their psyche, mind, or thinking. This alone is a flawed idea for the simple reason that the outer world should by no means be transferred to the inner world—rather, everything external in its interpretation is a product of our mind, more precisely, our *memories* and ideas (which are also suggestions of memories).[5]

Added to this is the fact that the word economy[6] is not used very precisely in everyday life because, at its core, it refers to the rational, that is, sensible and expedient use of something.[7] And that memories—as can be intuitively understood but will be explained in more detail—form the framework from which everything we consider to exist is built. They can be seen as a valuable

---

[4] The principles of economics refer to fundamental concepts and rules that guide the economic activities and decisions of individuals, businesses, and governments. These principles form the foundation of economics and serve as the basis for analyzing all socioeconomic processes, where economic activity is becoming an anthropological constant. Here are some of the central principles of economics that are particularly relevant to the concerns of the "internal economy":

1. Scarcity: This principle states that resources are limited. As the needs and desires of individuals are unlimited, societies and individuals must decide how to make the best use of limited resources.
2. Cost-benefit analysis: Individuals and organizations make decisions by weighing up the costs and benefits. They try to allocate their resources in such a way that they derive the greatest benefit from their investments.
3. Incentives: People react to incentives. Changes in incentive structures have a comprehensive influence on behavior.
4. Competition: Competition between entities promotes efficiency and innovation.
5. Specialization: The division of tasks and specialization enable entities to make processes more efficient.
6. Rationality: Most economic models are based on the assumption of rationality, according to which individuals make rational decisions in order to maximize their own interests.
7. Dynamic temporal preference structures: Individuals have temporal preferences, which means that they assess the value of resources and benefits in the future compared to the present.

See also Blum/Dudley/Leibbrand/Weiske (2015), p. 59ff. and Fehr/Schwarz (2002), pp. 11–27 and p. 49ff. as well as Leibbrand (1998), pp. 299–301.

[5] See also Benoit (2019), pp. 23–27.
[6] From the ancient Greek οἶκος *oîkos* "house" and νόμος *nómos* "law."
[7] See Blum/Dudley/Leibbrand/Weiske (2015), p. 43.

and far-reaching resource. These "building blocks of our thinking" will be discussed later—with far-reaching consequences and possibilities for the mind, feelings, and our own I (or our image of it).

In this universal sense, memories are economically valuable—one could even say they are the only things (meta-real as they may be) that have any value.[8] And they are valuable for any individual cognition and basic mental health; both, again, very valuable commodities, especially in modern, unhealthy times[9]

Dealing with memories is the ideal starting point for the development and exploration of thought, self-development,[10] and the fundamental realization of reality—probably even the only promising starting point. A heightened awareness of the basis of our thinking and the thinking processes themselves helps, on the one hand, to effectively counteract many psychological problems

---

8 A fundamental understanding of the economic significance of memories is based on their role in the creation and maintenance of social capital. Social capital refers to the networks, relationships, and norms that exist in a society and contribute to social co-operation. Memories can act as a link that strengthens social capital by preserving shared experiences, traditions, and cultural identities. In communities and societies where memories are actively cultivated and shared, they can promote cohesion and strengthen social bonds.

In the capitalist market economy, the economic significance of memories lies also lies in their role as a driver of consumer behaviour and brand loyalty. Companies have recognised that emotions and memories often offer stronger incentives to buy than rational considerations. Through targeted advertising and marketing strategies, companies seek to associate positive memories with their products or services in order to build customer loyalty and increase sales, as well as in their healthcare potential (which is a more central theme of this thesis).

Cf. Dessí (2008) and Erll/Rigney (2009), pp. 4–8.

9 In Germany alone, mental illness costs up to 45 billion euros a year; the economic potential for new findings and forms of treatment is enormous. See also Bödeker/Friedrichs (2011).

10 In this context, Jung in particular expanded psychological theory extensively; he speaks of the self "The self is not only indeterminate, but also paradoxically contains the character of determinacy, indeed of uniqueness." Jung (1944), p. 25.

In this, the process of self-development plays a decisive conceptual role; self-development according to C.G. Jung refers to the process of individual development and integration of different aspects of the personality in order to achieve balance and wholeness of the self. Jung considered the self to be the center of the psychic organism, comprising both conscious and unconscious elements. Self-actualization involves coming to terms with the shadow, the anima/animus, the archetypes and other aspects of the unconscious in order to develop an authentic and balanced personality. Cf. Kast (2014), pp. 39–65 and Jung (2022), pp. 69ff.

and, on the other hand, provides the basis for "going beyond" (in the sense of spiritual inner development)[11].

Accordingly, there are three pillars of economic-psychological knowledge:

1. **The material level of *homo economicus*.**[12] Economic activity is seen and defined as a basic human function.[13] It has an enormous impact on the psychological constitution and individual makeup; basic needs and fundamental insights into socioeconomic reality are seen as the basis for happiness, individual realization, and even transcendence. This view has become the central concept of liberal capitalism and has a strong impact on the psyche of the individual.[14]
2. **The immaterial level of the mind and psychology.** This is where images of mental processes emerge that obey their own rules and are not subject to physical logic. The concept of an "inner world" is based on this, which, as such, is also subject to its own rules and laws.

At this level, the human being and psyche are understood as a comprehensively researched conglomerate of mechanisms and intrinsic structures.[15] However, the mind is still bound to physical forms

---

11 Psychological approaches such as transpersonal psychology and humanistic psychology deal with this dimension of transcendence and emphasize the importance of self-transcendence for personal growth and psychological well-being. Cf. ibid.

12 *Homo economicus*, also known as "economic man," is a concept in economics that represents an abstract assumption about the behaviour of individuals in economic decision-making situations. This model is based on certain assumptions that characterize the behavior of *homo economicus*. The basic assumptions of *homo economicus* are rationality and consistency in decision-making processes, complete information, the pursuit of self-interest, transitive preferences and utility maximization.

It is important to note that *homo economicus* is an ideal concept and does not always reflect the actual behavior of people in the real world. In fact, many of these assumptions in behavioral economics and psychological economicswhich examine human behavioral deviations from these ideal assumptions. These areas of research have shown that in practice people are often influenced by emotional, cognitive and social factors and do not always act purely rationally.

See also Frey/Jonas/Maier (2007), p. 76ff.

13 See also Kirchgässner (2013), p. 113ff.

14 The frequently used concept of the "time-consistent expected utility maximiser" in particular has changed psychological processes permanently changed; see also Breyer et al. (2015), 191.

15 See also Billhardt/Storck (2021), p. 90 and p. 148.

(e.g., the idea of value and money in their physical representation), which it constantly seeks to expand (self-realization and striving for transcendence).
3. **The trans-material level of epistemology.** At this level, economization as a concept comes to the fore, as questions about the preconditions for knowledge, the emergence of knowledge, and other forms of conviction in the individual.[16]

The discourse of epistemology is a huge field in which universal basic elements and fundamental knowledge, which have been tested in a cultic, enlightened manner, can be brought to bear. Despite its abstractness, essential elements for individual cognition and self-development can be found here. Self-development can be found here;[17] a whole series of "theories of happiness" also come into play here.[18]

All three levels of cognition are located at the level of the individual mind. It follows that these insights can also be used to apply common basic principles; the economy of the inner world—the mind system—can take shape in this respect. These are ubiquitous and, therefore, suitable for gaining (synthetic) knowledge.[19]

This book is therefore dedicated to nothing more and nothing less than the ideal way of dealing with the (let's call them that for a moment) "building blocks of our thinking" and cognition. A simple and yet complex concern—with far-reaching consequences and possibilities for the mind, feelings, and our own I (or our image of it). So much for the title of this book.

In this universal sense, memories are economically valuable—you could even say they are the only things (meta-real as they may be) that have any value.[20] And they are valuable for any individual cognition and basic mental

---

16 Cf. also Luhmann (1988), pp. 87–89, p. 119ff.
17 Cf. Baumann (2006), p. 133ff.
18 Cf. Thomä (2004).
19 The ubiquity of systems means that they are ubiquitous or widespread and exist in different contexts; their complexity, structure, and adaptability enhance their quality. Cf. Baumann (2006), 232–236.
20 A fundamental understanding of the economic significance of memories is based on their role in the creation and maintenance of social capital. Social capital refers to the networks, relationships and norms that exist in a society and contribute to social co-operation. Memories can act as a link that strengthens social capital by preserving shared experiencestraditions and cultural identities. In communities and societies where memories are actively cultivated and shared, they can promote cohesion and strengthen social bonds.

health; both, again, very valuable commodities, especially in modern, unhealthy times.[21]

Dealing with memories is the ideal starting point for the development and exploration of thought, self-development,[22] and the fundamental realization—probably even the only promising starting point. A heightened awareness of the basis of our thinking and the thinking processes themselves helps, on the one hand, to effectively counteract many psychological problems and, on the other hand, provides the basis for "going beyond" (in the sense of spiritual inner development)[23].

As a professor of innovation management and psychology, I have spent the last few years working intensively on intra-psychological processes and my own exploration of the self. This journey began with a personal interest in the writings of great philosophers and thinkers, which inspired me to reflect on and explore my own inner discoveries. As I engaged with these works, I began to recognize patterns and connections between different disciplines and develop a multidisciplinary approach to the systemic exploration of the self.

In the capitalist market economy, the economic significance of memories lies also lies in their role as a driver of consumer behavior and brand loyalty. Companies have recognized that emotions and memories often offer stronger incentives to buy than rational considerations. Through targeted advertising and marketing strategies, companies try to link positive memories with their products or services in order to build customer loyalty and increase sales, as well as in their healthcare potential.

Cf. Dessí (2008) and Erll/Rigney (2009), pp. 4–8.

21 In Germany alone, mental illness costs up to 45 billion euros a year; the economic potential for new findings and forms of treatment is enormous. See also Bödeker/Friedrichs (2011).

22 In this context, Jung in particular expanded psychological theory extensively; he speaks of the self that "The self is not only indeterminate, but also paradoxically contains the character of determinacy, indeed of uniqueness." Jung (1944), p. 25.

In this, the process of self-development plays a decisive conceptual role; self-development according to C.G. Jung refers to the process of individual development and integration of different aspects of the personality in order to achieve balance and wholeness of the self. Jung considered the self to be the center of the psychic organism, comprising both conscious and unconscious elements. Self-actualization involves coming to terms with the shadow, the anima/animus, the archetypes, and other aspects of the unconscious in order to develop an authentic and balanced personality. Cf. Kast (2014), pp. 39–65 and Jung (2022), p. 69ff.

23 Psychological approaches such as transpersonal psychology and humanistic psychology deal with this dimension of transcendence and emphasise the importance of self-transcendence for personal growth and psychological well-being. and emphasize the importance of self-transcendence for personal growth and psychological well-being. Cf. ibid.

A central theme that runs through my work is the realization that many (or practically all) of man's problems and challenges lie within himself. This insight is reinforced by a cultural-philosophical background that encompasses different philosophical perspectives on the self. From existentialism to Buddhism, I have explored a variety of philosophical approaches, all of which emphasize that self-responsibility and self-dignity are central cornerstones of our existence.

Through this book, as well as my research and teaching, I hope to contribute to a deeper understanding of the human psyche and the self and the self and to support people in cultivating healthy self-awareness and self-leadership. My work is based on a holistic approach that combines psychological insights with philosophical thinking to paint a more comprehensive picture of the human being.

This approach is also reflected in the three overarching objectives of this book:

1. Introduction of a holistic approach to self-exploration, including accompanying and supporting methods and techniques.
2. It shows mechanisms to consolidate one's own inner world and, at the same time, identify and view problems more easily.
3. To develop the potential to experience memories fully and to value them as valuable inner resources. It is also crucial to harmonize your own imagination and language and to improve your own abilities in these highly human categories.

In summary, this book presents the essential cornerstones of economic cognitive therapy that strengthen one's own cognition and the resulting special mental abilities. The focus is actually on the practical handling of memory, an economic inner process that each of us practices but very often has not really consciously analyzed and examined for its effectiveness criteria.[24]

The connection and fusion of economy and psyche is obvious—and yet it is not. Most people will intuitively resist seeing their inner world, their thoughts, and even their memories as a system with economic rules, monetary values, and transaction mechanisms. Yet, many of the processes that take place in our mental system consciously and unconsciously are subject to such principles. It is not so much the case that the inner economy is a reflection of the outer economy—rather, the outer economy is a brainchild of our inner world.

---

24 Cf. also Quante (1993), p. 625ff.

The sometimes quite sober view of one's own inner harbors two major advantages:

> On the one hand, it gives you a very clear picture of what you can call the inner process landscape, the "transaction mechanisms," "resources," and "currencies" of our psyche.
> On the other hand, this view also provides relief and breaks through the phenomenon of self-preoccupation and self-observation often found in psychology—both can be useful but can also lead to nothing effective in endless loops. The introduction of a kind of inner efficiency concept into the psyche is ultimately nothing more than a relief and a cancellation of many pseudo-scientific and esoteric charges concerning our own mind. Our mind system is a system that *wants to* function; its many processes work (mostly unconsciously) hand in hand to ensure our well-being on various levels. With this simple background in mind, it should not be underestimated that every external value (which will be filled in further) is ultimately constituted in our mind.[25]

The findings in this book ultimately culminate in an economic theory of cognition and therapy that emphasizes the economic process and structural principles of the psyche and thus offers the individual a clear space for personal development—without too much metaphysical and depth-psychological baggage. After all, psychotherapy or analysis that is carried out for too long is often not necessarily the (potential) cure for the illness but rather symptoms and part of the cause of the illness.[26] In this respect, I would also like to see this approach as a further step toward a unified theory of the psyche that is based not only on subjective judgments but also on objective and transactional principles.

---

25 See also Wiest (2010), p. 89ff.
26 See also comprehensively Linden/Strauß (2018).

PROLOGUE II—INTRODUCTION AND OVERVIEW

Knowledge too belongs to the dross of cognition.[27]

In practically every doctrine of faith, every philosophy is about the source of human knowledge. This realization is usually seen as the key to understanding life itself.[28]

The role of cognition in human belief and life systems is a complex topic that is the subject of intensive research in both philosophy and psychology. Cognition—defined as the understanding of truth or reality—forms the foundation for individual belief systems and significantly shapes human behavior and the social and intersocial organization of life.

In philosophical terms, the nature of knowledge has been studied for centuries, with different schools of thought holding different views. From the rationalist emphasis on reason to the empiricist emphasis on sensory experience, there are numerous theories about how humans attain knowledge and understand truth. These philosophical considerations also influence spiritual traditions, as many belief systems are based on certain concepts of truth and knowledge.[29]

In psychology, the role of cognition in human belief and life systems is viewed from an empirical perspective. Psychologists investigate how people acquire knowledge, process information, and form their beliefs. Cognitive processes (such as perception, memory, and thinking) play a decisive role in their (often rather unstructured totality). In addition, cognition of psychological

---

27 Wilhelm von Humboldt, letter to Alexander von Rennenkampff, March 20, 1832.
28 Cf. Tillich/Siemsen (1965), p. 48ff.
29 Ibid.

concepts, such as self-perception, self-concept, and self-regulation, is becoming increasingly important in modern and postmodern times.

The interpretation of the role of cognition in human belief and life systems varies considerably depending on the cultural, religious, and philosophical context. Some spiritual traditions place great emphasis on the search for inner knowledge and self-realization,[30] while others rely more on external authority and tradition.[31] In addition, personal experiences, social influences, and individual differences can influence the way people acquire and interpret knowledge.

Nevertheless, astonishing correspondences and coherent approaches to knowledge can be observed among them; almost all of them want and say the same thing in different words. Faith realization is a key element of spiritual truth in many religious traditions as a form of realization or understanding of spiritual truths and principles can be achieved almost exclusively through prayer, meditation, the intensive study of sacred texts, religious practices, and spiritual experiences in general. This realization can serve as the basis of an individual belief, which in turn is itself part of knowledge.

So, what is a realization in that spiritual context? Essentially, there are four aspects and characteristics:

- **The concept of revelation:** In some belief systems, knowledge is considered to be the result of divine revelation. Believers receive divine wisdom and knowledge through direct communication with God or through prophets and saints who serve as intermediaries between the divine and humans.
- **Their role in establishing belief and doctrine:** Religious teachings and doctrines are often developed by (later attributed to) enlightened beings, saints, or prophets who claim to have received special knowledge or divine insights. These insights form the basis for the practice of faith and moral behavior within a (religious or social) community.
- **The individual search for wisdom and truth:** The search for knowledge also plays an important role in individual spiritual development. People can gain deeper insight into spiritual questions through philosophical reflection, inner contemplation, and the search for meaning and truth in their lives.

---

30 Cf. Knoblauch (2009), p. 25 and pp. 201–204.
31 Ibid, pp. 182–188.

- **The emergence of certainty of faith:** Knowledge can help to strengthen the certainty of faith in a reality. When believers, through their own experiences or study, have a deeper understanding of their faith teachings, this can help to dispel doubts and strengthen confidence in the faith.[32]

The importance of cognition is elementary for human self-development even in a purely psychological–philosophical context; after all, in many cases, the search for knowledge serves to deepen the understanding of the divine, morality, and spiritual as well as physical reality and to develop a more pronounced connection to the concept of the self.

Faith and (self-cognition have a long history of interference (and probably also of mutual skepticism) behind them.

I deliberately place this statement at the beginning of this introduction because I would like to emphasize that knowledge (and especially self-knowledge) always has a spiritual, even transcendental component on the one hand because of the obvious factual crossing of boundaries that is inherent in every realization (where something was diffuse or unconscious before, there is more clarity and structure afterward),[33] but also because of the epistemological proximity to the concept of faith. This is also an essential mechanism of action of cognition (which in sum modifies the perception and utilization of the entire spiritual system): It promotes the conviction of inner realities.

That is why cognition is the starting point and goal of an "economy of memory," an "inner economy," which has absolutely nothing to do with spiritualism but rather with practicality.

As absurd as you may find this as a reader, for me, the individual practicability of every inner realization is in the foreground when writing this book. There is a lot of talk about various theories, but all of them are only intended to help the individual psychologist better organize their own mental resources.

If you are more intensively involved with psychological (self-) theories of cognition and forms of discovering inner reality—be they spiritual-Buddhist or psychological—much of what has been written is impressive precisely because of its unworldliness or ignorance of reality. Many techniques or teachings are well formulated but require very radical measures in personal realization.

---

32 Certainty of faith is not least a reaction to the constant encounter with diversity (ambiguity) in today's pluralistic social structures. Cf. Klessmann (2018), pp. 37–41.
33 Cf. Malter/Rickert/Lask (1969), p. 89ff.

This is good in itself and can lead to insights, but it is hardly compatible with the complex reality of modern life.[34] Similarly, there are many rather off-putting elements that may be intellectually and emotionally understandable but are only socially recommended and practiced to a limited extent due to their overriding irresponsibility.

We must not forget that the idea of self-knowledge is, by its very nature, ultimately self-centered and egotistical. Therefore, it is also very important to me to pay attention to the social, interactive embedding of cognition. Because, like every economic system, our psyche also lives from multiple exchange and transaction processes with the outside, that is, the external world of reality and social interaction.

In the spiritual-Buddhist environment, people like to talk about enlightenment—in my experience, this is not necessary at all in order to recognize and understand one's own inner reality and to lead a better, calmer, and more conscious life; 20–40% of the "elements" of enlightenment are completely sufficient for this.[35]

Cognition is both a gradual and a binary process. In the classical conception, cognition is a gradual process in which people gradually gather information, understand it, and draw conclusions from it. This gradual approach to knowledge and understanding is reflected in everyday experience as individuals continually gain new insights and adapt their inner world accordingly.[36]

On the other hand, however, there are also moments of sudden realization or the "eureka" experience[37] that makes the cognitive process appear binary. These moments can occur unexpectedly and lead to a radical rethink or a fundamental change in perspective. This binary nature of cognition can be seen as a sudden transition from ignorance to knowledge.

---

34 See also Klessmann (2018), pp. 141–146.

35 This perspective is based on the idea that the practices and insights of Buddhism have a gradual and cumulative effect. The approach that 20–40% of the "elements" of enlightenment may be sufficient is based on the idea that even partial progress in spiritual practice can lead to tangible and lasting changes. This could mean that certain aspects of enlightenment—such as increased mindfulnessethical behavior and the acceptance of impermanence—already offer significant benefits for life and well-being. These partial aspects are achievable and realizable for many individuals without having to pursue the ideal of complete enlightenment.

Cf. also Kabat-Zinn (2003), p. 146ff.

36 In Chapter 6, these connections are discussed in more detail.

37 Heureka is ancient Greek (εὕρηκα or older ηὕρηκα) and means "I have found [it]." The exclamation has come down to us mainly in connection with Archimedes of Syracuse.

Interestingly, these two aspects of cognition can be compared with concepts from quantum mechanics. In quantum mechanics, particles can exhibit both wave and particle properties and behave both continuously and discretely, depending on how they are observed. Similarly, cognition can be viewed both as a continuous, gradual process characterized by the gradual integration of new information and as a discrete, binary process characterized by sudden insights or moments of enlightenment. This characteristic of cognition shows the multilayered and complex nature of the mental process behind it. Both aspects are part of these processes, and both will be conceptualized in this book. By integrating both gradual and binary elements, a more comprehensive understanding of the dynamics of individual psychological cognitive development becomes possible. However, this individual psychological and cognitive development is based on the use of mental resources, such as memories—channeled via various exchange processes in the mental system, such as narration or imagination.

This book will also deal in detail with accompanying techniques and methods for the presented concepts of the spirit system, mainly divided into narration (transcendental narration (TN)) and imagination (imagination reconstruction (IR)). Both are principles for climbing up the inner cognitive path for oneself and for expanding and developing inward in a targeted manner.

The development of the mental economy is flanked by support systems, often borrowed from spiritual and mental practices.[38] The supposed goals of spiritual practices (yoga, meditation, or even tantra) often quickly become completely overwhelming in everyday life. Therefore, the integration of simple but effective elements of these "support systems" into everyday life and our own everyday thinking is more effective and a central concern of this book. I emphasize the effects of these support systems on the individual mental economy; the most common practice of a "guru cult" specifically reinforces the impression of the metaphysical and the abstract and is, therefore, rather detrimental and unnecessary for one's own knowledge. And is therefore rather detrimental, unnecessary, and even counterproductive. Inner realization can be

---

In this context, cognitive science has shown that creative problem solving often involves a phase of incubation in which conscious thinking about the problem is interrupted, which can ultimately lead to a "eureka" moment (cf. moment (cf. Seifert et al. (1995)). Similarly, the sudden realization is related to specific neural activity in the brain, known as neural correlates; particularly in regions associated with insight and problem solving, such as the anterior temporal cortex (cf. Kounios et al., 2006).
38 See Chapter 5.

an everyday process that can be experienced in everyday life and only has to do with oneself.

A note on the structure of the book and the terminology: I make a relatively clear distinction between three different approaches (IR, TN, and holistic suggestion (HS)) for dealing with memory, along with different sets of appropriate methodologies and techniques. Ultimately, this only serves to improve understanding—and, of course, all approaches are not nearly so sharply separated in their practical application.

The objective of this book comprises three main approaches, all of which aim to create a closer link between psychological and economic aspects and to standardize and expand the theoretical framework of cognitive psychology:

- On the one hand, I would like to analyze the *construct of memory* more tangible and embed it clearly in an individual practice-orientated system of thought and spirit. The literature in this area is not very well developed and, in places, unspecific; to date, there are no truly comprehensive (meta-) analyses of the mind-system, including its functions, such as remembering or imagining, that can be used in (psychological) practice.[39]
- In addition, the aim is to merge the fields of *economics* and *psychology* on an individual level—precisely because the concepts of economics can also be of great value in dealing with thoughts and memories with regard to a kind of resource-based cost-benefit analysis. It can also be of great value when dealing with thoughts and memories.[40]
- As a final contribution, I would also like to give an *overview of the current state of knowledge on the interdisciplinary mind system*. This also includes the integration of research approaches or theoretical constructs from

---

39 Cf. also Rosenberg (2004) and Rosenberg (1999), p. 39ff.
40 The concept of shared receptivity is particularly interesting in this context; this is how economic values are constituted in the individual and transferred collectively. "A natural individual's receptivity is an element of its being that binds lower level individuals within it, making those individuals effective states relevant to one another in a direct way. As such, receptivity is an irreducible global property of a natural individual. The term 'irreducible' is not the sum, either linearly or nonlinearly, of the receptivity of its lower-level constituents. It is a novel element in the world, unique to the individual that it helps constitute." Rosenberg (1999), p. 43.

other scientific systems and cultural areas; Far Eastern philosophy, in particular, has made considerable, often little recognized, and frequently ignored contributions in this area.[41]

The individual, practical objective of the book is an expanded understanding of one's own mental processes and a more balanced relationship with one's own inner world, including a clearly structured approach to achieving insights.

This Book Is

- The quintessence of many years of working practice and self-exploration is, therefore, a matter of the heart.
- An integrated, scientifically based fusion of philosophy, psychology, and scientific theory.
- A comprehensive introduction to the complex and difficult-to-grasp world within us.
- A comprehensive appraisal of narration and imagination are the two most important abilities within ourselves.

This Book Offers

- A comprehensive model for exploring oneself within an insight therapy.
- Many methods and techniques at different levels of sophistication can specifically support cognitive therapy and reveal suitable complexes and nodes.
- Many suggestions for reflection and individual growth.
- A concept for learning from yourself about yourself.
- An explanation of how complementary support techniques (yoga, meditation, cultural immersion) can be used effectively.

---

41 See Walsh (1998), p. 679f. and Yates (2015), p. 192ff.

CHAPTER 1

THE WORLD WITHIN—IDENTITY, CULTURE, AND MEMORY

This remark provides the key to deciding the question of the extent to which solipsism is a truth. What solipsism means is quite true; it cannot be said, but it shows itself. That the world is my world is shown by the fact that the limits of language (the language that I alone understand) are the limits of my world. The world and life are one. I am my world.[42]

Each of us carries our own world within us, a world that only we can access ourselves. When I talk about the "world," I mean it quite literally: We, directly and indirectly, determine its rules, natural laws, and structures; we make the sunrise or comets fall.

What sounds rather exotic (or metaphorical) is actually a complex interplay of concepts that constitute our own I (or our idea of it). We are talking about identity, culture, and memory—three components that define the individual position within and without and co-create it in intersubjective, dynamic dependence.

Together, they form the basis of our spiritual system and its inner economy—the main reason why we must first deal with the inner world from this angle.

> **Overview: What Makes Up Our Inner World?**
>
> - **Identity—The pillars of the inner world:** Identity, the pillars of the inner world, encompasses the fundamental questions: What is identity? How is it formed? And what function does identity have in the inner world? Identity defines the self and shapes the perception of one's own person. It develops through individual experiences, social interactions, and cultural influences that shape and influence the self-image.
>
> *(Continued)*

---
42 Wittgenstein (2019), 5.62–5.63, p. 67.

- **Culture—The atlas of the inner world:** Culture serves as the atlas of the inner world, which comes from outside and shapes it, defining "boundaries" and "territories." It represents the collective unconscious and is selectively integrated into one's own world in a cascading process. Culture acts as a mediator between inside and outside and gives meaning to both the individual's self and the external environment. and the external environment by conveying and interpreting norms, values, and traditions.
- **Memory—Contents and entities of the inner world:** Memories represent the contents and entities of the inner world that form the spirit system. Forms are not static entities but rather changeable and actively modifiable concepts. Memories serve as building blocks of the mind system and are regarded as transactional goods that are formed through conscious experience and active processing. Through the process of remembering, experiences are processed, interpreted, and integrated into the self-image, thereby shaping the identity and the cultural imprint of the inner world.

Identity—The Supposed Pillars of the Inner World

I am what I appear to be and do not appear to be what I am, an inexplicable mystery to myself. I am at odds with my own self![43]

Identity refers to the understanding of the self and the ways in which individuals define themselves and relate to others and their environment. In this respect, it is a self-reflexive construct—this complex and multilayered construction often leads to misunderstandings within ourselves. Identity encompasses various dimensions, including personal identity, social identity, and cultural identity—all related to their aspect of the individual. Together, they accumulate in a concept of the self, which consists of many subcomponents and which sub-entities (often somewhat spasmodically)[44] try to hold together; the centrifugal forces are often strong.

---

43 Hoffmann (2022), p. 46.
44 Cf. Fetscher (1985), p. 243ff.

It is already important to emphasize at this point that many "pieces of the mosaic" are brought together to form the kind of identity; this correspondence will also be found later in the spirit system itself.[45]

In philosophy, there are numerous theories on **personal identity** that focus mainly on two questions: What makes a person who they are? How does a person maintain continuity over time despite all changes?

The discussion of this topic has filled numerous books and worn out scholars and laymen alike—for the purposes of this book, psychological continuity theory is the most relevant. This argues that personal identity is defined by the continuity of a person's psychological state or mental characteristics.[46] This includes aspects such as memories, personality traits, and beliefs that help to shape and maintain a person's identity. Psychological continuity theory assumes that a person's identity cannot be viewed as static or unchanging but rather as a dynamic process that develops and transforms over time. This perspective emphasizes the continuity of the self-concept, that is, the fact that people have a coherent idea of themselves that may change over time but still have a certain stability (the metastability of the ego will also play an important role in the mind system).[47]

A central aspect of psychological continuity theory is the emphasis on autobiographical memory as a mechanism for maintaining identity. Autobiographical memories are personal memories of past events and experiences that enable a person to reconstruct their past and identify with their former self. Through the process of memory (re)construction, individuals can develop a coherent narrative identity that enables them to understand their life story as a cohesive and meaningful unit—this process will be given much more attention in Chapters Two and Three.

In addition, psychological continuity theory emphasizes the importance of social interactions and relationships for the development and maintenance of identity. By being embedded in social groups and communities, people can identify with others and see themselves through the eyes of those around them. These social reflections and interactions help to shape and stabilize a person's self-concept by providing external validation of their identity.[48]

Another important aspect of the psychological continuity theory is the emphasis on developmental tasks in the life course. Here, all individuals go through certain developmental tasks or crises in the course of their lives,

---

45 See also Chapter 2.
46 See also Haußer (1995), p. 62ff.
47 Ibid., p. 32f., p. 46f.
48 See Schäfer (2012), p. 81ff.

which enable them to further define, confirm, or reject their identity. These developmental tasks are associated with certain phases of life and require active engagement and coping on the part of the individual in order to achieve a sense of continuity and coherence.[49]

In psychology, personal identity is often analyzed in the context of self-concept and identity development research. According to theories such as identity status theory, individuals develop a stable self-concept over the course of their lives, which consists of various dimensions (such as occupation, interests, relationships, and values).[50] These identity dimensions can change over time as the individual has new experiences and faces new challenges. Psychological research has shown that a stable self-concept and a sense of coherence are essential for psychological well-being and personal development.[51]

Personal identity, therefore, refers strongly to the individual characteristics, traits, and experiences that make an individual unique to themselves. This includes aspects such as personality, interests, abilities, values, and life history. The development of personal identity is a continuous, lifelong, and therefore never-ending process that is characterized by interactions with the environment and reflection on the self. This means that the individual (and their individuation)[52] is never finalized but remains an open concept in a permanent state of becoming.[53]

---

49 Cf. Erikson (1973), p. 43ff.
50 "Adolescents are classified into one of four identity statuses based on their level of exploration and commitment: Identity Diffusion, Identity Foreclosure, Identity Moratorium, and Identity Achievement."
These four identity statuses are
Identity diffusion: No clear direction or definition of identity; little exploration or commitment.
Identity foreclosure: Commitment to an identity without prior exploration, often based on the expectations of others.
Identity moratorium: Intensive exploration without final commitment, a phase of searching and experimentation.
Identity achievement: Successful exploration and subsequent commitment to a consolidated identity.
Cf. Marcia (1966), p. 554ff.
51 Cf. Marcia (1980), p. 181f.
52 Individuation is a central concept in the psychological theory of Carl Gustav Jung, which describes the process of self-realization and personality development. Jung coined this term to describe the complex path to an individual, authentic self that is characterized by the integration of various aspects of the psyche.
See Jung (2022), p. 69ff.
53 Ibid.

Social identity, which is somewhat less of the inner world, is somewhat less central to **social identity** and refers to membership in social groups and identification with these groups. This can occur at different levels, including family, friends, or nationality. An individual's social identity influences their behavior, attitudes, and interactions with others. According to social identity theory, the shaping and maintenance of the inner self-concept is decisive for social identity.[54] This happens primarily through social categorization. Individuals tend to categorize themselves and others in relation to certain social categories, such as gender, ethnicity, educational level, or profession. Through this categorization, they develop a group affiliation and identify with the socially trained and communicated characteristics and values of their group. Another process within social identity theory is social comparison processes. Individuals tend to evaluate their self-esteem by comparing themselves with others, both within their own group (internal comparisons) and with individuals from other groups (external comparisons). These comparisons can lead people to evaluate their group members more favorably and identify with them in order to increase their self-esteem.

In addition to this, there is also a (regionally differentiated) **cultural identity**, which refers to the values, norms, beliefs, customs, and traditions associated with a particular culture or ethnic group. These aspects of identity are shaped by the wider social environment and cultural affiliation and they influence an individual's behavior, communication, and worldview. Cultural identity can also be linked to the issues of integration and acculturation in multicultural societies and can lead to transindividual and societal identity conflicts.

It is important to note that identity is always made up of all three partial identities without being cumulative or free of contradictions.[55] Individual identity is not a static or uniform entity but is rather dynamic and situational. Identity can change over time, depending on life events, social relationships, and cultural influences—moreover, individuals can have different identities that are expressed in different contexts and can come into conflict with each other.[56]

Identity has one function above all: it is a mechanism of unification within the inner world in that it constructs the multiplicity of the mental system and all mental processes into a binding narrative—that of the ego. This function is the economic dimension of identity; otherwise, uncoordinated complexity is

---

54 Cf. Tajfel/Turner (2004a), p. 280f.
55 See Tajfel/Turner (2004a), p. 59f.
56 Ibid.

bundled and made identifiable.[57] At this point, the effect can be compared to that of a company—identity is a mental lighthouse to which all conscious and unconscious processes can orientate themselves and which makes an individual addressable and capable of acting in the first place.

Thus, individual identity is the framework within which our self can function and can function and work. It is a helpful construct without which the inner world could not exist in the long term.

The Three Key Messages

1. **Complexity of identity:** Identity is a multilayered construct consisting of various dimensions, such as personal identity, social identity, and cultural identity. These partial identities accumulate to form a concept of the self, which consists of many subcomponents and is often held together in the process of reconstruction.
2. **Psychological continuity theory:** Personal identity is defined by the continuity of a person's psychological state or mental characteristics. Autobiographical memories play a central role in maintaining identity by enabling a coherent narrative identity. Social interactions, life course developmental tasks, and the development of a stable self-concept are also important aspects.
3. **Dynamics and diversity of identity:** Identity is dynamic and situational and can change over time. Individuals can have different identities that are expressed in different contexts and can come into conflict with each other. Identity has the function of uniting the diversity of the mental system in a binding narrative and thus enabling a coordinated ability to act.

Culture—Mediator and Signpost between Identity and Memory

Culture begins in the heart of each individual.[58]

The relationship between culture, identity, and memory is central to understanding human experience and social cohesion. Culture not only serves

---

57 See also the description of the spirit system in Chapters 2 and 5.
58 Suzuki (1969).

as a mediator between individual identity and collective belonging but also acts as a guide for the construction and interpretation of memories.

What is culture? Culture can be defined in different ways, depending on disciplinary perspectives and theoretical approaches. In general, culture refers to the set of intellectual, material, emotional, and behavioral patterns shared by a society or social group and passed down through generations.[59] These patterns include norms, values, beliefs, customs, languages, art forms, religions, institutions, and other aspects of human life.

For the purposes of this book, a useful definition that encompasses these different dimensions of culture defines culture as "a pattern of basic assumptions—inventions, discoveries, and experiences—that has proved effective in solving problems of external adaptation and internal integration and that has enabled members of a group to adapt better to their environment."[60] If you want to emphasize the intersubjective context more, culture can be defined as "the collective programming of the mind which distinguishes the members of one group or category of people from another." Both definitions emphasize the common characteristics and norms that a cultural group shares, as well as their role in the constitution of the inner world, together with the importance of culture for adaptation to the environment and social integration, without ignoring the fact that it is a matter of mutual influence, that is, culture is also always the product of individual basic assumptions and experiences and is fed and also modified by these in the medium term.

Culture as an entity thus encompasses the shared values, norms, beliefs, traditions, and practices of a particular group or community. These cultural elements serve as the basis for the construction of individual identities, as they provide the framework for self-definition and belonging to a particular social group. Through the internalization of cultural norms and values, people identify with their cultural community and construct their identity in relation to this group—culture, therefore, acts as a mediator of identity.[61]

Cultural identity not only influences an individual's self-perception and self-concept of an individual but also shapes their behavior, attitudes, and world views. By identifying with their cultural identity, individuals seek community, recognition, and security in a world that is often characterized by divergence

---

59 Compare conceptually Thomas/Utler (2013), p. 41ff.
60 Schein (1985), p. 9.
61 Thomas/Utler (2013), p. 51f.

and complexity—individually experienced culture becomes a convergence factor for transpersonal identity.[62]

At the same time, culture interpersonally becomes a "signpost" for memories: Memories are not only individual situational representations of past events[63] but are also shaped and interpreted by cultural contexts and frameworks. Culture acts as a signpost for the construction and interpretation of memories in one's own inner world by contextualizing the meaning of events and experiences and placing them in a larger context. In addition, cultural narratives (which complement and transcend the individual narrative), as well as symbols, rituals, and traditions, serve as a means of maintaining and passing on formerly individual memories across generations.[64] By sharing common narratives and their interpretations and practicing cultural practices, individuals not only remember past events but also construct their identity in relation to their cultural affiliation.[65]

The interactions between cultural identity and memory are crucial for the mediating role of culture: culture provides the framework for the construction of individual identities and shapes the way people interpret and pass on their memories. At the same time, individual identities and memories also shape culture by bringing new perspectives and experiences and contributing to cultural diversity. Culture constitutes its own "collective unconscious."[66]

Taken together, the relationship between culture, identity, and memory illustrates the close interconnectedness of these concepts and their significance for the individual experience of reality and behavior. Acting as a mediator and signpost between identity and memory, culture enables not only the construction

---

62 Cf. Assmann (1988), pp. 10–12.
63 This aspect will be dealt with in detail later.
64 Cf. Assmann (2018), pp. 48–59 and p. 66f.
65 Ibid.
66 The concept of the collective unconscious was developed by Carl Gustav Jung and is a central component of his analytical psychology. Jung argued that in addition to the personal unconscious of each individual, which consists of personal memories, repressed desires, and individual complexes, there is also a collective unconscious that connects all of humanity. The collective unconscious consists of archetypal content that can be found in the cultural traditions, myths, symbols, and rituals of all societies. These archetypal contents are innate psychic structures that form the basis for universal human experience and behavior. They have developed in the course of evolution and are passed on from generation to generation.
Cf. Jung (2022), p. 19f., p. 58ff.

of individual and collective identities but also the preservation and transmission of intersubjective knowledge and the transposition of collective, transpersonal identity across generations.

Culture connects the outer world with the inner, experienced reality and makes it comprehensible in a context; it is the signpost on the complex terrain of the ego.

The Three Key Messages

1. **Central importance of the relationship between culture, identity, and memory:** The interconnectedness of culture, identity, and memory plays a crucial role in understanding human experience and social cohesion.
2. **Culture is a mediator of identity and a signpost for memories. Culture serves as a mediator between individual identity and collective belonging** while acting as a signpost for the construction and interpretation of memories.
3. **Interaction between cultural identity and memory:** Culture shapes individual identities and influences the interpretation of memories, while individual identities and memories, in turn, influence culture and contribute to cultural diversity. These interactions illustrate the close connection between culture, identity, and memory and their importance for the individual experience of reality and behavior.

The Constituent Function of Memory

We are set up in such a way that we can only enjoy the contrast intensely and the state very little. Our possibilities for happiness are therefore already limited by our constitution.[67]

One of the most important concepts in this book and for the inner economy is the mental resource "memory"; the economy within us revolves around it.

The central pivotal point for this inner economy is the spirit system—what is usually referred to as the psyche, personality, or inner voice. Without question, much has already been written about this—since ancient times, it has been a

---

67 Freud (2009), p. 43.

field in which people have been interested in many different ways—this is also where the term "memory" originated."[68] These were quickly regarded as a mediating or inherently meaningful resource that transposes impressions from reality into the soul.

The scientific study of memory began in the nineteenth century with pioneers such as Ebbinghaus, who conducted the first systematic experiment to research memory in 1885.[69] Ebbinghaus coined the term "retroaction" and developed the concept of "forgetting."[70] His work laid the foundation for the experimental psychology of memory—which he also considered to be of crucial importance for people:

> The knowledge of the existence of memory and its effects is accompanied by a manifold knowledge of the conditions on which the intensity of the inner afterlife and the fidelity and promptness of reproduction depend.[71]

These basic theories and models of memory have evolved over time, with important contributions coming from scientists such as James, Freud, Jung, and others. James, for example, described memory as a three-part process consisting of sensory memory, short-term memory, and long-term memory—a categorization that still enjoys a high profile in general knowledge today. At the same time, in his *"Principles of Psychology"* (1890), he established the depiction of the psyche as a process of consciousness, the concept of the *"stream of consciousness"*—an important starting point for the explanations in this work.[72]

This correlates with the concept of apperception by Wundt, the entry of content of consciousness into the field of attention, mediated by a number of functions that intervene in the process of consciousness.[73]

---

68 The concept of memory in (Western) psychology, the first significant approaches to questions about memory and how memory works can be found in Plato and Aristotle. In his concept of "anamnesis," Plato described memory as the process of reliving past impressions that the soul already knew. See also Huber (1964); pp. 20–41.

In Eastern philosophy, the roots of this interest in knowledge go back much further, see Borghardt/Erhardt (2016), pp. 227–268.

69 Cf. Ebbinghaus/Dürr (1913), pp. 224–242 and p. 303f.
70 Cf. Ebbinghaus (1885), p. 68 and p. 143f.
71 Ibid. S. 3.
72 Cf. James (1890), p. 179ff. and p. 245ff.
73 Cf. Wundt (1896), p. 134ff. and p. 187ff.

Freud expanded this model with the concept of the subconscious and unconscious memory, practically adding the "underside" of the basic model of consciousness, within which remembering is the most important function.[74]

Overall, the study of memory has come a long way in psychology (all the scientists mentioned wrote their works at the end of the nineteenth/beginning of the twentieth century) and remains a central topic for modern cognitive psychology and neuroscience—an expansion in the direction of "inner economy"[75] is merely the next logical step in researching the mind and its system.

The Three Key Messages

1. The mental resource "Memory" is at the center of the inner economy and is the central theme of this book.
2. The spirit system, referred to as the psyche or personality, forms the centerpiece of this inner economy and has aroused people's interest since ancient times.
3. The scientific study of memory remains a relevant topic and is consistently expanding in the direction of an inner economy.

The Structure of Memory and Its Role in The Mind System—A State of Research

A present is an object of perception, the future is a matter of expectation, the past an object of memory."[76]

Feeling the same today as yesterday means not feeling—remembering today what you felt yesterday, being today the living corpse of what was lived and lost yesterday.[77]

First, a brief outline of the neurological side of memory is provided.

From a psychological point of view, remembering is a process characterized by complex interactions, which are characterized and classified by cognitive,

---

74 Cf. Freud (1988), p. 266ff.
75 Contrary to the sometimes common use of the term in the context of the material side of human action and the economic order as an effect of psychological and spiritual aspects, this work would like to use the term as a rational inner handling of mental resources, see also Chapter 1.2.
76 Aristotle, Parva naturalia. De memoria et reminiscentia, Cap. I.
77 Pessoa (2008), p. 107.

neurological, and emotional mechanisms. The current research findings[78] can be briefly summarized as follows with regard to the functioning of memory:

Basically, memory is based on the interaction of different brain regions that are connected in a network. A central element of this network is the hippocampus, which plays a key role in the formation of new memories. The process of encoding, in which information from the environment is incorporated into long-term memory, often begins with the activation of sensory areas of the brain that process impressions, such as sounds, images, and odors. These sensory impressions reach the hippocampus, where they are processed and organized in neuronal networks. Emotional components play an important role here, as emotional events are often remembered more intensively and for longer periods of time. The hippocampus works closely with other brain regions, such as the prefrontal cortex, to consolidate and store memories.[79]

However, the phenomenon of remembering is not limited to the formation of new memories but also includes the retrieval of stored information. Various mechanisms, such as retrieval cues and associations, come into play here. Retrieval cues can be external stimuli or internal thoughts that are associated with a particular memory and facilitate access to it. And facilitate access to it. Interestingly, in neurological terms, remembering itself is not a passive retrieval of information but an active reconstruction process.[80] This means that memories are not simply stored and replayed but rather reconstructed on the basis of fragments and schemas stored in memory. This can lead to memories being distorted or falsified, especially over time or under the influence of external factors.[81]

Another important aspect of memory is its flexibility and plasticity.[82] Memory is not static; it can change over time and adapt to new information.[83] This process of memory plasticity enables experiences to be multidimensionally integrated, updated, and modified, which is a central mechanism for learning and adapting to new situations—memories are, therefore, changeable. They are, therefore, changeable.[84]

---

78 These are naturally extensive; only a small, condensed scope is presented.
79 Cf. in detail Thompson (2016), p. 45ff. and OECD (2005), pp. 64–71.
80 See Logie/Camos/Cowan (2020), pp. 4–9 and Baddeley/Hitch/Allen (2020), pp. 19ff. and Mauser/Pfeiffer (eds.) (2004), pp. 46–48.
81 Ibid.
82 See also Jäncke (2021), p. 19f., p. 43ff.
83 Ibid.
84 Ibid.

Overall, from a neurological perspective, remembering (as a function of the mental system) is a complex and dynamic process that is influenced by a variety of internal and external factors. However, these are non-situational—the individual is not stuck in the here and now: memory plasticity makes it possible to relive or even re-experience past[85] (or anticipate future[86]) experiences. From a neurological perspective, an individual is also able to go on "mental time travel" and thus influence decisions in the present.[87]

This now well-documented functionality of the mental system is reflected in cognitive psychology. A fundamental approach in cognitive psychology is the multistorage model of memory, which assumes that memory is divided into different systems or memories that process different types of information. It is divided into different systems or memories that process different types of information.[88] Working memory is a temporary store responsible for processing and manipulating information in the mind; long-term memory, on the other hand, is a more permanent memory that can store a wide range of information over a longer period of time.[89] The process of remembering begins with the encoding of information, in which sensory impressions are converted into formats accessible to memory.[90] Long-term memory is divided into different categories, including declarative memory, which comprises explicitly conscious memories such as facts and events, and non-declarative memory, which includes unconscious memories such as skills and habits.[91]

The retrieval of stored information from long-term memory is a crucial step in the memory process. This retrieval can be influenced by various factors, including retrieval cues, context, and emotional states.[92] For example, specific cues can contribute to the activation and retrieval of relevant memories.[93]

---

85 This process is understood as "narration."
86 This process is known as "imagination".
87 See Daniel/Stanton/Epstein (2013), p. 2340 and Schacter/Benoit/Szpunar (2017), p. 41f.
88 The three-stage model is a multicomponent memory model that is still one of the fundamental models of memory research today. Its exact functional principle is only of peripheral interest for this paper. Cf. Atkinson/Shiffrin (1968).
89 See Thompson (2016), p. 55.
90 Ibid.
91 Ibid. and Billhardt/Storck (2021), pp. 108–112.
92 Ibid, p. 276.
93 See Billhardt/Storck (2021), p. 124ff.

Another important aspect of remembering from a cognitive perspective is the reconstruction of memories. This means that memories can often not be regarded as an exact reproduction of past events but rather as constructions based on stored fragments and schemata.[94] This reconstruction can lead to distortions and errors, especially in the case of complex or emotionally charged events.[95]

Both perspectives show how central memories are as a mental resource—and how fluid the connection between memory and objective external reality is. In both models, memories are not a reflection of reality but are constructed on an individual basis. Therefore, a conscious preoccupation with memories (which can be changed and interpreted) is an individual psychological element that has a direct active influence on experience and the mental state—as Aristotle already put it in a nutshell: "The present is the object of perception future is a matter of expectation, the past an object of memory."[96].

The Three Key Messages

1. **Reconstructive nature of memories:** Memories are actively reconstructed and are based on stored fragments and schemas, which can lead to distortions or errors, especially in the case of complex or emotional events.
2. **Memory plasticity and flexibility:** Memory is flexible and plastic, which means that it can change over time and adapt to new information. This process makes it possible to integrate, update, and modify experiences, which is crucial for learning and adapting to new situations.
3. **Sensory impressions and recall cues:** The process of remembering begins with the encoding of sensory impressions, which are then stored in long-term memory. The retrieval of stored information is influenced by various factors, including sensory cues and associations, which can lead to relevant memories being activated and retrieved.

---

94 Ibid, pp. 156–163.
95 Ibid.
96 Aristotle (2021), p. 11.

Conceptual, Methodological, and Conceptual Foundations—The Terminology of Memory Psychology

Stulti autem malorum memoria torquentur, sapientes bona praeterita grata recordatione renovata delectant.[97]

To realize the objectives of this book mentioned at the beginning, it is necessary to clarify a few terms and theoretical and methodological frameworks in advance for a better understanding and classification of the following core statements.

Memory psychology is a complex, interdisciplinary field of research that investigates the processes by which information is stored in human memory. This is how information is stored, retained, retrieved, and modified in humans.[98] The central concepts of memory psychology offer an initial insight into the functioning of the mental system and help to understand the complexity of human memory. The following points briefly outline the concepts and terms of memory psychology that are important for this book.[99]

- Memory: Memory is the key concept in memory psychology. It refers to an individual's ability to store, retain, and retrieve information. Memory is not a static entity but a dynamic process that is influenced by various factors.[100]
- Memory systems: Memory is often divided into different systems or phases that have different functions and capacities. These include sensory memory, short-term memory, and long-term memory.[101] Sensory memory stores sensory impressions such as seeing or hearing for a short period of time. Short-term memory has a limited capacity and duration and is used for the temporary storage of information. Long-term memory has an almost unlimited capacity and stores information for the long term.[102]

---

97 "But while the foolish torment themselves with the memories of bad things, the wise enjoy past happiness, which they visualise in their memories. visualise in their memories."
Cicero, Tusculanae Disputationes, Liber V, 40.
98 See Wentura/Frings (2013), pp. 101–125.
99 At the same time, it is also worth taking a look at the detailed glossary for all technical terms.
100 Ibid., pp. 118–122.
101 See Billhardt/Storck (2021), pp. 90–106.
102 See Wentura/Frings (2013), pp. 120–125.

- Explicit and implicit memory: Long-term memory can be further divided into explicit (declarative) and implicit (non-declarative) memory. Explicit memory comprises facts and events that can be consciously recalled. Implicit memory refers to the knowledge about skills and behavior, which often takes place unconsciously.[103]
- Forgetting: Forgetting refers to the inability to recall information previously stored in memory. There are several causes of forgetting, including interference, disintegration, and lack of depth of encoding.[104] Forgetting is a natural and normal part of the memory process.[105]
- Memory distortion: Memory distortion occurs when memories are altered or distorted by various influences. This can happen through suggestive questions, personal interpretations, or prejudices.[106] Memory distortion can lead to false memories and has important implications for the mind system as a whole.[107]
- Memorization: Memorization refers to an individual's ability to recall and reproduce information. The ability to remember can be influenced by various factors, including repetition, elaboration, organization, and context dependency.[108]

The central concepts of the psychology of memory provide an initial framework for the development of a dedicated economy of memory. The mental memory processes are based on these concepts. The mechanisms that can lead to memories being changed or re-evaluated.

ONE: The Three Key Messages in Brief

1. Identity, culture, and memory determine the framework and boundaries of our inner world.
2. Our inner economy depends on our mental system, which includes all mental resources and processes.
3. Memories are an essential mental resource.

---

103 Ibid., pp. 182–184.
104 See Pritzel/Markowitsch (2017), pp. 18–22.
105 Ibid.
106 Ibid., p. 19.
107 Ibid., p. 20.
108 See Billhardt/Storck (2021), pp. 116–119.

CHAPTER 2

THE CORE OF BEING—CHANGE, FLUIDITY OF THE EGO, NARRATION, AND COGNITION

> The ideal beauty, though indivisible and simple, shows in various respects both a melting and an energetic quality; in experience, there is a melting and an energetic beauty. So it is, and so it will be in all cases where the absolute is set within the bounds of time and ideas of reason are to be realized in humanity. Thus, the reflecting man conceives virtue, truth, and bliss, but the acting man will merely practice virtues, grasp truths, and merely enjoy blissful days. To lead these back to those—to put morality in the place of morals, knowledge in the place of knowledge, bliss in the place of happiness—is the business of physical and moral education; to make beauty out of beauty is the task of aesthetic education.[109]

The first approach to the functioning of the spirit system and the inner economy now goes into more depth.

There are two main aspects to this: First, I would like to differentiate the inner economy further and make it understandable and usable as a concept, as well as lay the foundation for cognitive therapy. Second, I would like to explain the spirit system in total; in my opinion, it is essential to develop a precise understanding of such a complex tool as the spirit system in order to be able to use it effectively. Most people spend a lot of time thinking about how technical devices or applications work, but very few people think about how their own minds are structured and work.

The further development of the inner economy and the development of a concept for cognitive therapy are also important focal points. This is not only

---

109 Schiller (1903), p. 192.

about researching how the human mind works but also about the practical application of this knowledge to promote inner growth and the efficiency of the mind system.[110]

The inner economy refers to the efficient utilization of an individual's mental resources, including memory, mindfulness, resilience, and (general) cognitive capacity. By developing this concept further, we can develop a better understanding of how we can optimize the use of our mental resources to achieve goals, overcome challenges, and improve decision-making processes. This can help to increase efficiency in thinking, feeling, and acting, solve mental health problems, and create a balance between the different, often conflicting aspects of our lives.

An Initial Overview

- Insight therapy is ultimately based on the idea that our insights and beliefs have a decisive influence on our conscious psyche and our actions. By developing insight therapy, we can identify ways in which we can actively influence our thought patterns and beliefs to bring about positive change. This will include identifying and overcoming irrational beliefs, fostering self-compassion and self-acceptance, and developing more constructive thinking and action.
- In addition, it is crucial to develop a precise understanding of the spirit system at work within us. This system includes complex processes such as perception, memory, emotions, motivation, and self-regulation. By explicitly visualizing and exploring this mind system, we can develop a deeper understanding of ourselves and identify effective strategies for self-regulation and self-development. This can help us to utilize our mental resources more effectively, promote emotional well-being, and lead a more fulfilling life.

The Economy of Memory

Insight cannot be learned from others. Knowledge must come from one's own self.[111]

If you want an "economy of memory," the first step is to agree on the elements and active components that are contained in memories and the

---

110 Cf. Kaiser-El-Safti (2001), p. 259ff.
111 Zhuangzi, quoted from Watson (1968), p. 237.

memory process itself. This will be the first focus in this main section, creating a framework for consideration.

In the second step, this makes it possible to take a new look at remembering (and imagining—as future-oriented recollection) as an intrapersonal process and to demonstrate mechanisms that make an individual holistic approach possible under economically meaningful conditions. This approach to be developed is interspersed with elements of traditional (cognitive) psychology as well as elements of other scientific traditions.[112]

In the end, the whole thing comes together to form a model of an inner economy whose concrete psychological implications and derivations are discussed in the following chapter.

Economic Aspects in Individual Psychology: A Reconstruction

> The worry cupboard, the holy of holies of the innermost soul economy, which is only opened at night. Everyone has their own.[113]
>
> Of course, we must all try to make use of our present moments, and this would not be so difficult, for we should only do what we like best every moment. But who does not realize that we would soon lack the material for it if two years were spent like this, all future ones would be spoilt? Every present moment is a mirror of all future ones; our present pleasure, compared with that which will become a future one, can become a greater one.[114]

By way of introduction, it is useful to take a closer look at the important mental concept of reconstruction,[115] as this plays a key role in the mental system and, at the same time, contains the first close and obvious links to economic aspects.

The role of reconstruction in the psyche and the mental system, especially in the context of memories, is a concept that forms the basis of our understanding of identity, perception, and behavior.[116] Reconstruction refers to the process by which our mind takes information, experiences, and events from the past, rearranging and reinterpreting them to create meaning and coherence.

---

112 In particular, the Far Eastern scientific tradition of Buddhism and Zen Gnosticism.
113 Lichtenberg (2017), p. 17 [A 43].
114 Lichtenberg (2017), p. 17 [A 43].
115 See Westermann (2013), p. 70f.
116 See ibid. and Bohleber (2019), pp. 69–73.

This process is fundamental to the way we understand ourselves and how we interpret the world around us—conceptually, symbolic interactionism.[117] Memories are an essential component of the reconstruction of the psyche.[118] They are not simply static records of past events but are shaped and distorted by a variety of factors as they are processed and reproduced in memory. The memories we have are not just the result of objective replay of past events but are strongly shaped by situational and socio-historical factors. An important aspect of the role of reconstruction in the psyche is the way in which we form our identity. Our memories of past experiences significantly influence how we perceive ourselves and how we interpret our lives. By reconstructing past events, we create a narrative structure (narration) that gives meaning to our lives and enables us to develop a coherent picture of ourselves. However, these narratives can also be distorted or selective, as we tend to select and interpret events and information that are consistent with our self-image and beliefs.[119] Similarly, we create an imaginative future from the now, which is derived from the past (imagination). These are the essential mind functions of narration and imagination[120]; both are to be defined as economically active concepts, as both contribute centrally to the function of the mind system and, thus, also to its inherent value.

The consideration of economic aspects in connection with the reconstruction of the mental system will show how individual and collective psychological processes interact with economic principles.

Although the term "reconstruction" will be considered more from a psychological perspective, further economic considerations relate to the following aspects:

- **Resource allocation and internal opportunity costs:** In the mind system, reconstruction can be seen as a process that requires resources such as attention, cognitive capacity, and (emotional) energy (also referred to as well).[121] Individuals (and groups)[122] must decide how to allocate these limited resources[123] to reflect on past experiences, process new information to reflect on past experiences, process new

---

117 See also Drüe (1963), p. 255ff. and Winter (2010), pp. 83–85 and Sutter (2013), p. 65ff.
118 Cf. ibid.
119 Cf. e.g., Neumann (2005), pp. 172–178.
120 Cf. Gregorio et al. (2024), pp. 78, 145ff. and 220–228.
121 Cf. Eccles/Wigfield (2002), p. 114ff.
122 Which is not the focus of this paper.
123 See Christie/Schrater (2015).

information, and prepare for future challenges. Like the economy, the mind system faces opportunity costs: By focusing on a particular type of reconstruction, it may forgo other potentially valuable processes or insights. This needs to be understood and anticipated.

- **Investing in inner growth and development:** Individuals invest time, energy, and other (mostly non-physical) resources in their inner development and remembering themselves. Like (macro-) economic investments, these investments in the spirit system can yield long-term returns in the form of improved well-being, greater resilience, and a deeper understanding of self (inner world) and outer world.[124]
- **Externalities and interpersonal effects:** The reconstruction in the mind system often has not only intrapersonal but also interpersonal effects. The way in which people interpret their memories and reflect on their life experiences influences their interactions with others and the development of social norms, values, and institutions.[125] Similar to economic externalities, these interpersonal, collective effects can be positive or negative and can reach far beyond the individual.
- **Efficiency and optimization:** The spirit system is also subject to a system-inherent optimization potential. This means that resources can be used to reflect on developmental processes and develop further to realize efficiency gains in the inner world.[126] This is also about the optimal utilization of (mental) resources.
- **Risk assessment and decision-making:** In the reconstruction of experiences and memories in the mental system, risk assessment and decision-making play an important role. The mind system must find a basis for evaluating memories and imaginations in order to be able to modify them. Like economic theory, these decisions are often based on system-inherent assessments of risk and reward as well as on individual preferences and values.[127]

---

[124] See Greene/Galambos/Lee (2004), p. 76ff. and Southwick (2014), p. 25339ff. and Cyrulnik (2009), p. 22f.

[125] Cf. Hummell (1971), pp. 68–74.

[126] External techniques such as mindfulness training, cognitive behavioural therapy or creative self-reflection should be mentioned here in passing; however, this is only of secondary relevance for dealing with the mind system itself, however, this is only of secondary relevance.

[127] See Küchle (2012), p. 188f.

The basic economic framework—transferred to the mental system, which will be discussed in detail in the next chapter—therefore contains a nested hierarchy of partial aspects that can subsequently be applied to the overall mental process. Figure 1 illustrates this once again.

It should be noted that the economization of the function of reconstruction in the mental system quasi-subordinates it to the economic aspects listed above. This is a process that should clearly lie in the realm of consciousness. More details are provided in the later chapters.

In addition, the reconstruction of memories plays an important role in overcoming traumas, complexes, and other stressful events.[128] The mental system has the ability to reconstruct traumatic memories and mold them into a form that is more compatible with the situational experience. However, this process can lead to certain aspects of the memory being distorted or suppressed in order to modify negatively perceived emotions associated with the trauma. In some

FIGURE 1 Economization of the mental system.[129]

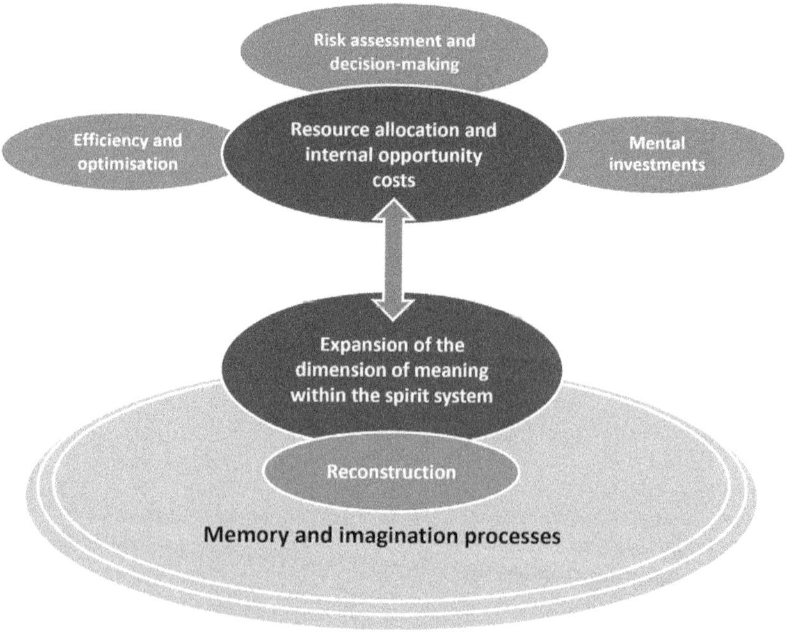

---

128 See also Dieckmann (2013), p. 38ff.
129 Own presentation.

cases, this can lead to fragmentation or distortion of the memory, resulting in an inconsistent or unreliable representation of the event—an inefficient process in an economic sense.[130]

The reconstruction of memories is also closely linked to the way in which the mind system processes new information and experiences into memories. When it processes new information, it is interpreted through preexisting mental filters and concepts. In this way, the reconstruction becomes a dynamic process that continuously changes the meta-processual perception of the inner world and the mind system, as well as the inner world and the mental system itself. By mirroring the mechanisms of reconstruction on economic aspects, this perception can be more strongly objectified and thus better influenced at will by the conscious part of the mind.[131]

The Three Key Messages

1. **Reconstructive nature of memories:** Memories are not static but are actively reconstructed each time they are recalled. This means that they can be influenced by current experiences, emotions, and circumstances, which can lead to distortions or changes.
2. **Memories as constructive processes:** Memories are not simply recalled but actively constructed. This process can lead to details being added, omitted, or changed based on cognitive biases, expectations, or other influences.
3. **Influence of emotions and motivation:** Emotions and motivation play an important role in the reconstruction of memories. Emotional events are often remembered more intensely and in greater detail, while memories of events associated with strong emotions can be distorted or amplified.

Economic and Psychological Systems—Identity and Memory

All memory is the present.[132]

This leads to the question of what exactly memories are within the "economized" mind system and what role they play in detail because the central starting point

---

130 See Dipper (2016), p. 124ff. and Komes, J./Wiese, H. (2013), p. 42.
131 Cf. Küchle (2012), p. 67ff.
132 Baron von Hardenberg (1960), p. 196.

for the economization of the mind system is the realization that memory as a resource has a reality-constituting effect both internally and externally.[133]

The psychic mind system as a concept is a dynamic and complex network of mental processes and states that comprehensively (and at least conceptually conclusively) describes the human experience, behavior, and thinking. It encompasses the various components of the mind, including cognitive processes, emotional reactions, motivational drives, and consciousness. As a system, it forms the foundation for the individual perception of the world, social interaction, and introspective self-reflection.[134]

A central component of the psychic mind system is consciousness. It refers to the state of awareness and attention in which we are aware of our surroundings, our thoughts, and our feelings. Consciousness enables us to process sensory impressions, analyze information, and make decisions.[135] A multitude of dependent and independent cognitive processes are organized around consciousness.[136] These include the mental activities associated with acquiring, storing, retrieving, and processing information in order to perform functions of the mental system, such as perception, memory, thinking, language, or problem-solving.[137]

The psychic mind system (Figure 2 shows a schematic) forms the basis for understanding the human mind and the basic behavior of an individual.[138]

An economic system, on the other hand, is initially a complex structure of institutions, rules, and patterns of interaction that regulates the production, distribution, and consumption processes of a group of individuals. It forms the foundation on which economic activities are organized and significantly influences the level of prosperity of society as well as the distribution of (individual and collective) resources and opportunities[139]—it is, therefore,

---

133 See Dipper (2016), p. 187ff.
134 See Leipner (2018), p. 130f.
135 See Chlupsa (2016), pp. 33–37.
136 Emotions and motives act as mediators and catalyzers between the mental processes, which are also an integral part of the mental system, but are less the focus of this work.
137 See Billhardt/Storck (2021), p. 201ff.
138 See Zauner (2018), p. 310.
139 In the external world, economic systems vary according to the situational political, social, and historical parameters of a society. They can range from market-orientated capitalist systems, in which supply and demand are the main mechanism for allocating resources, to planned-economy socialist systems, in which state institutions are the central decision-makers. See Deimer (2017), p. 42ff.

FIGURE 2 Schematic representation of the psychic mind system.[140]

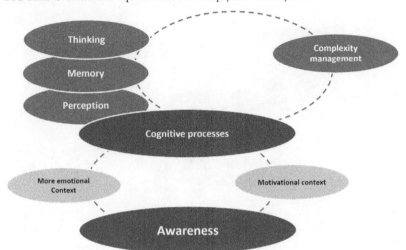

an intersubjective construct of a collective consciousness. of a collective consciousness.[141]

A fundamental characteristic of economic systems is their ability to mobilize and allocate resources (production factors such as labor and capital as well as natural resources) in order to meet the needs (perceived as such) of the constituent individuals globally[142]—a process that is defined as economic efficiency.[143] It is only through the allocation of memory resources that reality is constituted in the case of the internal economy to the constitution of reality—which, in a further step, leads to a multitude of mental transaction processes. Figure 3 illustrates the model.

In the following, all three levels are examined in more detail and harmonized with a meta-analysis of the spirit system itself.

---

140 Own presentation.
141 Ibid.
142 Ibid.
143 Ibid.

26 THE MIND ECONOMY

FIGURE 3 Schematic representation of the economic mind system.[144]

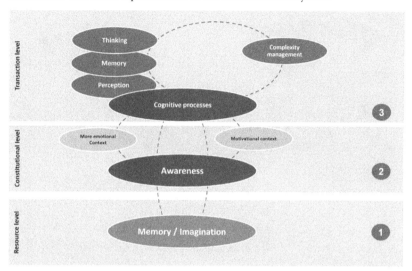

The Individual-Psychological Approach to Memory as a Decidedly Economic System

First, the resource level of the mind system is the level of memory (and imagination). Memory is an abstracted, purely subjective mental[145] representation of a specific past, the expression of which is defined both by its

---

144 Own presentation.
145 The question of whether memories have a physical component in the brain is being intensively researched in neuroscience. Current scientific knowledge suggests that memories in the brain are represented by complex neuronal networks made up of a multitude of synapses, neurons, and neurochemical processes.
  The formation of memories begins with the acquisition of sensory information by the sensory organs. This information is then processed and interpreted in different areas of the brain. In the hippocampus region of the brain, which plays a key role in memory, new information is temporarily stored and processed before it is stored in the brain for the long term. Long-term memories are encoded in the brain through structural and functional changes in the synaptic connections between neurons. This process, known as synaptic plasticity, involves the strengthening or weakening of connections between neurons based on their activity and importance to the individual.
  The physical basis of memories in the brain has been uncovered through various experimental techniques and studies, including imaging techniques such as functional

emotional content and by its individual information (facts, events, emotions, and sensory impressions).[146]

Memory can, therefore, not simply be regarded as a static record of past events but as a dynamic and complex construction of the mind system itself.[147]

The organization of memories is not a one-dimensional process. It is continuous and situational, whereby memories not only exist as isolated units but are closely linked to other thoughts, emotions, and experiences. This can lead to complex and often contradictory interpretations that cause the mind system to constantly re-evaluate and reflect on memories as part of the *narration of events*. By structuring memories in the form of (continuously perceived) history, the mind system gives them context, emotional meaning, and individual significance—and, thus, a self-constituting effect.[148] Emotionality is an essential component of memories. Emotional reactions can lead us to reinterpret events, retrospectively and see them in a new light. As a result, memories are not only seen as objective images of past events but also as subjective constructions that are characterized by individual experiences and perspectives.[149]

---

magnetic resonance imaging (fMRI) and electroencephalography (EEG), as well as neurophysiological studies in animal models. These studies have shown that different brain regions are involved in the storage and retrieval of memories, with the exact involvement depending on the type of memory and the associated cognitive processes.

See von Kutschera (2014), p. 32ff. and Rugg/Vilberg (2013), pp. 257–260, Alberini (2005), p. 55 and Squire/Zola-Morgan (1991), p. 1380ff.

146 Ibid.

147 Ibid.

In this context, it is important to note that remembering and forgetting are not opposites, but rather two sides of the same coin, one could also speak of anti-memory. In fact, the question arises as to whether it is even possible to forget something. Even if memories may be temporarily buried, they can resurface through certain stimuli or contexts. The mental system has numerous mechanisms to store and retrieve information, even if it appears to have been forgotten.

See also Trigo (2011), p. 13ff.

148 The process described in this way not only takes place in a past-preserving way, but also in a future-orientated constructive way – narration becomes imagination; imagination as an anticipation of future memories. By imagining how we would like to remember certain events, we unconsciously influence our memories and the way in which we interpret them.

See also Cyrulnik (2021), pp. 138–142.

149 Ibid.

With this resource-based approach, it is important to recognize that there can be no objective memory. Every event is immediately fragmented into countless individual memories, which are all colored by the situation. This makes it possible to consciously deal with memories as a valuable personal resource, as this is what makes them influenceable and, therefore, changeable. The "objective" past is self-chosen and self-constructed by the mind system. There are always several, even contradictory, interpretations of an event possible.[150] The process of narration turns memory into a mental resource with which the mind system can work efficiently. Through an economic understanding of the organization and handling of memories, the narrative processes can be understood and coordinated differently and thus further differentiate the structure of the memory resource.

The unifying element of the narration is the illusion of the continuity of the inner and outer world (self and environment) and their synchronicity. A large part of the idea of the "self" is based on a complex illusion of the continuity of a core being and the environment surrounding us.[151] The surrounding environment, reality, is subject to comprehensive, continuous change—but this is ignored due to its complexity and the associated uncertainty. The same applies to the core of our being—which is a variable set of memories that are also continuously exchanged and reinterpreted. As a result, there are effects of numbness and alienation of one's own memories and a suppression of (necessary) changes in the self.[152] Nevertheless, the idea of continuity has become firmly anchored in the (western liberal) worldview and is hardly ever questioned, with many complex, negative effects on the psyche.[153]

Memory is constituted in this network; Figure 4 shows a corresponding model.

---

150 There are also phenomena such as alternate memory, where memories change or new details are added. This emphasizes the dynamic nature of memory and the impermanence of memories over time.

At the same time, it should be noted that it is certainly the subject of scientific debate whether the past (as such) really exists at all or whether there is even a present in the physical sense. In this respect, the individual construction process is of particular importance. Cf. also Münster (2022).

151 Cf. Wils (2023), p. 20ff.

152 One can also speak of a wave character of memories and self. One is not the same person in the present as in the past—these are different people with a different set of memories. See also Newell (1994), p. 121ff.

153 Comprehensive ibid.

FIGURE 4 The inner structure of memory.[154]

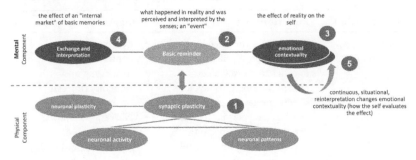

Decisive for the economic, mental system is the continuous, situational, (re)interpretation of reality through the emotional contextuality of the self (which is either projection or distraction)[155]; the past, even the objectively real past, is more a construction of the self than a factual inner reality. Thus, this mechanism is the equivalent of the external (economic) market mechanism since values are constituted in a complex, interdependent system of interpretation.[156] This structure of memory provides the economic framework of the mind system and defines memory as a resource.

The Spirit System: Narration, Imagination, and Will as Economic Exchange Processes

> Thus, the cognition of every mind, at least of the human mind, is cognition through concepts, not intuitively but discursively.[157]

In addition to the basic memory as a mental resource, the processes of exchange and interpretation of memories are part of an economic, mental system. Three mental processes are primarily used here: narration, imagination, and (conscious and unconscious) will. These are summarized and explained in Table 1.

The term "exchange" is to be understood in a transactional sense: All three types of processes are based on using the resource memory (or imagination) to

---

154 Own presentation (with (content) use of Pohl (2007), pp. 82–90).
155 Ibid. and p. 104ff.
156 Cf. Frey/Benz (2001), pp. 24–29 and p. 44f.
157 Kant (1787), B93.

TABLE 1 The three economic exchange processes.

Designation	Functionality	Impact
(Self-) narration[158]	Narration is the selection and organization of information in order to convey a certain interpretation. This involves selecting relevant events, emphasizing certain mental details, and structuring the narrative into a meaningful sequence of cause and effect. Through this process, we give meaning to events and convey them in a specific situational context.[160]	• Self-narration as a contingent experience • (Narrating and remembering self)[159] • Structure of memory • Narration is the construction of knowledge and reality
Imagination	Imagination is the reverse process of remembering; it feeds on visualization of the past and its projection into the future (remembering future events as anticipation of the future). Memory complexes from the past are transferred to the future. Dynamic imagination comprises various mental operations, including imagination, visualization, abstraction, and fantasy.[161]	• Complexities of the past are perpetuated and not transformed; cycles emerge, even indeterminate action • Emotional regulation and mental well-being • Creativity, problem solving and planning

(*Continued*)

---

158 Cf. also the comments on narration in Cyrulnik (2021).
159 Ibid.
160 See Schöpf (2014), chapter 4 (n.p.)
161 See Newell (1994), p. 111ff.

TABLE 1 (*Continued*)

Designation	Functionality	Impact
Will	The will includes the ability to set intentions, make decisions, and initiate actions to achieve specific goals. It involves the conscious management and control of thoughts, emotions, and behaviors in order to fulfill our personal needs (derived from the individual narrative) and desires (derived from the imagination) to realize them.	• Self-regulation and self-determination • Past-related compensatory behavior • The central exchange process between narration and imagination transfers all processes of the mental system into active visualization.

modify or expand it or to change its orientation.[162] Narration and imagination (in all their forms) are always also a reflection in the visualization and thus an inventory of memories, feelings, and ideas in order to understand one's own actions and being, a critical "analysis of the moment."[163]

As a result, the transactional character of the processes merges the being/self that one is for oneself with those as seen from the outside; the dualistic nature of inside and outside can thus be transformed into a momentary equilibrium; this is metastable and subject to continuous change, which makes it "economically active" (in the sense of a market mechanism).[164]

Both narration and imagination are processual upstream of the will.[165] The exchange character of imagining results, above all, from a mental anticipation of a future in the present and the resulting self-reinforcement of (potential) realization; imaginary experiences are practically equivalent to lived experiences within the framework of an economic model of the mental system.[166] Narration is, therefore, the basic process. Imagination is only a derivative of narration.

---

162 Cf. also Schlegel (1995).
163 In classical psychological theory, the externally imposed social framework and external goals give rise to systemic self-reproach, which in an economic interpretation can be compared to a misallocation of resources. Cf. also. Groeben/Scheele (1977), p. 140ff.
164 In addition to this transitory equilibrium, there is also the equilibrium between one's own self and the self of others, which leads to a dualism between the self and the self as a product of what others perceive in it; the "objectifying gaze of the other." Cf. de Beauvoir (1947), p. 65ff. and Drobe (2016), pp. 488–491.
165 See Scheidt (2015), pp. 26–38.
166 Cf. Kast et al. (2010), p. 164f.

The economic value of memories is thus also reflected in the external world since the decisions of individuals are based on narration, imagination, and the situational memories constituted by them.[167] Imagining is a strongly situationally dependent process and is constantly shifting; only the transfer into a narrative memory objectifies people and their relationships with them.[168]

There are, therefore, basically two transaction levels:

1. The situational agreement with one's own self is, therefore, not a state but an "evaluative activity"[169] (self-transaction of the self).
2. Emotional–rational transactions between the inside and the outside world; this exchange make the contingency of the self possible in the first place in dualism to the necessities of the self and the utilization of its abilities. (Transactions between self and environment; see also Figure 5).[170]

Both levels are economic in nature, as they aim to optimize the use of limited (mental) resources and thus create an equilibrium that is as sustainable as possible; many psychological complexes arise in this area of tension.[171] The individual psychological choice point of the equilibrium is an essential question of the inner economy[172]—as well as the entire mental system itself.[173] The self, with its contents of consciousness, defines the individual (and thus also the absolute) reality as well as the relationships to the outside world—both are

---

167 In this context, reference should also be made to the being-acting theorem, according to which decisions are not only made once, but are part of a continuous continuum of decisions. Every decision is thus "constantly in the process of becoming; they are repeated every time one becomes aware of them. [...] Action in action is confirmation of the self." This emphasizes the importance of economic schemata. Cf. Lagneau (1925), p. 61f.
168 See Scheidt (2015), p. 28f.
169 Bergson (1903), "activité d'évaluation."
170 See also Newell (1994), p. 26ff.
171 Every equilibrium in the psyche is inevitably also a betrayal—of oneself or of the other; the efforts to achieve inner balance can lead to the suppression or negation of aspects of the self that do not match the desired image.
   See Kernis/Goldman (2006), pp. 291–310.
172 Cf. Headey/Wearing (1989), p. 736f.
173 The economization of the mind leads in its basic features to a position that can be interpreted as close to solipsism. Solipsism (a philosophical position that assumes the existence of only one's own mind or consciousness and at least questions the reality of other persons and things) has significant implications for the economization of the mind.

FIGURE 5 The memory cascade of the spirit system.[174]

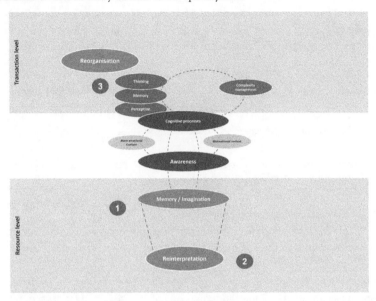

A central aspect of the economy of the mind is the distribution of mental resources. In the solipsistic worldview, there is a tendency for individual resources to be strongly focused on the self as the existence of other existences (and objects) is not seen as a given. This can lead to a one-sided allocation that can be detrimental to the mental system.

Furthermore, solipsism influences the evaluation of values and priorities in the mental context. If reality is limited to one's own consciousness external factors may not be considered relevant. This can lead to a lack of appreciation for collective concerns such as community, environment or social justice. The focus on the self can lead to individual goals and desires being prioritized over community or global concerns, which can be detrimental to the development of a sustainable and just society—both of which contradict the outward-facing transactional level.

Another aspect of the economy of the mind that is influenced by solipsism is the evaluation of information and knowledge. In a solipsistic view, it may be difficult to accept the validity of external information as the existence of other sources of reality is denied. This can lead to a lack of openness to new ideas and perspectives as they do not seem to fit with one's own limited world view. Rejecting external knowledge can limit the ability to innovate and solve problems and hinder intellectual development.

Finally, solipsism can interfere with co-operation and the sharing of resources. In a solipsistic perspective, it can be difficult to develop trust in others or find common ground for co-operation as the existence of others is questioned. This can lead to a lack of co-operation, which can affect efficiency and productivity.

See also Straus (2013), p. 35f., pp. 56–59, p. 185ff.

174 Own presentation.

to be understood as a double process of exchange and modification; memory and self are in a "permanent process of irreversible becoming," the self is not a momentary state, but an active, economically relevant development from the narrative and imagination conducted with oneself.[175]

Memory Is a Process of Accumulation and the Nucleus of the Inner Economy

Nullius non origo ultra memoriam iacet.[176]

The economy of the spirit system is guided by the same principles as external economic systems.[177] These would be at the core:

1. The accumulation principle[178]
2. The rational (i.e., effective) use of scarce resources with individual value
3. Striving for individual gain (or happiness)[179]

All of this also applies to our own way of dealing with memories with the inner economy as a framework for action and memories (mediated by narration and imagination) as a primary, personality-constituting resource.

Dealing effectively with memories involves both the construction and deconstruction of memories; both are valuable experiences that define the individual's approach to remembering. Together, they form the memory cascade of the mind system (see Figure 5), which reinterprets existing memories according to the situation and thus, in turn, modifies the underlying resources and thereby reorganizes the transaction elements.

---

175 Cf. ibid.
176 "The origin of everyone lies beyond memory."
    Lucius Annaeus Seneca, Letters to Lucilius (Epistulae morales ad Lucilium), 44th letter.
177 This is one reason why capitalism fits so natively into the human psyche, indeed why practically no alternatives can be thought of. See also Herrmann (2022), p. 85ff.
178 Conceptually, this also contains another physical representation of memory namely the use and (accumulation) of objects as materialized memory, especially in the context of symbolic self-completion. Objects often have strong specific moments of memory and reflect the longing for holism. and complete comprehension, which are accumulated in the mind system. Thus, real, external transactions also have a direct influence on the spirit system. Cf. also Gollwitzer et al. (2002), p. 193ff.
179 Cf. Frey/Jonas/Maier (2007), in particular p. 95ff.

The reinterpretation and reorganization of memories is a mental process that contributes significantly to mental health.[180] Reorganization, in particular, is central, as the evolution of the self depends on both processes (construction and deconstruction of memory).[181] This reorganization also follows basic economic rules; memory serves as a resource for development and cognition.

Thus, the individual concept of "value" (and thus the basis of the external economy) is constituted out of this mechanism of the mind system; memory is the only source of the concept of "value."[182] Economic value, therefore, fundamentally has two universal components:

1. The intersubjective construct of itself, that is, imagination in collective form in the context of the spirit system.
2. The individual memory and its situational reinterpretation.

Memories are thus also carriers and mediators of value; they become the central economic property, whereby they are subject to volatile, continuous change via the transaction mechanisms described—which ultimately represents an internal market mechanism in consciousness and subconscious/unconscious. We will soon realize that the construction (especially the conscious construction) of memory requires both material resources and immaterial resources are necessary even if the processes behind them are behind it are perceived as secondary.[183]

The emergence of memories leads to the automatism of accumulation; emotional patterns[184] in the reorganization of memories lead to a lifelong accumulation of this resource.[185]

---

180 See Heinz (2016), p. 45f. and p. 93ff.
181 Particularly, negative events must first be meaningfully integrated into the existing mental system and then interpreted; this is where the greatest individual development potential lies. Cf. ibid.
182 See Herles (2011), p. 111ff. and Frey/Jonas/Maier (2007), p. 131ff.
183 Ibid.
184 See Holland/Kensinger (2010), p. 92ff.
185 From a psychological point of view, there are different types of memoriesthat are based on different processes and mechanisms in the brain:

  1. Sensory memory: Sensory memory stores short-lived sensory impressions such as visual, auditory, or olfactory stimuli for very short periods of time, typically only a few seconds. It serves to hold and process information during perception and process it before it is either forgotten or transferred to working memory.

36 THE MIND ECONOMY

This also makes it possible to consciously "invest" in memories; they are ultimately the only source of realization about oneself—memory is the nucleus of the inner economy, its center of gravity.[186]

The Three Key Messages

1. **Memories as a constituent force of the mental system:** Memories have a reality-constituting effect and play a central role in the psychic mental system. They are not just static records of past events but dynamic constructions that are constantly re-evaluated and reflected upon.
2. **Narration, imagination, and wills economic exchange processes: The processing of memories takes place through three primary mental processes:** narration, imagination, and volition. These processes are closely linked and serve to organize and interpret memories and place them in a situational context. Through these processes, memory becomes a valuable personal resource.

(*Continued*)

---

2. Working memory: Working memory, also known as short-term memory, is a temporary store for information that is currently being actively processed. It plays an important role in the performance of cognitive tasks such as reading, arithmetic and problem solving. Working memory has a limited capacity and information is often quickly forgotten if it is not actively maintained.
3. Explicit (declarative) memory: Explicit memory comprises conscious memories of past events, facts or experiences. It can be divided into two sub-categories: episodic memory, which relates to personal experiences and events, and semantic memory, which stores facts and concepts. Explicit memory enables people to remember and think about specific events or information.
4. Implicit (non-explicit) memory: In contrast to explicit memory, implicit memory refers to non-conscious or automatic memories and skills. This includes, for example, motor skills such as riding a bike or swimming, as well as cognitive processes such as recognizing faces or playing melodies on a musical instrument. Implicit memories are often formed through repeated practice or experience and are difficult to describe verbally.
5. Emotional memory: Emotional memories refer to events or experiencesthat are associated with strong emotions. These memories can be particularly vivid and detailed and often have a strong influence on behaviour and decision-making. Emotional memories can be both explicit and implicit and are closely linked to the limbic system of the brain. Cf. Goldenberg (2007), p. 21ff.

186 Cf. Koch/von Rosenstiel (2007), p. 761ff.

3. **Memory as a process of accumulation and nucleus of the inner economy:** Memories are seen as the primary resource of the internal economy. They are subject to similar principles as external economic systems, such as accumulation, rational use of resources, and the pursuit of individual profit. The construction and reinterpretation of memories is an essential contribution to mental health and the development of the self. Ultimately, memories are the only source of insight about oneself and form the core of the inner economy.

Personality-Internal Constitutional Mechanisms and their Function

Responsibility begins in dreams.[187]

In the next step, a whole range of cognitive processes are integrated into the economic and mental systems. These complete the economic flow and the model introduced. To this end, it is useful to first define the building blocks of mental contingency in more detail in order to then link the cognitive core processes of narration, imagination, and suggestion.

Mental contingency and fluidity of the self

The first point of contact in the economized mental system is the processual contingency theory of memory[188]: Memories form a single continuum in their contingency, and each individual memory also forms a continuum in itself, that is, the memory as such is initially free of contradictions and stringent.[189]

This creates the impression of the self. It would not be arbitrary and would fit into the perceived and felt continuity of personality. At the same time, however, what we remember is extremely contingent and not subject to any objective controlling authority, that is, memories do not have to bow to a subordinate context and are only subject to conscious mental influence to a limited extent. Memory is thus formed from an interplay of continuity construction and contingency.[190] Both are economically active components in

---

187 Yeats (1916), p. 172.
188 See also Luhmann (1975), pp. 39–50.
189 Cf. Cermak (2014), p. 277ff.
190 Ibid.

the economically active components—both have an economic function. The continuous integration of memories leads to the perception of a self, which makes transactional processes possible in the first place. Processes:[191] the contingency of memory in itself allows for an (inner) market system in the first place, as this introduces the possibility of reinterpretation and dynamics into the system.

At the same time, this leads to a paradox: memories constitute the momentary self in subjective continuity—but the permanent disruption of individual memories through reinterpretation, and reinterpretation means that no objective past can exist in the present; the "fluidity of the self" emerges.[192] This alternating field between dissolution and new formation in the present of the self leads to the economic dynamics already described and delimits the field of the essence core.[193]

The self can rather be seen as the situational interpretation of the given set of memories and mental processes of thought and cognition—in a metastable framework; the mind nevertheless requires the illusion of self-continuity in order to maintain its supposed integrity and sustain its inherence.[194]

As change can also be regarded as a constant, the ability to consciously change memories in a controlled manner becomes essential. This is how development and realization take place.[195] The same applies to the relationship between the essence core and the environment, which emphasizes the importance of social elements in memory and their high degree of interconnectedness.[196]

---

191 Ibid.
192 See Knoblauch (2019), p. 240f. and Priddat (2017), p. 7ff.
193 The essence core can be seen as the essential element that embodies the fundamental meaning or main thought of an individual. It is the core idea or central concept that underlies and can define the term. It is an abstract idea that is characterized by its flexibility and versatility, as it does not have a fixed outline but can change depending on context or interpretation.

An idea as a concrete element of the inner world is a concept or notion that exists in the mind of an individual. It can include thoughts, beliefs, dreams, or goals that influence an individual's thoughts and actions. In contrast to the essence, which represents the essence of a concept, an idea represents a specific notion or conception that is characterized by individual experiences, values and beliefs. However, despite its concreteness, an idea can also be fluid and change over time or through various influences.
194 In this context, it should be noted that even the physical self has no real continuity.
195 See Zauner (2018), p. 305f.
196 See Bovensiepen (2019), pp. 51–58.

When memory and its associated transactional processes (narration, imagination, will) are economically active components, their gain is the realization.[197] The fluidity of the ego ensures that the individual's relationship to themselves is never finally defined and can only be transformed through the ability to learn from the (self-constructed) past. Both must, therefore, play a central role in cognitive processes. (Self-)narration provides access to the past and is, therefore, a central human ability; language and cognition are, therefore, very closely linked. Language can be seen as an important universal tool for accessing narration and imagination and can be trained as a mediating carrier medium.[198]

As with all transactional processes, this leads to a mutual influence; narration has reality-modifying effects on the process of imagining itself; imagination also changes the perception of reality.[199] This has the following most important effects on the economization of the mental system:

- Events in the spirit system are not random and arbitrary but exclusively situation-related (whereby the initial situation or the acute event can be changed); they have an economically constitutive effect.[200]
- Even a wilful endeavor (more precisely, the action of will as an inner transactional process) to bring about change can bring about change. The transformation of the self is an autonomous function of the spirit system.[201]
- The mind system and its narratives and imaginations are part of the individual reality and can, therefore, also be actively influenced via the transactional processes.[202]

Influence and control over the transactional processes of the mind system change the mind itself and its patterns, which amounts to a real change in reality.

The further development of memories is, therefore, a central component of an economized mental system; memory and external reality often diverge

---

197 Cf. on the economic concept of profit Wegmann (1970), pp. 24–31.
198 See also Kempert/Schalk/Saalbach (2019), p. 179ff.
199 Cf. Achtziger et al. (2014), p. 55ff. and Kosslyn/Ganis/Thompson (2013), pp. 198–203.
200 See Potter (2005), p. 60f.
201 See Geimer (2012), p. 232f.
202 Cf. Storp (2009), pp. 33–40.

or merge into larger complexes.[203] In this context, the mind system resilience[204] is a further economically active resource (Table 2 provides an overview), which works antagonistically to the permanent reinterpretation of memory and dampens the fluidity of the ego.

Resilience processes change one's own perception of reality and, as a consequence, enable the concept of self-efficacy[205]—the subjective meaning of experiences defines how we deal with them and generates their meaning.

TABLE 2 Resilience as an economically active resource.

Designation	Functionality	Economically active aspects
Resilience[206]	Anticipation and immersion of transactional relationships between the inner and outer world.	• Resilience factors • Vulnerability factors • Imaginary and real parts
Memory/Imagination as part of the transactional mind system	Remembering itself is a newly created version of the past that no longer corresponds to external reality since memories evolve in contrast to the (assumed) external reality.	• Change processes generate defenses and fears • These are usually assigned an internal value that is too high
Resilience processes	Self-narration and its interpretation build up a specific, topic-related resilience, which can also be transferred into a general (summarized) resilience. These processes cascade (primarily) in the subconscious.[208]	• Language and personal narrative • Physical representation, e.g., via symbolic self-completion[207]

---

203 Cf. Bohleber (2004), p. 44f. and Bohleber (2007), pp. 298–306.
204 Resilience is derived directly from a high level of mental contingency; see Cyrulnik (2021), p. 140f.
205 See Henninger (2016), p. 159ff. and Ong/Bergeman/Bisconti/Wallace (2006), p. 734ff.
206 Ibid.
207 See also Cyrulnik (2009), pp. 22–25.
208 See Hoffmann (2020), pp. 36–38.

The Core of Being—Change, Fluidity of the Ego, Narration, and Cognition

The processualism of meaning attribution occupies a central position within the cognitive framework, as it plays a decisive role in the construction of a subject's individual reality and identity. This significant process is fundamental to the acquisition and processing of sensory impressions and their subsequent integration into an individual's cognitive schema. The attribution of meaning takes place via complex neurocognitive mechanisms,[209] which are based on both intrinsic cognitive processes and extrinsic environmental factors. Here, individual experiences, mental representations, and cultural influences interact with each other to form a subjective reality that acts as the basis for identity formation. The continuous creation of meaning enables the individual to shape their self-perception and social interactions and to locate themselves in their social environment.[210] In this sense, the attribution of meaning is an essential part of the cognitive process and contributes significantly to the construction of individual reality. Figure 6 concludes the basic economic spirit system.

Mental contingency is thus a constitutive, inter-mental act in which memories are transferred into a situational equilibrium via resilience and language as

FIGURE 6 Equilibrium of the fluid ego.[211]

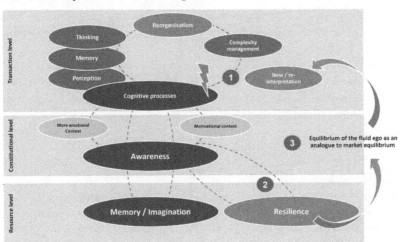

---

209 See McKenzie (2022), p. 125ff.
210 Ibid, pp. 126–132, p. 23.
211 Own presentation.

a mediating function.[212] The parallels with the economy make it possible to consciously influence the mental system in a further step.

The functions and techniques of narration, imagination, and suggestion

The observation of the economic and mental system accumulates at the constitutional level of consciousness; only here do subjective and intersubjective constructs such as value or emotion arise.[213] In this respect, narration, imagination, and suggestion[214] form the basic prerequisite for emotionality; most emotions (especially stressful ones such as fear, worry, etc.) result from these two mental transaction processes.[215]

These bring the individual past or future into the present, where emotion arises specifically from the comparison, either from a perceived abundance or lack or the unwillingness to adapt.[216] Strong emotionality rarely arises solely from the present; there is always an underlying (positive or negative) expectation or regret, both phenomena that have their origins in the past or future.[217]

The individual psychological approach to narration and imagination also determines the happiness or suffering felt in the present. The present, as such, does not offer nearly as many opportunities to favor a broad, deep spectrum of emotions; on the contrary, it is considered to be rather uneventful.[218] This circumstance has a number of implications for the economy of the mind system:

- The economic handling of the transaction mechanisms of the mind system can enhance the present through suitable narrative and imagination techniques; self-perception and self-reflection on one's own suffering and happiness, as well as the subsequent cognitive processes,

---

212 Cf. Stein (1996), p. 260ff.
213 Cf. Plutchik (1980), pp. 4–21 and Lazarus/Kanner/Folkman (1980), pp. 192ff.
214 Suggestion refers to the process by which an individual is encouraged to accept or adopt certain thoughts, feelings, or behaviors, often due to the influence of an external source. It is a form of influencing an individual's mental state or behavior through suggestions, instructions, or implications made directly or indirectly—which may well be self-reflexive.
215 Ibid.
216 Ibid.
217 Cf. Traue/Kessler (2003), p. 21ff.
218 Ibid.

are also favored. Self-reflection on one's own suffering and happiness and the subsequent cognitive processes are also favored.[219]
- Analytical meditations (to anticipate the effects of imagination and the inner evaluation of events) becomes a concrete depth-psychological instrument, as the present can be understood as the sublimation time of the self.[220]
- Mental resources such as resilience and the ability to adapt to or accept reality are enhanced and strengthened within the framework of one's own mental system.

Narrative and imagination techniques, in turn, act as mental mediation processes. There are five basic orientations for these processes. Table 3 provides an overview.

TABLE 3 The five basic types of intrapsychic narrative and imagination techniques.

Designation	Characteristics	Economically active aspects
Analytical narration	Learning and improvement-orientated approach to memory	• Fact-based • Transactional-weighing
Syntagmatic narration	Synthesis of individual narratives	• Formation of a common (emotional) syntax • Uncovering similarities • Networking
Paradigmatic narration	Individual memory with high subjective emotionality and its situational emotional evaluation	• Mental beacon of the individual narrative
Native, directed imagination	Subjective projection of potential, mostly general experience	• Low focus on benefits • Often, it only considers partial aspects
Synthetic, holistic imagination	Action- and decision-orientated imagination	• Neutral observation of reality • High potential for decision-making

---

219 See Brüllmann/Rombach/Wilde (2014), p. 8ff.
220 Cf. Flatscher (2010), p. 51ff.

First, the general interpretation of all mediation processes from the perspective of psychodynamic theories,[221] which already understand inner-psychic narration as an economic process. This broader perspective makes it possible to understand more effectively how mental resources are managed and how they affect an individual's behavior, emotionality, and (psychological) well-being.[222] Essentially, the following five economically active aspects have been established here:

1. **Energy allocation:** Psychodynamic models postulate that the psyche has limited energy at its disposal, which must be allocated to various mental processes. The inner mental narrative requires attention and cognitive resources that compete with other mental processes, such as problem-solving, emotion regulation, or perception. Therefore, the psyche must decide how much energy is allocated to inner narration and which other processes can be neglected.[223]
2. **Cost-benefit analysis:** Like economic decisions, the inner-psychic narrative often contains an implicit **cost-benefit analysis**.[224] The psyche evaluates the advantages and disadvantages, often in an "inner monologue." For example, ruminating on past events or imagining can be seen as useful for problem-solving or self-reflection, but it can also lead to mental resources being used inefficiently if they are used too excessively or destructively.
3. **Efficiency and self-regulation:** An efficient inner-psychic narrative enables effective self-regulation and adaptation to the environment. If these are productive, they can help to set goals, maintain motivation, and regulate emotions. However, inefficient narrative processes can lead to psychological complexes.
4. **Resource management:** Narrative processes require not only mental energy but also other resources such as time, mindfulness, and attention.[225] Everyone must decide when and how to utilize their inner

---

221 See also the concept in Kuhn (2016), p. 233ff.
222 This approach is also clearly reflected in other psychological reference systems, cf. for example, Dalai Lama (2002), pp. 122–129.
223 See Raab (2023), p. 304ff.
224 See Pfister/Jungermann/Fischer (2010), p. 187ff.
225 Mindfulness in the psychological context refers to conscious, focused and non-judgmental attention to the present experience of the (experiential) moment. This practice originates from the Buddhist tradition and has been adapted as a therapeutic technique in Western psychology. Mindfulness training includes various practices such as meditation,

thought processes based on their current needs and priorities. This requires meta-psychic management to ensure that resources are not wasted and the most important goals are achieved.[226]

5. **Investment and dividends:** As with economic investments, the inner-psychic narrative can yield long-term dividends. For example, investing time and energy in self-reflection and self-understanding can lead to better emotional well-being and personal growth in the long term.[227]

The most common type of narrative in terms of individual psychology is the *analytical narrative*. This is characterized by an objectifying approach to memory. It endeavors to focus on experienced facts. It is fact-based; remembering initially collects the most comprehensive facts possible for a specific narrative, and these are subsequently analyzed by the mental system and its transactional processes. And its transactional processes; cognition is based on the comparison of facts with the theoretically possible and the actually experienced options for action. In general, analytical narration enables a learning- and improvement-orientated approach to memory; insights can be gained, particularly when a lot of information from different perspectives is available about memory, and this can be completed and relived. The various sub-forms of analytical narration[228] are particularly helpful for learning purposes when experiencing content and retracing early decision-making patterns. The narrative is broken

---

breathing exercises and body awareness, which serve to increase awareness of the present moment and to draw attention away from stressful thoughts or emotions.

In psychological practice, mindfulness is often used as an intervention technique to reduce stress, anxiety, depression, and other psychological problems. Through mindfulness training, people learn to consciously focus on their present sensations, thoughts, and emotions without evaluating or judging them. This can help to achieve greater emotional regulation, improved stress managment, and increased life satisfaction.

Research suggests that regular mindfulness practice may be associated with a variety of psychological and physiological benefits, including a reduction in anxiety and depression, improved cognitive function, greater resilience to stress, and positive changes in brain structure and function.

See also Baer (2010), p. 45ff., Soucek et al. (2018), p. 130ff. and Hofmann/Sawyer/Witt/Oh (2010), p. 173f. and Yates (2015), p. 153ff. and pp. 473–477.

226 Ibid.
227 Cf. also Weil (1976). S. 387.
228 Cf. the methodology of narrative analysis (Biegoń/Nullmeier (2014): p. 43ff.)

down from the stream of experience into individual elements, which are analyzed in a pattern of interdependence (cause-effect principle) and from different perspectives.[229]

In contrast to this, the *syntagmatic narration* is orientated toward a connective approach to individual narratives; individual memories are organized along common thematic complexes and processed into a single narrative from various individual experiences based on commonalities in inner experience and memory.[230] Cognition is based here on the remembered commonality in action or thought; experiences are primarily connected along the emotional memory, and patterns in past actions and thoughts are clearly worked out (these can be consciously interpreted and recalled in the context of a syntagmatic narration). In this way, present situations can be seen (and revisited) in the mirror of a unified past. This type of narration connects different streams of memory via a common (emotional) syntax and thus binds memory regarding inner emotional experience; the cognitive effect lies in the commonalities of the individual strands of memory.[231]

Paradigmatic narration forms the conceptual antithesis of this. It is characterized by the detailed (individual) handling of memory and its orientation toward the inner experience in (formative) specific situations. Paradigmatic narration is based on individual memories with a high degree of subjective emotionality; remembering is orientated toward the situational emotional evaluation.[232] The knowledge gained from this is, in turn, based on the emotional density of the narratively processed and utilized experiences; this can contain a beacon character for the momentary experience. The situational specificity of past actions and thoughts is emphasized. The comparison between the current experience and the paradigmatic memory opens up new (non-objectified or objectifiable) options for action and thought.[233] The narration is based on the intensity of past experience and its momentary (emotional) significance; the narration is used as a "mental beacon."

---

229 Ibid.
230 Ibid.
231 Ibid., p. 122ff.
232 See Groeben/Christmann (2012), p. 310ff.
233 Ibid.

With future-directed narration (i.e., imagination techniques), the *native, directed imagination* is the primary type. This is a subjective projection of potential, mostly general experiences into the future, without taking into account specific framework conditions.[234] It is the most unspecific type of mental transaction.[235]

In contrast to this, the *synthetic, holistic imagination* is an action- and decision-orientated imagination.[236] It is an observation of reality that is as neutral as possible through a pre-assessed collection of facts, which are used to construct decision scenarios that can create a completely new framework for action. The decision and action parameters are then concretized; consciously allowing the built-up imagination to seep into the present leads to decision and action.[237] Imagining here is an anticipation of an expectable future in the present and, at the same time, functions as a reinforcement of the achievement of precisely this imaginative future.[238]

Through the sequencing of narration and imagination, the mental system is transformed into an order of transaction processes. Thoughts always have a clear temporal sequence; their simultaneity is excluded.[239] At the same time, these transaction processes also have a connecting effect with regard to the outer world; through them, external circumstances and the mental reactions of the mind system flow into the inner world.[240]

---

234 In psychology, the term "native, directed imagination" refers to a form of mental imagination that is consciously controlled and focused. In contrast to spontaneous or uncontrolled thoughts and images, native directed imagination is a focused mental activity in which a person intentionally creates or manipulates certain images, scenarios, or concepts in their mind. This type of imagination is often used in various therapeutic approaches such as cognitive behavioral therapy, imagination work, or trauma therapy. It can also play a role in creative processes such as art, writing or problem solving.
   See also Moulton/Kosslyn (2009), 1275f. and Holmes/Mathews (2010), p 350ff.
235 Cf. ibid.
236 See also Pearson/Deeprose/Wallace-Hadrill/Burnett Heyes/Holmes (2013), p. 4ff.
237 Ibid, p. 18f.
238 Ibid.
239 See also Schmidt (2003), p. 891.
240 Cf. Kellermann (1980), pp. 355–367.

These functions and techniques lead to the following consequences in dealing with memory:

- An "objective truth"[241] as such (in the sense of actual events in concrete physical reality[242]) does not exist in memory because memories are handled flexibly and are permanently and systematically reinterpreted and re-evaluated. Likewise, an objective experience is only possible at the moment, the present, in which narration and imagination take place (convergence of narration and imagination in the now[243]), but even here, it only plays a subordinate role, as remembering is not "calibrated" to this category.[244] Our own narration constitutes the past as a construct and can, therefore, change it incrementally and alter it through re-evaluation or reinterpretation. Therefore, there is no such thing as a collective, conscious past; it is fragmented into any number of subjective pasts that can change.[245]

---

241 The idea of objective truth in psychology is often caught between realism and constructivism. Realists argue that there is an external reality that exists independently of human perception and interpretation. This external reality can be captured by objective measurements and methods, and the task of psychology is to depict this reality as accurately as possible. On the other hand, constructivists argue that perception and interpretation are strongly influenced by individual experiences, cultural influences and social contexts. From this perspective, there is no objective reality that exists independently of human construction. Instead, knowledge and truth is shaped by social interactions and cultural narratives. In clinical psychology, this could mean that diagnoses and interventions can be based not only on objective indicators, but also on the subjective meaning that people attach to their experiences.

Cf. McNally (2005), p. 27ff. and Gergen (2009) on the idea of the social construction of knowledge and truth in psychology (and other social sciences).

242 However, whether physical reality actually exists is a philosophical-metaphysical question.

243 Claude Bernard already wrote about the natural mental limitations of man: "Notre esprit est, en effet, tellement borné, que nous ne pouvons connaître ni le commencement ni la fin des choses; mais nous pouvons saisir le milieu, c'est-à-dire ce qui nous entoure immédiatement." (Our mind is indeed so limited that we can know neither the beginning nor the end of things; but we can know the centre, i.e. what immediately surrounds us.); Bernard (1865), p. 63.

244 Cf. Casey (2000), p. 48ff. and p. 262ff.

245 In this regard, we should once again refer to the duality between being oneself and how one is seen from the outside. Every individual is situated in a certain context (existing place, time, network of possessions); this situation characterises the ability to imagine one's place in the world.

Cf. conceptually also Fouillée (1890), p. 124ff. and Sartre (1964), p. 87ff. as well as Schmidt (2000), p. 150ff. and p. 196ff.

- For the imagination of the future, this principle makes relatively simple sense to us; the social perception of the past is still characterized by a scientistic view of the world, which simply does not apply to our individual experience and memory.[246]

For the economy of the spirit system, this results in four fields of action:

- At the interface between individual memory and collective memory, the abstract idea of possession, as well as that of property, arises; the individual mental system works toward the preservation of the current status quo.[247]
- Both narration and imagination lead to a series of drafts of the self. Because of this multiplicity, action itself can become a problem since the mind system is more focused on one's own resource management. One's own actions are the central means of self-development and the ultimate connection to the external world. All designs of the economic self[248] require other people (and therefore other spirit systems) for their successful realization.[249]

---

246 Intentions play a central role in economic intentionality, as they function as concretized imaginations and represent products of economic will formation. The will acts as a mediating force between the imaginative ideas and the intentions to act, which have a forward-looking orientation.

The connection between imagination and intention is of particular interest, as imaginations are often regarded as precursors to intentions. Individuals can imagine certain actions and then translate these imaginations into concrete intentions. This link demonstrates the close relationship between mental representations and goal-directed behavior. An essential characteristic of intentions is their future-oriented element. They are orientated toward events or states that have not yet occurred and guide actions with the aim of bringing about or avoiding these states. Intentions act as concretizing functions that make it possible to transform vague ideas and wishes into specific goals and action plans. In addition, intentions have a will-forming dimension in that they mobilise and channel the will of the individual. They influence the selection and organisation of options for action and make it possible to use one's own resources and abilities in a targeted manner in order to achieve the desired goals.

Cf. in detail, Husserl et al. (1980), p. 24ff and Husserl et al. (2004), p. 105ff.
247 Cf. Husserl et al. (1968), p. 65ff.
248 The economic self is both an empirical concept and a therapeutic postulate; it is the unity and wholeness of all psycho-economic phenomena in a person as an overall personality. See Helsper (2013), pp. 23–114.
249 Ibid.

- A dualism arises between imaginary experiences and lived experiences. For the transaction processes themselves, there is only a downstream difference; both are ultimately equivalent to the constitution process of consciousness and cognition. Ultimately, of equal value. It follows that both categories of experience have an economic value.[250]
- The transactional character makes it clear that consciousness is to be understood as a phenomenal, mental awareness of individuality.[251] This view, therefore, forms a basis for economic thinking, experience, and action; without the psycho-economic translation in the mental system of narration, these phenomena could not be transferred to the external world.[252]

Thus, the internal concept of economy can also be understood as an archetype, that is, part of the collective unconscious, and represents a fundamental, mediating, transactional function of the mental system. The outlined internal and external perspectives of the respective transaction processes form two essential access routes to economic consciousness, each of which encompasses different aspects of perception and experience. The internal perspective refers to the direct, non-symbolic experience of consciousness, which is often referred to as intuition.[253] This type of perception manifests itself as the direct experience of sensations, emotions, and thoughts without intermediary cognitive processes. In contrast to this is the external perspective, which focuses on the symbolic description of consciousness by the intellect. Here, the experienced phenomena are translated into cognitive concepts and language in order to understand and communicate them. This symbolic representation makes it possible to analyze, interpret, and share experiences with others.[254]

The realization of economic reality thus takes place on both levels, with the internal perspective offering an immediate and intuitive experience, while the external perspective enables a structured and reflective approach.

---

250 Cf. Bürmann (1997), pp. 193–196.
251 This definition of consciousness includes the perception of mental stimuli (phenomenal), the experience of thoughts as memories, expectations, etc. as well as the meta-consciousness of precisely these individual phenomenal and mental processes in differentiation from other living beings.
   See Westerkamp (2023), p. 181ff. and Hansch (2013), p. 153ff.
252 In addition, every experience with high emotional or intellectual content changes the physical structure of the brain itself, cf. ibid.
253 Cf. DePaul/Ramsey (1998), p. 45ff. and Berne (2005), p. 33ff. and 191–199.
254 Ibid.

Both approaches complement each other and contribute to a comprehensive understanding of economic awareness.

The phenomenon of remembering (borne by narration and imagination) represents a complex cognitive, economically active process that goes far beyond the mere recapitulation of past events. Rather, it is a continuous reconstruction of the past in which memories are actively reconstructed and interpreted.[255] During this process, certain aspects are emphasized while others fade out or are distorted. This selective reconstruction can lead to contradictions and distortions that shape the individual memory image—this is precisely where the economization of the mind system comes into play, as it makes these transaction and translation processes easier to grasp in terms of individual psychology. This is precisely where the economization of the mental system comes into play, as it makes these transactional and translational processes more comprehensible from an individual psychology perspective and reveals more comprehensive, neutral points of influence—the individual functions as a kind of "meaning machine," which endeavors to assign metamorphic, transitive meanings to past events and embed them in a coherent narrative framework. This meaning-making process serves to shape the self-image and identity of the individual[256] and, as shown, is in its nature subject to economic principles.

The Three Key Messages

1. **Reconstructive nature of memories:** Memories are actively reconstructed and interpreted, whereby certain aspects are emphasized, and others are suppressed or distorted. This continuous process of reconstruction can lead to contradictions and distortions that characterize the individual memory.
2. **Economization of the mental system:** The economization of the mental system enables better recording and influencing of these reconstructive processes. The mind system functions as a "meaning machine" that endeavors to assign meanings to past events and embed them in a coherent narrative framework to shape and consolidate the individual's self-image and identity.

(Continued)

---

255 See Pilard (2018), p. 68f.
256 Cf. Lucius-Hoene (2000), Art. 18 (above).

3. **Transactional processes and their effects:** The transactional processes of narration, imagination, and suggestion play a central role in the reconstruction of memories and the shaping of the individual self. They enable an active engagement with the past and the future, whereby different techniques and orientations have different effects on individual experience and behavior.

Excursus: The Mental Spirit System in Detail

'Nothing' denotes the absence of what we seek, what we desire, what we expect. If one actually assumed that experience ever offered us an absolute emptiness, it would be limited, have outlined, i.e., still be something.[257]

The highest knowledge does away with knowledge; highest love forgets to love. The highest virtue is not virtue.[258]

The following description of the mind system goes into much greater depth with regard to the model of consciousness and the generation of experience and memory. It is astonishing that the *model of the moments of consciousness* is ultimately based on ancient texts[259] but can nevertheless be harmonized extremely well with the latest neurobiological findings.[260]

I am deliberately presenting this model in a separate excursus, as it contains a whole series of logics based on spiritual principles (which is probably quite good for something called "spirit system," which is presumably also quite good) and thus ventures strongly into the realm of meta-psychology. Nonetheless, I find the model of moments of consciousness extremely helpful in understanding the complexity and workings of our mind as fully as possible. At the same time, it is based on individually tangible mental reality, which we can become aware of even without the theoretical superstructure. For these reasons, I have decided to include this model, as it significantly influences the approach to the inner economy presented in this book and (in its formalism) has significantly influenced it.

---

257 Bergson (1948), p. 116.
258 Lü Bu We (1928), p. 296.
259 The so-called "complete picture of consciousness and mind" is anchored in the Abhidhamma of the Buddhist Theravada tradition and the Yogacara philosophy.
260 The following presentation is based in part on the presentation in Yates (2015).

In the beginning, there is the illusion of a continuous flow of experiences—be it thoughts or sensations—as we experience them every day. On closer observation, it becomes clear that these are individual moments of consciousness that occur one after the other. These conscious "mind moments" are so short and numerous that they only appear to form a continuous and uninterrupted stream of consciousness.[261]

Consciousness is thus made up of a series of separate events and is therefore not continuous, as only one piece of information coming from one sensory organ can be conscious at any one time. Each moment represents a separate mental event with unique content, and no two experiences can occur at the same time. It can occur simultaneously[262]; the high speed of the mental system merely creates the impression of simultaneity.[263] No change takes place within individual moments; they are static. Thus, every conscious experience consists of brief moments with a single piece of static information. Each mind moment is only a single and unique object of consciousness, comparable to pearls of a particular "color," depending on the type of sensory impression, and accompanied by a series of moment-specific mental factors and information.[264]

There are seven types of moments in total: *Five senses* (sight, hearing, smell, taste, touch), the *sense of mind* (for mental objects such as thoughts and emotions), and the *attachment consciousness*, which integrates the information provided by the other senses as a whole.

The somatic sense—particularly complex—is made up of many individual senses, including touch, pressure, vibration, temperature, pain, proprioception, the sense of acceleration, rotation, balance, and gravity, as well as visceral sensations.[265] Similarly, the sense of mind is a complex system consisting of a variety of mental processes, such as memories, emotions, and abstract thoughts.[266] Thus, no two pieces of information from somatosensory categories or moments of mind can share the same moment of consciousness, which means that there are far more than five types of senses.

The same applies to the spiritual sense, which also forms its own complex system from a multitude of mental processes that share the same moment

---

261 See Yates (2015), p. 192f.
262 For example, a moment of visual consciousness must be completed in order to enable a moment of spiritual consciousness (about what happened before).
263 See VanRullen/Koch (2003), pp. 207–210.
264 Ibid.
265 See Yates (2015), pp. 226–228.
266 Ibid.

of consciousness and can, therefore, only enter consciousness singularly as a spiritual moment. as a moment of mind.

The integration of the individual, self-contained moments of consciousness takes place in a kind of working memory of the mind, in which the combining binding consciousness brings these moments together and projects the product of this integration into consciousness. This combining binding consciousness moment represents an independent type of mind moment and serves to create integrated, situational perceptions that bring together information from the six senses and give them a complex overall context of perception and thinking focused on one moment.

Every conscious experience is filtered either through *attention* or *awareness*,[267] which are two different ways of perceiving and recognizing the world. All conscious experiences consist of seven types of mind moments, each of which can take the form of either an attention moment or an awareness moment. In particular, the moment of peripheral awareness is holistic, comprehensive, and inclusive[268]; it perceives many objects simultaneously and requires little mental processing. In contrast, a moment of attention isolates certain aspects of the experience for analysis and interpretation, perceiving only a few objects at a time and requiring thorough mental processing.

---

267 Awareness is defined in scientific psychology as a state of conscious experience in which a person is aware of present experiences, thoughts, feelings, and sensory impressions without judgment or reaction. It is a comprehensive, nondiscriminatory awareness that focuses on the present moment and simultaneously registers a wide range of internal and external stimuli.

Some essential aspects of awareness include:

Non-judgmental perception: Awareness is characterized by an open and accepting attitude toward all thoughts, feelings and sensory impressions that arise, without judging or analyzing them.

Present focus: It refers to the conscious experience of the present moment, with attention focussed on the here and now rather than on past events or future expectations.

Vastness and inclusivity: Awareness encompasses a holistic perception in which a multitude of stimuli are perceived simultaneously and in their entirety, in contrast to focused attention, which concentrates on individual aspects.

Increased mindfulness: It involves a high level of mindfulness in which individuals are aware of their surroundings and their inner states, which is often promoted through mindfulness training or meditation.

Reduced cognitive processing: Awareness requires less-intensive cognitive processing compared to focused attention, as it is more about passive experiencing than active analyzing or reacting.

268 See Schmidt (2019), p. 104ff.

These moments of mind organize subjective reality in its entirety by filtering and conceptualizing different types of perceptions.[269] Attachment moments, which are associated with either attention or awareness, organize these sensory impressions into a coherent experience of the present. Sensory impressions are often already conceptualized in peripheral awareness, and these concepts are then further analyzed and interpreted in moments of attention. In these moments of attention, it is no longer the sensory impressions themselves that are further elaborated but the concepts that have arisen from them. Moments of attention thus generate more complex concepts that are constructed and further developed from the simpler concepts of peripheral awareness. Moments of awareness tend to originate more frequently from the physical senses, while moments of attention come more frequently from the mental sense and are more strongly oriented toward conceptualizing and condensing various concepts. The mental processing of these conceptual formations is more intensive here.[270]

In psychological and neuroscientific research, the term "non-perceptual moments of mind" is used to describe potential, non-actual moments of consciousness. These moments are real mental events, but they do not involve perception as they are not supplied with information or content by the sensory organs. Although they do not process external stimuli, they replace perceptual moments of consciousness and are often associated with a pleasant feeling. These non-perceptual moments of mind are interspersed in the continuous sequence of moments of consciousness.[271]

Each moment of consciousness is endowed with a certain type of mental potential (or energy). However, non-perceptual moments of consciousness contain less energy, resulting in a state known as dullness. The energy level of the mind depends anti-proportionally on the number of non-perceptual moments of consciousness.

---

[269] For example, moments of auditory attention are used to filter the sound of a voice, while moments of peripheral awareness allow the multitude of background noises to enter consciousness.

[270] Mindfulness training helps to develop introspective awareness. This means that the moments of peripheral awareness of mental activities and objects are increased, and moments of attention are also increasingly focused on sensory impressions. Through such training, individuals can learn to better organize their conscious experiences and gain a deeper insight into the workings of their mind.

[271] See Yates (2015), p. 199f.

Perception itself is regarded as a passive momentum of moments of consciousness, while (conscious) intention is regarded as an active momentum. Intention unconsciously determines the objects of subsequent moments of consciousness and is a component of all perceptual moments. The awareness of this intention is usually subliminal unless the intention is explicitly made the object of a moment of consciousness. The intention also influences the number of perceptual moments of consciousness.[272] Non-perceiving moments of consciousness have no intention and are, therefore, non-intentional moments of consciousness.[273] Scientific research into these phenomena shows that the balance between perceptual and non-perceptual moments of consciousness and the role of intention are essential factors for the energy level and clarity of the entire mind system.

The model of the mind system based on the moments of consciousness does not describe the mind as a single entity but as a complex network of numerous, highly interconnected, and interdependent processes with specific functions. These processes are individual, and each has specific functions as well as autonomous sub-hierarchies that form the entire mind system. The model divides the mind into two main components: the conscious mind and the unconscious mind.[274]

The *conscious mind*, also known as consciousness, is the part of the mind system that can be experienced directly. This means that the content that we consciously perceive is projected directly into our consciousness.[275] These contents comprise the seven moments of consciousness, which are made up of the six categories of sensory experience (visual, auditory, olfactory, gustatory,

---

272 The assumed empirical figures for the number of moments of consciousness range from 14 to 70 units per second. See also Norretranders (1997) and Lutz/Greischar/Rawlings/Ricard/Davidson (2004), p. 16370ff.

273 All truth values in everyday life are therefore degrees of various stable subtle dullness. In meditation, where only a few stimuli and thoughts are allowed, the increased number of non-perceiving, non-intentional moments lead to a progressive subtle dullness that can develop into strong dullness.

274 The mind is aptly described as a collection of many thousands of highly networked but individual processes which all have a specific function and run in parallel. The individual processes are linked together in an increasingly complex hierarchical order.
Cf. Minsky et al. (1985), p. 35ff.

275 Conscious awareness is not to be equated with awareness in the general sense or with consciousness the conscious mind usually forms the subconscious awareness. This includes processes and objects that an individual does not perceive at the level of subjective experience but would be perfectly capable of doing so.

somatosensory, and mental) and the moments of attachment. These seven moments of consciousness represent the entire conscious mind. The experience of these moments is passive, while intention functions as the active component. These intentions can be subliminal or become the object of attention themselves and serve as precursors to mental, verbal, or physical actions, such as conscious intentions and directed attention. Thus, all moments of consciousness contain intentions.[276]

The *unconscious mind* is not directly accessible but can only be experienced indirectly through inferences or conclusions. It consists of many subgroups and can be further subdivided into the sensory mind and the discriminating mind.

The *sensory mind* processes the information coming from the five physical senses and creates moments of seeing, hearing, and other sensory experiences.

The *discriminating mind*, on the other hand, is the largest component of the thinking and emotional mind. It generates moments of consciousness with mental objects such as thoughts, emotions, logical thinking, and analysis.[277]

There is a constant transactional exchange of information between the conscious and unconscious mind. The conscious mind is fed by the mind's sense of objects, such as memories and ideas, and the intentions they contain. For example, we can consciously think back to something, whereby these memories and ideas enter our consciousness via the sense of mind. To summarize, the model of the mind system shows a dynamic interaction between the different parts of the mind, whereby the conscious mind is only a small part of the overall mind system. The unconscious mind system is dominant in many aspects, controlling basic sensory and cognitive processes and thus forming the foundation for the conscious and actions.

The human mind must, therefore, be seen as a highly complex system made up of numerous autonomous subgroups that act simultaneously, and each fulfills specific tasks for the overall system as a whole. These subgroups can be roughly divided into the sensory mind and the discriminating mind, whereby both fulfill different but complementary functions.

The *sensory mind* comprises several subgroups, each of which deals with its own sensory field, such as the visual or auditory mind.[278] Each of these subgroups deals exclusively with the corresponding sensory phenomena, forming specific

---

276 See Yates (2015), p. 239f.

277 Differentiation means that concepts and symbolic representations are used integratively in order to be able to differentiate.

278 A percept is basic sensory information from which perceptions and concepts are formed. Percepts are usually composed of a variety of sensory impressions.

cognitive domains. Within these domains, the raw information from the senses is processed into "percepts," which are the mental representations of the stimuli. This basic sensory information is recognized, categorized, analyzed, and evaluated before it is passed on to the conscious mind. The percepts are actively organized and interpreted in the sensory mind before being projected into the peripheral awareness as aggregated percept constructs.

From there, they can become the object of a moment of attention, although most percept constructs remain in an unconscious awareness. In addition, each sensory subgroup generates a feeling (pleasant, unpleasant, neutral) with each percept and anchors reflex reactions. The end products of this process are, therefore, percepts, the associated feelings, and automatic responses that are provided as input to the discriminating mind.

The *discriminating mind* integrates the percepts and percept constructs into complex mental images, which are called *perceptions*.[279] Perception is a complex, unconscious process that involves both top-down effects of remembering and expecting as well as bottom-up processing of sensory inputs.[280] This transforms the inputs into specific conceptual objects.

However, the discriminating mind also creates purely conceptual images such as thoughts, ideas, and feelings without direct sensory input, which accounts for a large part of its function as a thinking and emotional mind. The discriminating mind also consists of many specific subgroups that work autonomously and only select, analyze, and project back the information relevant to their specific task from the stream of consciousness. Each subgroup develops its own constantly evolving model of reality. In addition, each subgroup generates feelings of pleasure or displeasure as a reaction to the information processing, which in turn can trigger desire or aversion. This process can only be avoided through equanimity and insight if no craving arises and no attachment occurs.[281]

> To summarize, the human mind is a dynamic, multilayered system in which the sensory and discriminative minds interact closely. These subgroups work together autonomously and simultaneously to produce a coherent and functional mental experience.

---

279 Cf. Euler (2004), p. 14ff.
280 Thus perception is is the process that organizes and interprets perceptions. As a complex function of the discriminating mind, it is completely outside of consciousness and therefore works completely effortlessly.
281 See Germer/Siegel (2014), p. 23ff.

In the psychological model of an individual's mental structure, the individual subgroups of the mind result in different intentions, which in turn result in physical, linguistic, and mental actions. These intentions often lead to inner conflicts, as the various subgroups that make up the differentiating mind pursue their own emotions and goals. Each subgroup strives to make the overall system—the self—happy, but each has a different idea of how to achieve this goal.[282] The spirit system itself has a structurally dysfunctional organization.

Within this differentiating mind, there is a hierarchical order of subgroups. Personal values and self-image often dominate other subgroups and significantly influence the decisions and actions of the overall system. The activities of the subgroups determine how sensations, thoughts, and emotions are perceived and direct the individual's attention through their respective intentions, which can sometimes be stronger and sometimes weaker.

In this model, the conscious mind acts as the central interface for the communicative interaction and cooperation of the unconscious subgroups. It serves as a universal receiver of information and processes a continuous stream of moments of consciousness, the content of which originates from the unconscious subgroups and is projected into the conscious mind. This projected information is made available to all subgroups, resulting in constant interaction via the conscious mind.[283]

The *conscious mind* can be seen as the "supreme discussion body" of the spiritual hierarchy, a passive space of discussion and decision. Although it does not perform any active actions itself, it is essential for the central interface of interaction. Everything that appears in consciousness originates from the unconscious mind, which makes the conscious mind a crucial platform for the communication and integration of information.[284]

The *executive functions* of the mind are crucial in certain situations, especially when higher cognitive tasks that go beyond pre-programmed behavior are required. These higher-level, semi-collective mental functions include regulating, organizing, inhibiting, planning, and correcting actions, as well as problem-solving. They are particularly necessary for novel or complex situations in which conditioned behavior is not sufficient. The executive functions coordinate the activities of the subgroups, communicate information, differentiate between contradictions, decide on conflicting intentions, and integrate new information.

---

282 See Yates (2015), p. 225ff.
283 Ibid, p. 224.
284 Ibid.

They program new behavioral patterns into individual subgroups, which can lead to automatic behavior. These executive functions are the result of the collective performance of many subgroups acting in a cooperative and consensus-oriented manner and not the work of a single subgroup. The simultaneous access to information in consciousness enables this coordinated performance.[285]

Information projected into consciousness by the sensory subgroups includes percepts, percept constructs, feelings of pleasure or discomfort, and intentions that originate from the sensory subgroups. Perceptions, concepts, thoughts, ideas, mental states, emotions, and intentions, on the other hand, are projected by the differentiating subgroups. Each of this information is made accessible in a different mental unit, whereby all information is available simultaneously.

On an individual level, the subgroups can react differently to this information. They can modify their own information, project new information, and activate their own reaction programs. However, they can also participate in executive functions in the collective and develop new actions or concepts with other subgroups. In this way, common conscious intentions emerge that guide the individual's behavior and decision-making processes.

On a collective level, the subgroups of the mental system use the information projected into the consciousness to interact with each other and thus jointly generate and execute the executive functions; they map the entire process of these functions. These subgroups jointly modify existing response programs or create completely new automatic, unconscious behaviors.[286]

Information can either enter the consciousness or into peripheral awareness and be projected. Intentions play a central role here, as they guide everything we feel, do, and say. They determine our paths of action and decisions and can be both conscious and unconscious. All intentions arise in the subgroups of the unconscious and only become conscious when they are projected into the conscious mind.

In consciousness, different subgroups can then either support or oppose a specific intention before taking action. An action that arises from a conscious intention (top-down process) requires an upstream consensus of subgroups. In contrast, actions arising from unconscious intentions are automatic; we only become aware of these actions after they have already been initiated (bottom-up process). These unconscious actions often have their origin in a single subgroup of the unconscious.

---

285 Ibid, p. 234ff.
286 Ibid.

This dynamic interaction between conscious and unconscious processes shows how complex the control of human behavior is and how close cooperation between different subgroups of the brain is necessary for the execution of actions; this interplay between conscious and unconscious intentions is a central aspect of transactional decision-making and action processes. These findings emphasize the importance of neuronal networks and their interactions for understanding cognition and behavior.[287] Within this complex system, certain objects or even entire sensory fields can be marked as particularly important, which influences attention and prioritization.

In the individual mind system, decisions are made by consensus among unconscious mind groups.[288] Conflicting intentions initially lead to internal conflicts in which the participating subgroups present their arguments until a consensus is reached. This process is similar to voting, with each subgroup contributing its perspective. The *decision-making process*, which is ultimately controlled by the executive functions, can be seen as a form of group decision-making. Conscious decisions and deliberate actions are, therefore, the results of a collective decision-making process at an unconscious level.

Decision-making processes are often open, which means that the inner, unconscious discussion can continue even after the decision has been made. Actions can, therefore, be interrupted or changed. Every decision and action results from the interaction of the entire mental system. The input of certain sub-groups is particularly relevant; if some of them do not contribute to the decision-making process, the quality of the decision decreases. The best decisions involve the whole mind system, which emphasizes the value of increased mindfulness. By avoiding rash decisions, more subgroups are given time to participate in the decision-making process, which improves the quality of decisions. This demonstrates the positive effect of indecision and conflicting tendencies, as mindful observation of mental processes allows new information to emerge in the subgroups.[289] Figure 7 illustrates the connection between the different levels of consciousness.

Every inner conflict must be decided as soon as it becomes conscious. Subjectively, this is experienced as a conscious decision of the self, which leads to a conscious act of attention and action. Yet this decision is actually the result of a collective decision of the majority of mind groups on an

---

[287] See Ryba (2018), p. 109ff.
[288] Cf. Jung (1954), pp. 30–31 and Freud (1946), pp. 264ff. and Kahneman (2011), pp. 20–22.
[289] Cf. Damasio (1994), pp. 165–167.

FIGURE 7 The connection between different levels of consciousness.[290]

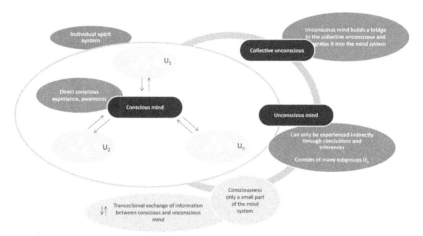

unconscious level, indicating deterministic behavior. Prolonged action requires sustained, uninterrupted consensus, which emphasizes the notion of the non-self and the human being as an open, dynamic system in which actions are not predetermined. To establish consensus more effectively, the subgroups train through executive processes.[291]

The *transactional exchange of information* in consciousness and its feedback leads to learning processes in the subgroups involved. The human mind can thus radically change its own programming; self-modification of behavior is possible to any extent, right down to subtle mental and physical reactions. Subgroups of the unconscious mind are guided in their learning process by conscious intention. These subgroups are highly receptive to conscious intention and unite for thoughts with strong intention. A common strong intention has a significant programming effect on the individual subgroups.[292]

Acting out of a *strong intention* is evaluated positively or negatively by the thinking and emotional mind, depending on the outcome, which leads to a feeling of well-being or unhappiness as an emotional reaction that is projected into consciousness. This feedback strengthens or weakens the activities or intentions of the subgroups and thus influences the probability of future action. Conscious action with a repeated conscious intention leads to automatic action,

---

290 Own presentation.
291 See Yates (2015), p. 234ff.
292 Ibid.

creating habits that no longer require conscious intentions. Preprogrammed responses are faster and more effective than conscious action, which underlines their adaptability and efficiency in human behavior.[293]

Every new ability and every new action result from the complex interactions of the entire mental system in the execution of executive functions. Within this system, different subgroups act collectively in consciousness during the learning process to generate new programs that are integrated into the individual subgroups. Repetition creates automatic activity that leads to the efficient execution of the learned skills.

A special role within this process is played by the *narrating mind*, a subgroup of the discriminating mind, which has a special meaning and an essential function in the mind system.[294] The narrating mind takes all the information projected by the other subgroups, combines, organizes, and integrates it into a meaningful, holistic compilation. This activity creates a special mind moment, a *bonding mind moment*, which is a subtle but essential component of the mind system.

The narrating mind weaves the content of the conscious mind into episodes in a continuous story, each episode being projected back into the conscious mind as a binding moment of consciousness. This creates a continuous chronicle of the ongoing conscious activities of the mind that is accessible to the entire mind system.

During all activities of attention, a chronology of experiences is created by the narrating mind, which provides a coherent description of our environment and ourselves. This chronology is made up of different episodes—similar to an edited film—and projected back. The narrating mind provides the causal link in which sensory information, cognition, and feeling become one. The *I* is created by the narrating mind as its narrative construct. It serves as the *organizing and structural principle* of the memories and experiences in the mental system. Our self-concept is, therefore, our own narrative "I"; analogously, the "it" is such a construct that represents the other persons and objects in our environment.[295]

In truth, however, we never have direct experiences that correspond to the "I" or "it"; they are merely images and emotions that arise in our consciousness. It is only the narrating mind that gives these constructs of order an apparent, purely fictional (i.e., narrative) reality. The fictitious "I" of the narrating mind

---

293 Ibid.
294 Ibid, p. 526.
295 Cf. Heiner (2008), p. 292f. and Kraus (2000), p. 56ff.

becomes the ego-self of the discriminating mind, while the "it" is seen as the cause of the emotions that arise. This fundamental misperception of the "I" leads to intentions that evolve into desire or aversion.[296]

The sequence of causally linked episodes is expanded to include a "fictitious I": "I" wanted "it" […]." The discriminating mind processes this stored information as the output of the narrating mind and uses it to develop the story of the ego-self and a description of the external world, a cyclical reinforcement of the ego-self. Reference to these complex constructs triggers craving, aversion, and emotional responses aimed at protecting and promoting the well-being of the ego-self.[297]

The narrating mind takes up this process again and weaves it into a new story. This creates a cyclical process that leads to the reinforcement of the ego-self. Contents of the conscious mind are, therefore, always only mental constructs, sensations that arise from the information processing of the subgroups, just like feelings, thoughts, and emotions. The "self" and the "world" also consist entirely of such mental constructs. The intuitive feeling that these are real results from a misinterpretation of the discriminating mind, which misinterprets the output of the narrating mind.[298]

Desire and aversion are also mental constructs designed to stimulate "self-oriented behavior; the resulting intentions and outcomes also depend on how the mind system. This creates a self-reinforcing cycle of perception and reaction that characterizes subjective experience and interaction with the world.[299]

The transactional nature of the mind system and its economy offers a profound understanding of how our consciousness and our sense of self arise and function. The mind system can be viewed as a dynamic network in which constant interactions and transactions take place between different subgroups of the brain. These transactions are the basis for the emergence of consciousness and the experience of the sense of self.

Each of these subgroups contributes specific information and functions to the spirit system. This information is continuously exchanged and re-evaluated, whereby a collective consensus is sought. The decisions and actions attributed to the ego are, therefore, the result of complex negotiations and agreements between these unconscious subgroups. This network operates according to a kind of economic principle in which mental resources such as attention,

---

296 See Weber (2017), p. 14f.
297 See McDowell (2023), pp. 440–453.
298 See Yates (2015), p. 234ff.
299 Ibid.

memory, and cognitive capacities are distributed and utilized to make the best possible decisions.

The *transactional nature* of the mental system is reflected in the way in which information is processed and integrated. Every mental activity, be it a thought, an emotion, or an idea, arises from the exchange of signals and information between the subgroups. These processes are not isolated but take place in a constant flow and interplay, resulting in a dynamic and self-organizing structure.[300]

From an economic point of view, this means that the mind system constantly weighs up on which information and activities should be prioritized. This is done to utilize the limited cognitive resources efficiently and ensure the functionality of the entire system.

These transactions and the resulting economy of the mind system allow us to experience a coherent and continuous sense of self, even though our mind is made up of many different, often competing subgroups. The sense of self is thus a kind of emergent property of the mind system that arises from the collective and coordinated activities of these subgroups. Figure 8 provides an overview of the spirit system.

It is precisely the transactional character of the mind system, and the economy based on it illustrates how our consciousness and our sense of self are created through a complex interplay and constant exchange within the mental system. These processes are designed to maximize the efficiency and effectiveness of the mind system to cope with the demands of life and maintain a coherent sense of self-perception.[301]

At this point, it should also be pointed out that a mind system recognized and understood in this way, of course, represents both a starting point and an end point of an individual mental economy—since the concept of a self basically begins to dissolve and merges into a meta-concept between the individual and the (broadly understood) collective. Since the concept of economy requires the individual concept of value, it leads to an absurdum if there is no longer a self in the end. Ultimately, there is a philosophical, spiritual question behind this that lies beyond psychology and economics.

---

300 See Yates (2015), p. 232ff.
301 Ibid, pp. 250–258.

THE MIND ECONOMY

FIGURE 8 Overall visualization of the spirit system.[302]

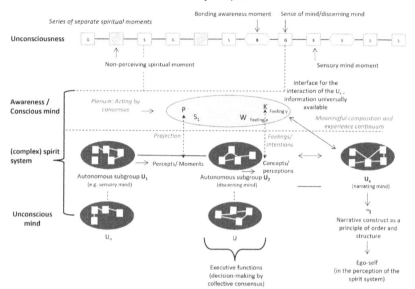

Excursus: The Five Key Messages in Brief

1. **Model of the moments of consciousness:** The model is based on the idea that consciousness consists of individual, very short, and static moments of consciousness that run one after the other and thus create the impression of a continuous stream. Each of these moments is associated with specific content from one of the seven senses (visual, auditory, olfactory, gustatory, somatosensory, mental, and binding).
2. **Conscious and unconscious mind:** The mind system is divided into the conscious mind, which can be experienced directly, and the unconscious mind, which can be accessed indirectly through inferences. The unconscious mind processes sensory and cognitive information, while the conscious mind integrates and processes this information.
3. **Interaction and integration:** Moments of consciousness are brought together in attachment consciousness to create a coherent

(*Continued*)

---

302 Own presentation.

and functional mental experience. The conscious mind serves as an interface that receives and processes information from the unconscious subgroups, resulting in a continuous exchange of information and constant adaptation.
4. **Executive functions:** These are responsible for regulating, organizing, and planning actions as well as solving problems. They coordinate the activities of the subgroups of the mind, which is particularly important in novel or complex situations where pre-programmed behavior is not sufficient.
5. **The narrative mind:** A special subgroup that integrates all projected information into a coherent story. This leads to a continuous chronicle of conscious activity that creates the self-concept and ego-consciousness by causally linking sensory information, cognition, and feeling.

CHAPTER 3

WORKING WITH THE SPIRIT SYSTEM—TRANSFORMATIVE PROCESSES

> Recognising external objects is a contradiction; it is impossible for man to go outside himself. We cannot actually recognize anything in the world except ourselves and the changes that take place within us. In the same way, we cannot possibly feel for others; as the saying goes, we only feel for ourselves. The sentence sounds harsh, but it is not if it is understood correctly. We love neither father nor mother nor wife nor child, but the pleasant sensations they give us always flatters our pride and our self-love. [...][303]

The study of the extended mind system is central to understanding the complex interaction between individual consciousness and the surrounding world.

While traditional approaches often limit the mind to the brain and its neuronal activities, specific aspects of the extended mind system open up a broader view of the role of environment, culture, and social relationships in shaping human experience. Social relationships shape human experiences and actions.

Thus, a complementary point in consideration of the economized mental system is the realization that mental processes do not only take place in the brain but are also shaped by interaction with the environment and other people. This approach is in the tradition of the philosophy of externalism,[304] which

---

303 Lichtenberg (2017), p. 200 [H 151].
304 Another aspect of externalism is the idea of extended cognition, which states that the mind is not limited to the brain as an isolated unit, but extends across the body and the environment. This means that mental processes often take place in close interaction with the environment and can be supported by external resources and structures. At the same

emphasizes that mental states and processes can also be influenced and shaped by external factors. Specific aspects of the extended mind system include various phenomena that show how individual mental states and abilities can be enhanced by external artifacts, psychosocial practices, and cultural contexts.

But there are also forms of narration when looking inward and imagination, which are particularly efficient in terms of conscious interaction with one's own mental system (or its own interaction with its subprocesses). These forms act as transformative and even transcendental processes that can lead an individual to a more conscious use of mental resources. Narratives within the self are not purely external narratives but internal constructions of meaning and sense. They help organize experiences, shape identity, form identity, and develop personal life stories. By consciously shaping these inner narratives, an individual can influence their self-perception and behavior.[305]

Imagination also plays a decisive role in inner exploration and transformation. Through the ability to visualize the past, present, and future and their respective interpretations, an individual can explore new possibilities and create alternative realities. This imaginative process makes it possible to free oneself from limiting beliefs and find creative solutions to personal challenges. The conscious application of narration and imagination holds considerable potential for profound change and further development of the individual mind system. Narration, as a design principle for narrative structures, influences retrospective experience through the dynamics of memory construction. Imagination, on the other hand, as a dynamic process, opens up access to the essence of individual concepts and provides insights into the inner structure of the psychic economic fabric. By consciously directing these processes, the individual can not only reevaluate their past but also actively shape their future. By using narrative and imaginative techniques in a targeted manner, individual resources can be mobilized and (creative) potential released. This conscious examination of one's own narrative and imagination makes it possible to rethink deeply rooted beliefs and behavioral patterns and develop new perspectives. In this way, individual growth processes can be triggered, and the mind system can be strengthened in its flexibility and adaptability.

---

time, the emphasis is on the social dimension of the mind. For example, language and communication can serve as external tools to express and convey thoughts, and cultural norms and values can shape a person's thinking and behavior.
Cf. Andy/Chalmers (1998), pp. 10–19 and Clark (2008), pp. 10–45.
305 See Weber (2017), p. 14ff.

An Initial Overview

- The polar division of being from the perspective of the individual into an inside and outside creates the basis of all cognitive processes; a preoccupation with bridging this division precisely is the background to all experiences.
- When contemplating the inner world of an individual, narratives and imagination become essential tools that enable conscious interaction with one's own mental system. These inner processes can be seen as transformative and even transcendental experiences that can lead the individual to a more conscious use of their mental resources.

Basic Motifs of IR, TN, and HS

It is not in the realization lies happiness, but in the acquisition of knowledge.[306]

Narration and imagination represent essential instruments in the human domain of cognition, which also act as basic architectural elements of the economic experience of the world. Imagination, a dynamic process, opens up access to the essence of individual conceptions and thus provides insights into the inner structure of the psychic economic fabric. Narration functions as a design principle for narrative structures and thus influences retrospective experience through the dynamics of memory construction. This process of memory and experience manifests itself in a complex interaction that requires a comprehensive conceptualization.[307]

In this context, the introduction of a framework is a good idea, which includes extended key components of narration and imagination with specific concepts—namely IR, TN, and HS—and integrates them. Together, these components form a comprehensive framework for the exploration and application of narrative and imaginative processes in an economic context.[308] At the same time, the framework offers individual-psychological starting points for the targeted economic of the mental system in a targeted economic manner.

The subsequent introduction of the concept of insight therapy expands the understanding and scope of the application of these framework components.

---

306 Poe (1849), p. 464.
307 Cf. Bamberg (1999), p. 221, p. 225f. and Kraus (2000), pp. 159–182.
308 See also conceptually Lucius-Hoene (2000), Art. 18 (o.Sz.) and Kraus (2000), p. 241.

Insight therapy is a methodology that uses the extent and scope of insights as a catalyst for change processes. Not only the possibilities but also the limitations of this form of therapy are considered and analyzed.[309]

As cognitive processes constitute narration and imagination of individual and collective reality—they can be seen as central economic processes that influence the construction and shaping of individual and collective socioeconomic external factors.[310]

At the same time, they offer individual-psychological access to the (dynamic) core of our being—the narrative of the economic and mental system is thus itself dualistic in nature; the structure of narratives determines our memory and thus also our retrospective experience.[311] One's own narrative, that is, the structure and flow of thoughts of the self-narrative, allows one to actively shape one's own reality in an economic sense.[312] It belongs to the core of the constitutional level of consciousness.

Of course, the concrete manifestation of individual narratives is comprehensive and diverse; however,[313] particularly effective components or techniques for the mind system (which enable it's economic (which enable economical use of resources) can be systematized in the following framework: Figure 9 provides an overview.

---

309 Knowledge serves as a catalyst for change processes; see Chapter 4.

310 The joint interaction of individuals through language and communication shapes reality; narration and imagination play a central role here by creating shared stories and cultural narratives that influence collective reality. The ability to imagine defines not only individual perceptions, but also social interactions and collective ideas. Imagination is therefore an essential component of the construction of shared (internal and external) realities.

Cf. comprehensively Berger/Luckmann (2023), p. 96ff. and Abraham (2015), pp. 249–255 and Abraham (2018), p. 35ff.

311 The connection between remembering and experiencing lies in their mutual influence. On the one hand, past memories can can influence our present experience by shaping our perception, interpretation and reaction to current events. This happens, for example, through the activation of associations, emotions or behavioral patterns associated with past experiences. Experiencing refers to the active process of perceiving and interpreting current events, situations, or environments. It encompasses the entire range of human experiences, including sensory perceptions, emotional reactions, cognitive evaluations, and behaviors.

Cf. Hartmann (1998), p. 134ff. and Polkinghorne (1988), pp. 17–21, pp. 105–113 as well as Polkinghorne (1996), p. 367f. and Polkinghorne (1998), p. 16ff.

312 Cf. on the function of narratives in detail Goldie (2013), p. 190ff., Goldie (2003) and von Contzen (2018), p. 20ff.

313 See Goldie (2003), pp. 303–307.

FIGURE 9 Basic motifs of economic narratives.[314]

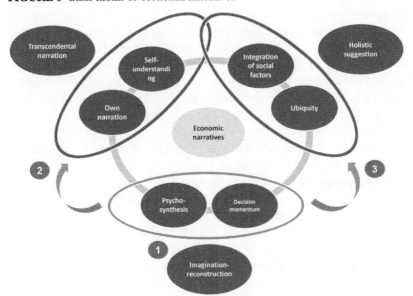

IR provides the basis for the economical utilization of the mental system; it is a fundamental technique for activating intrapersonal transaction and translation processes by specifically shifting the imagination narrative in the direction of synthetic imagination.

The other two techniques are economic techniques of the spirit system that build on this, namely TN and HS. The former offers a particularly effective method of self-narration, and the latter integrates mental resources particularly effectively into transaction processes of the mind system.

Imagination reconstruction

The method set of IR has a direct effect on the individual imagination narrative and leads to efficient synthetic imagination in narrativization. At the same time, it is the unifying aspect between TN and HS.[315]

---

314 Own presentation.
315 Cf. Bude (1991), p. 106f.

Imagination is a unique human ability that is both a union of senses[316] and imagination and is based on a common cognitive mechanism. This power of imagination makes it possible to grasp something that either no longer exists or has never existed.[317] The capacity for imagination can be categorized into different forms, including reproductive, productive, and creative imagination, all of which are based on psychic energy (as an economic resource). Carl Gustav Jung, for example, considers the "creative imagination" to be the only accessible psychic primal phenomenon and the only immediate reality:[318]

> Imagination is the reproductive or creative activity of the mind in general, without being a special faculty, [...] Fantasy as imaginative activity is for me simply the direct expression of psychic vital activity, of psychic energy, which is given to consciousness in no other way than in the form of images or content, [...]." consciousness other than in the form of images or content, [...].[319]

The importance of imagination, therefore, extends far beyond its definition and demonstrates its profound impact on various aspects of economic activity. The human mind and brain inevitably and automatically engage with the inner world on all sensory levels in the absence of external tasks.[320] Imagination itself manifests in different ways, including visual, auditory, olfactory, gustatory, and somatosensory, and bringing them together is crucial to fully utilize this ability.[321]

The imagination plays a decisive role in determining and constituting our inner world. Conscious control over this ability enables the individual

---

316 Cf. Kraus (2000), pp. 168–182 and Merleau-Ponty (1974), pp. 196ff.

317 Compare the fundamental statements by Immanuel Kant: "Imagination is the ability to visualise an object even without its presence in the mind." (KdrV B.151) – Imagination can therefore be seen as the ability to imagine an object (or an abstract concept) that is no longer present or has never been present (thus imagination differs from conceit in that physical presence is not a criterion here).

318 In a letter to Dr. Kurt Plachte dated January 10, 1929, C. G. Jung wrote: "I am indeed convinced that creative imagination is the only accessible primordial phenomenon of the soul, the actual soul essence, the only immediate reality…" Jung (2001a), p. 86.

319 Cf. Jung (1921), §869.

320 Cf. Erreich (2016), p. 484ff.

321 See Schönhammer (2013), p. 240, 247f.

to understand their own life comprehensively, to make their own actions comprehensible, and to reveal hidden potential; an active lifestyle and health can, therefore, be promoted through the conscious use of the imagination.[322]

Imagination can (in addition to the future orientation) also be used for the reconstruction of one's own experience—that is, *de facto*, the reexperiencing of the past[323]—can also be used; for this purpose, guidance in the consciousness at the constitutional level of the self is necessary.[324] In principle, imagination thus partially and situationally cancels the division of life into a before and after; the present is strengthened as the only decision-making momentum.[325] The episodic memory, which is concerned with remembering past events and emotions, plays a decisive role at the transactional level of the mental system, especially when an individual falls into native imagination (or syntagmatic or paradigmatic narration).[326] In such moments, one's own past can appear unassociated and enigmatic, and it seems as if the causes of all complexes lie in this past time.

Through the technique of structured IR, it is possible to allow the mind system to carry out an organized interpretation and reevaluation of the past.[327] This enables the past elements to be actively shaped.[328] IR thus serves as a means of transporting problems of the self into the present, where they can be understood, comprehended, and processed by the spirit system. However, reliving past events can often be exhausting and stressful as it is associated with strong emotional reactions.[329] Nevertheless, the technique of IR offers an important mechanism for coping with and processing past experiences and emotions as well as dealing with them internally. Emotions and the inner

---

322 Especially the synthetic imagination.
323 Cf. Tulving (2002), p. 3ff.
324 Cf. Mummendey (2006), p. 115ff.
325 Ibid, p. 18f.
326 Colloquially also referred to as "superficial thinking" or "brooding," see Schlager (2020), p. 86ff. and Kast (2017), pp. 219–223.
327 This technology can also be used in a forward-looking manner, for example to develop scenarios or identify potential development paths.
328 It is important to note, however, that there is also the countervailing process by which reality can attenuate or weaken our imagination weaken or weaken our imagination, especially when expectations or emotional colouring (e.g., the role of longing) comes into play. Cf. Scheibe/Freund (2008), pp. 126–131.
329 Cf. conceptually also Will (2018), p. 377ff.

handling of psycho-economic claims to wholeness (such as the longing for the absolute, which can also turn into concrete material ideas or wishes).[330]

At this point, reference should be made to the connection between imagination and identification, as the latter can effectively interrupt the reconstruction of IR; memories should be perceived as a neutral transaction process and not be associated with the self.[331]

Ultimately, the IR ends in the imaginative and narrative holism of psychosynthesis.[332] The imaginary aspect of psychosynthesis refers to the individual's ability to explore new possibilities and potentials through imagination and to utilize mental resources economically.[333] This process goes beyond traditional therapy in that it aims not only to treat psychological problems but also to promote creativity,[334] self-efficacy,[335] and spirituality.[336] By engaging with our inner world and actively shaping it, we can organize our lives more consciously and creatively. The narrative aspect within the framework of psychosynthesis focuses on the construction and interpretation of individual life stories. By means of IR, alternative narratives of the past are explored,

---

330 Reconstruction as a mental technique is a universal technique for exploring the inner world and promotes its universalism. For detailed information on how it works, see Kast (2010), p. 75ff.

331 Imagination and identification play a decisive role in remembering and in the construction of an individual's inner reality. When an individual remembers past events, they become witnesses, as it were, who view their own past like a film and detach themselves from the form of the self at that time in order to assume the position of the neutral observer, who takes on a new form that is not identical with the current self. In order to avoid identification, it is crucial not to allow oneself to be drawn into remembering. A whole range of techniques can support the mental processes here. Becoming a witness can also be transferred to the present, making emotional reactions more controllable, especially when it comes to strong emotions such as anger, which are often associated with identification. Through this process, the individual can recognize the uninterpreted form of reality of the inner world and find the core of the past. In this way, the past can be released and resolved and serve as a source of insight and growth. This even enables a kind of "conscious dying" of the past and a letting go of old burdens. Cf. Fromm (1991), pp. 122–128 and Kast (2010), p. 109ff. and p. 159ff.

332 Cf. Assagioli (1933) and Assagioli (1937) and Hardy/Whitmore (1990), p. 45ff. and Hardy (1987), p. 31ff.

333 Ibid.

334 Cf. Frey (2007), p. 825ff.

335 Cf. Egger et al. (2015), p. 289ff.

336 Cf. Bucher et al. (2014), p. 24ff., pp. 133–145.

which makes it possible to view past experiences in a new context and to open up new meanings. This process of structured, systematic reevaluation and reinterpretation evokes a profound understanding of individual self-perception and the development of personal life history. And the development of personal life history by uncovering and eliminating limitations in the form of outdated beliefs and behavioral patterns.[337]

Ultimately, the practiced reconstruction of the imagination within psychosynthesis leads to an integrative and comprehensive narrative holism.[338] This holistic approach allows the individual to mobilize their inner resources in order to lead a life that is perceived as fulfilling and authentic.[339] This concept integrates the physical, mental, and spiritual spheres of the individual and helps to deepen the understanding of one's identity and purpose in life. The creative shaping of the imagination and the active reshaping of the life story thus open up the possibility of developing and realizing personal potential on a deeper, economically relevant level; conscious and unconscious aspects of the self (often particularly fragmented and difficult to integrate due to social aspects)[340] can be brought together to form a whole within themselves.[341]

All in all, IR is an intrinsically immersive technique in which one's own past becomes a "dream." Reality and individual desires[342] recede; the mental system is alone with itself and its form, creating new perspectives for action. In economic terms, IR is, therefore, a primary mental resource that supports important connection points in the transfer system of the mental system.[343]

---

[337] Cf. Hermans/Hermans-Jansen (1995), pp. 31–71 and Keupp et al. (1999), pp. 45ff.
[338] See also the transcendental narration and holistic suggestion which build on this.
[339] Cf. Lucius-Hoene (2000), Art. 18 (above).
[340] See Storck (2022), pp. 54–71.
[341] Ibid.
[342] The idea that desires project the past into the future can be explained in cognitive psychology by the fact that desires are part of a cognitive process in which an individual uses information from the past to construct ideas about future states or events. The cognitive schemas and expectations about what is possible or desirable are shaped and influenced by past experiences. On this basis, individuals can imagine future scenarios that are (exclusively) based on past experiences and wishes, that is, that do not incorporate a real (different and independent) future. Thus, the wish can turn into an intrapsychic utopia.
   See also Baltes (2008), p. 79ff.
[343] Cf. also Hermans/Hermans-Jansen (1995), p. 22 and p. 198ff. and Hermans (1999), p. 1201f.

Transcendental narration

Building on the IR, there are two narrative techniques that effectively support the economization of the mind system. The TN is an effective method of self-narration.

The concept of the continuity of the self is seen in the transcendental narrative as an elaborate process that is manifested through a complex network of multiple individual narratives. In this context, life is understood as a multilayered mosaic in which nodes of narration are woven in order to organize and structure memories. Organise and structure memories.[344] These nodes, which often take the form of key memories and key dreams, play a central role in the construction and maintenance of the individual life story (i.e., identity[345]), the primary function of TN.[346] In contrast to other forms of narration, the blurring of the boundary between memory and narrated experience emphasizes those transgressive elements that effectively shape the narration.[347] The driving and inhibiting force within these narrative constructions lies in the active, passive, or inactive longings, as well as in the feelings of shame, guilt, and the desire for change and realization. These psychological elements shape and influence individual life stories in subtle ways, shaping the experiences and actions of each person.[348]

The narratives are mainly characterized by the first and last events,[349] which exert a significant influence on the overall life narrative. The dynamics of life transitions and the segmentation of the narrative into before and after episodes create an individual transitional structure. This structure makes it possible, through TN, as a continuous process of change and development.[350]

---

344 Ibid.

345 The philosophical term of personal identity contains a diachronic and a synchronic component. In the context of the discussion about synchronic identity, the question is how the many aspects and characteristics of a person are summarized into a single unit at one point in time. The diachronic identity of persons refers to the identity at different points in time. Neither of the two technical terms includes everyday language terms. The latter can rather be summarized by the concept of individuality.

See Brand (2013), p. 181.

346 Cf. ibid. p. 182ff.

347 Cf. Polkinghorne (1998), p. 87ff. and Polkinghorne (1991), p. 143ff.

348 Ibid.

349 Cf. Freeman (2006), p. 80ff.

350 The transcendental narration itself is in turn a dynamic process that continuously changes and develops over the course of a lifetime.

See Brand (2013), p. 181 and p. 190.

Through this continuous reflection and the expansion and integration of the individual narrative experiences, a condensed psychological truth emerges that deepens the individual's self-understanding: The connection between narration and the situational influence of the self leads to a change in the emotionality of the individual memory. This interaction allows the boundaries of individual narratives to be removed, allowing nodes to connect with each other and the connections of the individual's inner world to become clearer.[351]

Different topoi of narratives[352] influence this emotional resonance and interpretation of memories; the individual sense of self-feeling is the result of all existing narratives and the subjective experience of the individual in the reality of the external world. These narratives play a crucial role in the construction of identity and self-esteem, as they contribute to the continuity and coherence of the individual self. The transcendental narrative can even become a dialogue with oneself that enables a reflective examination of one's own experiences.[353]

The distinction between truth and untruth[354] is relativized in this perspective, as the truth lies in the subjective narration. Memory does not necessarily correspond to the concrete experience at the time but is characterized by a high, often overemphasized emotional component.[355] This can lead to a fragmentation of the narrative, whereby all narratives are adapted to the current self-image, and a fusion of memory and fiction can take place in the narrative, which is reinforced by the cultural resonance of certain memories.[356]

The transcendental component can put difficult memories in a more positive light and vice versa. The search for a narrative that you can live with better enables a deeper understanding of the past and your own motives for past thoughts and actions. Reconciliation with the past and a deeper understanding

---

351 Cf. Kölbl/Straub (2010), p. 22ff.

352 Like redemption stories and contamination stories, see Kast (2010), p. 33ff.

353 Cf. Kölbl/Straub (2010), p. 36f. and Atkinson/Shiffrin (1968), p. 139ff.

354 The opposite of truth is usually untruth (or falsehood). Untruth refers to the absence of truth or the (objective) non-conformity with reality. It can involve deliberate lies, deceptions or false statements that do not correspond to the objective facts. Untruth can also arise through error or misinterpretation if information is incorrect or incomplete. Since ipso facto no objective verification of truth (or falsehood) can take place in self-narration, the term is based on this.

Cf. conceptually also Heidegger (1988), p. 131ff.

355 Cf. Lazarus/Kanner/Folkman (1980), p. 192ff.

356 Cf. ibid. and Rosa (2018), p. 347ff.

of the self can be achieved through emotional remembrance in the narrative.[357] TN is, therefore, the decisive process for recognizing oneself, which in turn is one of the economically active components of the mind system, as the transaction processes can be made much more effective. Figure 10 illustrates the integrated process of TN.

The exploration of the self marks the initial step in a process of self-acceptance. This process implies that individuals visualize themselves and define their identity through a synthesis of individual experience and creative imagination. Central to this is the integration of the self into the larger context of the world and the recognition of its belonging to a more comprehensive whole.[358]

This process of anchoring and continuously maintaining the self in the world in the world can be effectively supported by various methods such as immersion and meditation.[359] It is crucial to emphasize that this means not acting against the self and avoiding unrealistic ideals.

By immersing oneself in deeper layers of individual existence through TN, the foundations for personal development and the unfolding of abilities and

FIGURE 10   The integrated process of transcendental narration (self-knowledge and self-acceptance)[360]

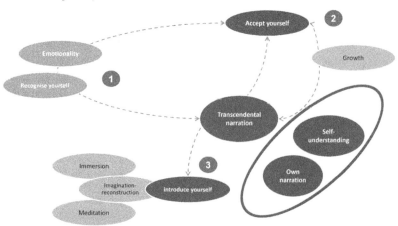

---

357   Cf. Hermans/Hermans-Jansen (1995), pp. 14–30.
358   Own presentation.
359   See also Mühling (2020), p. 361ff.
360   See also Borghardt/Erhardt et al. (2016), p. 232f.

realizations can be created. This recognition and integration of the self into the world[361] enable individuals to connect to their true potential and thus create a stable foundation for personal growth and self-realization, both of which are functions of the economic spirit system.

Holistic suggestion

In contrast to the two previous basic economic motives, the effect of HS is fueled by another mental resource from a further mental resource—that of the individual will. HS integrates mental resources particularly effectively into the transaction processes of the mental system.

The HS functions as the decisive interface between the individual narrative and the external reality. In this context of interaction, culture acts as a mediator, channeling, and interpreting both the meaning and the purpose of the individual's inner world. In this context, culture represents an essential resource for the development of the individual's creative expression.[362] A comprehensive definition of culture,[363] including its multiple subcategories, allows for an in-depth analysis of the connection between cultural aspects and the individual. In particular, it emphasizes that cultural identity forms an integral part of individual identity. Through processes such as imitation, identification, and combination,[364] the suggestive and influential power of cultural elements has an immediate effect on the inner world of the individual, initiating a dynamic exchange process.

---

361 Many external conflicts arise from a lack of transcendental narration because here the alignment of the self with social, societal narratives comes into competition or conflict. Transcendental narration always refers to an individual's ability to integrate their personal life story into the wider context of cultural and social narratives. If this integration is not successful or if individual and social narratives come into conflict with each other, this can lead to internal tensions and external conflicts.

Cf. Bruner (1987), pp. 25–32 and Erikson (1968), pp. 208–231 as well as McAdams (1993), p. 26, pp. 103ff.

362 Cf. Hany/Heller (1993), p. 108ff.

363 Overall, culture can be can be understood as a dynamic system of symbolic meanings, rituals, traditions, values and norms that shapes the behavior and perception of the world of a group or society and shapes its identity. Cf. the definitions by Geertz (1973) and Triandis (1994).

364 Ibid.

The concept of the cultural unconscious[365] plays a significant role here. Cultural patterns open up the possibility of a reinterpretation of individual nodes and a reorientation of self-image.[366] Symbolic processes that are rooted in the culture act as catalysts and transitional objects that have a direct impact on the inner world by transposing the suggestion.

The HS now offers deliberate suggestions[367] for the individual life situation and conveys a cultural heritage of significant individual value and meaning. At the same time, social constructions and intersubjective entities determine a second aspect of external reality, which also has a direct impact on the inner world of the individual.[368] Social ties and entanglements manifest a considerable suggestive power for the cognitive processes of an individual's inner world. Through social interactions and shared experiences, these bonds convey implicit and explicit expectations and values that decisively shape an individual's behavior and perception. The social narrative and the individual narrative play a central role in the construction of identity and self-image.[369]

A comprehensive understanding of the outer world and the embedding of its social, cultural, and historical dimensions in the spirit system acts as an important catalyst for the development of the inner world—HS takes on the role of an interpreter of the individual will, which is strongly characterized by those same cultural factors.[370] This type of suggestion influences the perception and interpretation of the environment by individuals and thus forms the basis for individual experiences and actions, which gives the processes of the mental system an additional economic framework. The power of suggestion, which emanates from social ties and interdependencies, is individually and situationally variable.[371] The decisive factor in this addition to individual narration is the integrating factor: the HS is able to channel the will as a mental resource—socially channeled and distorted by the socially evoked concepts of shame

---

365 Cf. Kast (2014), pp. 23–38 and Kast (1995), pp. 28f.
366 Cf. Hannover/Kühnen (2003), p. 214ff. and Mummendey (2006), pp. 45–49.
367 See Thomä (2007), pp. 290–314.
368 Cf. Chrudzimski et al. (2013), p. 68ff.
369 While the social narrative represents the collective history and identity of a group or society, the individual narrative reflects the personal experiences, memories and convictions of an individual.
   See Viehöver (2011), p. 194ff.
370 See also Hannover/Kühnen (2003), p. 220f.
371 See Schaeffler (2019), pp. 31–44.

and guilt[372]—effectively embed it precisely in this socioeconomic discourse and therefore translate it more effectively (measured against external factors) into the external world.[373] The intrapsychic suggestion also influences the cognitive processing of information by promoting or inhibiting certain thought patterns and interpretations. By creating (positive or negative) embedded suggestions, an individual can directly influence their perception of reality and their reactions to it.[374] HS as a component in the mind system is, therefore, a factor for its ubiquity and flexibility, which significantly improves the use of resources.

The Three Key Messages

1. **Basic architectural elements of the economic experience of the world:** Narration and imagination are fundamental tools in the human cognitive domain and function as basic architectural elements of the economic experience of the world. They shape the retrospective experience through the construction of narrative structures and enable the reevaluation of the past.
2. **An extended framework:** A framework extends key components of narration and imagination with specific concepts such as IR, TN, and HS. These form a comprehensive framework for the exploration and application of narrative and imaginative processes in an economic context and offer starting points for the targeted economic orientation of the transaction processes of the mind system.
3. **Better utilization of mental resources:** The use of IR enables an organized interpretation and reevaluation of the past, while TN and HS establish a connection between individual narration and external reality. These processes contribute to deepening self-understanding, self-acceptance, and personal growth, and they provide important economic resources for the mind system.

---

372 See Cyrulnik (2018), p. 57ff. and Rinofner-Kreidl (2009), p. 144ff.
373 Cf. Hermans/Hermans-Jansen (1995), p 165ff.
374 In addition, the inner psychological suggestion also influences also influences the emotional experience of an individual. Self-suggestion can increase positive emotions such as self-confidence, motivation, and joy or reduce negative emotions such as fear, stress, and insecurity. By giving themselves positive affirmations or focusing on positive memories and experiences, an individual can and experiences, they can improve their emotional well-being and maintain a positive emotional state. See also Mandler (1980), pp. 236–239.

Memory Is a Central Resource of the Mental System

An hour is not just an hour; it is a vessel filled with scents, with sounds, with plans and climates. What we call reality is a certain relationship between sensations and memories.[375]

The concept of the economization of the mental system is well established by psychological research in its partial aspects (as described); the perspective itself is new—and brings with it a whole series of theoretical and practical implications.[376]

The mental system of an individual can be understood in its essential partial aspects and partial processes as an economic system that operates with mental resources and is, therefore, also accessible for economic resource utilization (see the summary in Figure 11). As a result, the handling of these resources becomes

FIGURE 11 Overview of the economic spirit system.[377]

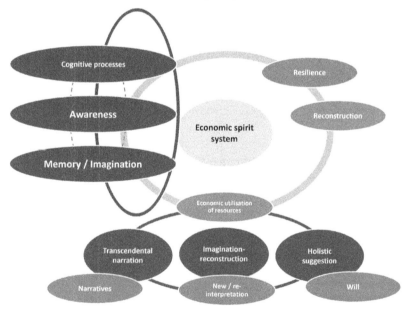

---

375 Proust (2000), p. 3976.
376 These are discussed in detail in Chapter 4.
377 Own presentation.

a central aspect of the psyche.[378] The economic perspective shows that the transaction processes, in particular of narration and imagination (which assign the mental resources to the individual processes in the mental system and at the same time co-constitute them),[379] are decisive for the effective utilization of mental resources.

A deeper understanding of the mental ecosystem also provides approaches for therapeutic interventions; targeted measures such as mindfulness, cognitive restructuring, and emotional regulation can strengthen the resilience of the mental ecosystem and improve the individual's perceived well-being.[380]

The reinterpretation/reinterpretation of memories, the associated narrative, and the integration of volitional (i.e., conscious, controlled) processes create an intermental system within which resources can be allocated particularly efficiently using various instruments. This enables an individual to utilize the conscious aspect of their mental system in the perceived sense of self and, at the same time, strengthen their mental resources. The holistic integration of different psychological schools and philosophies from an economic perspective, therefore, creates a unified theory of the benefits of the mind system. In this, memories and the individual psychological handling of them form the central starting point; one can speak of memories as the central transfer unit in the mental context.[381]

The Three Key Messages

1. **New perspectives:** The concept of the economization of the mental system is well established by psychological research and offers new perspectives with theoretical and practical implications.
2. **The spirit system is an economic system:** The mind system of an individual can be regarded in its partial aspects as an economic system that operates with mental resources and is accessible for

(*Continued*)

---

378 One could also speak here of a "management" of one's own psyche, whereby this corresponds to the numerous subconscious and unconscious processes in the mind system, which would not do justice to the numerous subconscious and unconscious processes in the mental system and would be too active in nature.

379 Cf. Schubert (2012), p. 208ff.

380 See also Hofmann/Sawyer/Witt/Oh (2010), pp. 172–180 and Southwick et al. (2014), p. 25340f. and Beck et al. (2011), p. 30 and p. 36ff.

381 Memories are therefore to a certain extent the "currency" of the mental system, see also Ricœur (2014), pp. 122–160 and Schacter (2002) and Damasio (2000), p. 383f.

economic resource utilization. The transaction processes of narration and imagination are decisive for the effective utilization of mental resources.
3. **Expanded intervention options:** A deeper understanding of the mental ecosystem enables therapeutic interventions that can strengthen resilience and improve an individual's perceived well-being by utilizing targeted interventions such as mindfulness, cognitive restructuring, and emotional regulation.

The Economic Handling of Mental Processes as a Basis for Therapy

There is always something hidden in the present, the emergence of which could change everything; that is a dizzying thought but a comforting one.[382]

Individual psychology has always been concerned with the inner processes of the human mind. In addition to analyzing behavior and emotions, it also looks at the structure and functioning of thought and memory. In this context, the economical handling of mental processes plays a particularly important role, as it is decisive for the efficiency and effectiveness of individual psychological mental activities.

The economic aspect of individual psychology refers to the efficient utilization of various mental resources such as attention, memory, and cognitive capacities. And cognitive capacities.[383] These resources are limited and must, therefore, be managed economically to achieve optimal results.

A central aspect of the economical handling of mental processes is the conscious control and prioritization of individual mental activities within the mental system. Teaching a form of therapy to allocate mental resources effectively (i.e., making this economic approach comprehensible) can not only resolve psychological complexes in a targeted manner but also contribute to individual well-being and the development of resilience.

Theoretical implications

Memories are more than just ephemeral moments that linger in the individual mind. They shape identity, influence behavior, and shape our entire way of life.

---

382 Hofmannsthal (1979), p. 207.
383 Which also represent an external value factor, see Schubert (2012), p. 202ff.

Remembering itself is not a peripheral or unguided process but a complex, self-evident economic dynamic that must be consciously shaped.[384] The creation of memories is, therefore, not a trivial issue but an economic process that requires the use of resources. Similar to a market, memories are also subject to a selection process. Not all memories can "survive" or remain relevant in the long term. There is a kind of supply and demand for memories, which is shaped by our experiences and lifestyle.[385]

Due to limited resources and selective mechanisms, it is impossible to preserve as many or as differentiated memories as desired. To preserve.[386] It is, therefore, an individual psychological necessity to develop a kind of internal catalog of criteria that helps us to consciously decide which memories are important and which are not. Actively shaping this process has so far been neglected too much in psychological theory—but precisely because of the economic approach, it is evident that it is of great importance for mental hygiene.

It follows that memories are not just abstract entities but represent real goods that arise from the reality of the specific situational experience and have a monetary component.[387] This way of looking at memories reveals a complex dynamic that cannot simply be fitted into traditional economic models.[388] Rather, a hybrid strategy manifests itself that combines several theoretical economic models for the individual-psychological shaping of memories. First, from the economization of the mental system, it must be recognized that memories (as well as other mental resources) cannot be viewed in isolation but rather in a continuous interplay between individual experiences, cognitive processes, and interpersonal relationships. Cognitive processes and the intersocial meta-environment. Traditional economic models, which are often based on rational decisions and utility maximization, cannot capture this complexity on their own. A hybrid strategy must, therefore, integrate concepts from behavioral economics and psychology.[389] By taking emotions, heuristics, and cognitive biases into account, a more realistic model of how memories are formed, evaluated, actively organized and can ultimately be created. These statements reflect the diversity

---

384 Cf. Kast (2010), p. 57ff.
385 As on a physical level, see Deco/Rolls (2005), p. 240ff.
386 Ibid.
387 Cf. Schacter (1996), p. 317ff.
388 Ibid.
389 Cf. Roediger III/Dudai/Fitzpatrick et al. (2007), p. 222f. and p. 339ff.

of mechanisms and influences that affect memory itself—and offer scope for further research at the interface between internal and external economics.[390]

Overall, looking at mental resources[391] from an economic perspective shows that it is important to consciously control and shape the inner processes and mechanisms in order to create a rich and meaningful inner world. Memories are not just passive remnants of past events but active building blocks of our identity and lifestyle that need to be cherished and valued.

Another field of theory is the impact of the economization of the mental system on the inter-collective materialism of liberal humanism, which is prevalent in postmodernism.[392]

Materialism, especially in its aggressive form,[393] characterizes the worldview of many individuals and entities. It is the conviction that all thinking and consciousness are ultimately based on a material (possibly also pecuniary)[394] and procedural foundation. This view, often described as functional atomism,[395] sees the world and the mind as a collection of functional parts that are considered interchangeable. According to this worldview, the mind is nothing more than an arbitrarily influenceable, repairable entity made up of individual parts, as are its processes and products.[396]

However, this materialistic approach leads to a distortion or even misjudgment of the reality of mental cognitive processes—especially in an economic context. It undermines the effectiveness of mental-inactive processes and can grow into a potentially dangerous ideology, as has happened in the case of behaviorism. This reduction of the human mind to purely material aspects

---

390 Ibid.
391 On the concept of mental resources, see also Ricœur (2014) and Schubert (2012), p. 193ff.
392 Cf. von Kutschera (2003), p. 25ff.
393 Cf. ibid.
394 Cf. Churchland et al. (1989), p. 351ff. and Gazzaniga (2005), pp. 63–87.
395 Functional atomism in psychology refers to an approach that breaks down human behaviour and mental processes into their smallest functional components. This approach assumes that complex psychological phenomena can be explained by analyzing and understanding the basic functions and processes that make them up.
Cf. Fodor et al. (1983), pp. 36–45, pp. 88f. and conceptually Tulving (2011).
396 An image that is often used to illustrate this view is that of the metaphysical television: although the quality of the picture and sound depends on the condition and functioning of the individual components, these have no influence on the programme that you can watch. If you don't like the programme, the argument goes, the problem lies at the material level of the system and not in its immaterial aspects. See Fodor (1983).

harbors the danger of negating the ubiquitous human capacity for reflection, introspection, and self-understanding.[397] It is important to emphasize that the human mind is non-materialistic and cannot be understood within a purely material framework. Rather, the mind exists within its own mental ecosystem, which is characterized by mental and spiritual discipline.[398] This discipline can be applied individually to explore and better understand the deeper dimensions of human consciousness and provide a holistic view of cognition and memory beyond the purely materialistic paradigm.

Overall, materialism is a problematic factor in cognition and memory, and there is a need to develop alternative approaches and perspectives in order to achieve a more comprehensive understanding of human nature and its mental processes.[399] It is crucial to recognize that the mental spirit system is more than the sum of its material (and immaterial) parts (processes) and that a purely materialistic view is contrary to the economy of the mind system.[400]

Finally, it should be added that the topic of a unified theory of the mental system and the human psyche (including its own economic system) has accompanied the philosophical-psychological discourse since the beginnings of research into the mental system and the first theories (which attempt to explain the complex phenomena of consciousness, emotions, and behavior).[401] One common thread is the realization that the human mind cannot be viewed in isolation but is anchored in a broader context of cultural, social, spiritual, and economic influences.[402]

---

397 The danger lies in the fact that emphasizing purely physiological or neurological processes cannot fully capture the complexity of the human mind and its abilities.

398 Cf. Knoblauch (2012), p. 96ff. and Essen (2012), p. 115f.

399 At the same time, individuals who are materialistic and consider material possessions to be important tend to have lower levels of psychological well-being and life satisfaction. These results suggest that an excessive emphasis on material values and goals can lead to a loss of inner well-being.

Cf. in detail Richins/Dawson (1992), p. 308ff.

400 Cf. Ryan/Sheldon/Kasser/Deci (1996), p. 11ff.

401 Cf. in detail the concepts of Newell (1994) and Kahneman (2011).

402 In modern psychology and neuroscience, various approaches have attempted to develop a unified theory of the mind system that considers the biological as well as the psychological and social aspects of the human mind. Some of these approaches emphasize the neural basis of consciousness and mental processes while others focus on psychodynamic or cognitive models. Nevertheless, the challenge remains to integrate these different perspectives and achieve a holistic understanding of the mind.

See also Churchland (1989), Newell (1994), and Baars (2002), p. 47ff.

The inclusion of the intermental economic system in this discourse is of crucial importance, as it allows the interactions between individual behavior, economic structures, and psychological transaction processes to be taken into account for the first time. The economized mental system influences not only the material reality but also the psychological and spiritual well-being of an individual.[403]

In all (standardizing) theories, the economical use of mental resources (which are relevant practically in every theory)[404] has always been at the forefront of a wide variety of approaches—without explicitly working toward an economy of the mind.[405] This gap can be further closed in future research, and the aspects mentioned can be further elaborated and refined. By expanding the understanding of the human psyche to include intraindividual economic principles, new insights into the dynamics of the human mind can be gained, and new approaches to the promotion of mental resources (such as resilience) can be developed.

Basic principles of economic cognitive therapy

The approach of an economic mind system also has numerous implications from an application-oriented perspective. Taken to its logical conclusion, the economization of the system amounts to an individual psychological transformation of the overall nexus of thinking and feeling (i.e., also of the own narrative)[406], which can be described as "economic cognitive therapy"[407] (OEK). The following four elements are of particular relevance:

---

403 See also Richins/Dawson (1992), p. 311f.
404 See Newell (1994), p. 35f.
405 See also the "Concept of the free energy principle" in Friston (2010).
406 Cf. Neisser (1994), pp. 10–18 and Winogard (1994), pp. 246f.
407 Insight therapy itself is based on the principles of cognitive psychology and cognitive behavioural therapy and aims to identify and change a person's thought patterns, beliefs, and perceptions in order to improve their emotional well-being and change their behaviour. In combination with the findings from the economization of the mental system, economic cognitive therapy focuses on the conscious design of mental transaction processes and the use of the resources of the mind. It focuses on recognizing dysfunctional resource allocations and thought patterns and replacing them with an adaptive narrative. This is done through a series of techniques and strategies (such as transactional analysis (TA)) that aim to correct the cognitive distortions and irrational beliefs that cause a person's emotional suffering. Cf. Borghardt/Erhardt (2016), p. 361ff. and Chopra (2023), pp. 17–49 and Kast (2010), pp. 159–178 and the appendix.

1. Conscious thinking forms the basis for all human cognition.[408] This is a constant process that develops in a certain pattern.[409] The first step in economic cognitive therapy is to systematically build up an understanding of one's own mental system. in which the conscious mind is understood as a tool, strengthened, and its mechanisms (of imagination and narration) are understood and trained.
2. The application of the derived basic motifs of IR, the TN, and HS lays the foundation for extended, holistic experiences with more differentiated narratives and makes it possible to interpret them better.
3. Together, these insights enable a transformation of the mind system (and its self-perception of it) itself. Thinking can be modified and recedes more into the background, while feeling, which can be seen as transcended thinking,[410] comes to the fore—precisely because mental transaction processes can run more effectively and are therefore less resource-intensive.
4. The immanent processes of the spirit system continue to change until the conscious mind plays a subordinate, pluralistic role. Alternatives emerge in current thought and action, opening up the space for further insights.[411]

Memories and imaginations also consist of different components. On the one hand, there are future-oriented parts—wishes[412]—which represent the cognitive and intellectual components of conscious thought.[413] These wishes are the result of conscious thought and imagination. On the other hand, there are desires, which represent the intuitive component of feeling.[414] They arise from emotional impulses and deeper, mostly unconscious longings.[415]

---

408 This view is shared in all psycho-philosophical orientations, see also Winogard (1994), pp. 243f. and Yates (2015), pp. 43–60.
409 Ibid.
410 Cf. Plutchik (1980), p. 9f.
411 The process is not necessarily consecutive.
412 See Heckhausen (2013), p. 2ff. and Dörner (2013), p. 240ff.
413 Cf. ibid.
414 Feeling is often described as "thinking with the heart." It is a different form of consciousness, a translingual form of interpersonal interaction that differs from purely rational thought processes. Despite these differences, feeling is a similarly complex process to conscious thinking and has its own mapping system. Cf. Kast et al. (2017), pp. 29–34.
415 See Kanfer (2013), pp. 291–296.

The essential message of economic cognitive therapy is that memories and insights must be managed. First and foremost, this means consciously dealing with them, nurturing and utilizing them to enable further growth and development.

Interestingly, the basic principles of the management of memories and knowledge, and knowledge can be compared with those of economics (especially in the context of practices such as meditation, yoga, and tantra)[416]; these would be

- Conscious use of resources[417]: This implies the need to use existing resources carefully and efficiently. This means that decisions should be made on the basis of sound analysis in order to minimize waste and achieve the greatest possible benefit.
- Mindfulness and focus on processes (flow principles)[418]: This concentration emphasizes the importance of all current activities and processes. By consciously paying attention to every step of a process, efficiency and quality can be increased, leading to better results.
- The scientific basis of both systems,[419] including the principles of verifiability, repeatability, and the value of experimentation, is essential for informed decisions and strategies. By applying scientific methods and collecting empirical data, hypotheses can be tested and theories validated, leading to informed decisions and innovative solutions.[420]
- A long-term focus[421] ensures the achievement of sustainable goals. By taking long-term effects and consequences into account, short-term gains that could lead to negative consequences in the long term can be avoided.
- The principle of abstraction requires the ability to simplify complex problems and grasp the essentials. By identifying patterns and correlations, complex situations can be better understood and managed, leading to more effective solutions.

---

416 These practices emphasize the conscious use of resources, mindfulness and a focus on processes. They are based on a scientific foundation based on verifiability, repeatability, and the value of experimentation. These practices also have a long-term orientation and utilize the principle of abstraction to understand and apply complex concepts. Cf. Yates et al. (2015), p. 13ff. and p. 388ff.
417 See Schubert (2012), p. 210ff.
418 See Pietsch (2020), p. 178ff.
419 See Schlicht (2007), pp. 2–4.
420 Ibid.
421 See Osranek (2017), p. 29ff.

These similarities clearly show that the "economy" (i.e., the external economy as an economic system) is itself primarily a product of the human mind and is based on the foundations of collective memory and cultural practices.[422] Through a conscious and mindful use of our inner resources, an individual can specifically promote personal growth and spiritual development.[423]

To summarize, economic cognitive therapy aims to identify and modify the formation mechanisms of individual narratives in order to support a more economical use of mental resources, which can lead to improved emotional stability and increased well-being.[424]

The application of the abovementioned cornerstones forms the basis for successful therapeutic intervention in economic cognitive therapy (to be developed further).[425]

The Three Key Messages

1. **Structure and functioning of thinking and remembering:** In addition to behavior and emotions, individual psychology also looks at the structure and functioning of thinking and remembering, whereby the economical handling of mental processes plays a decisive role in increasing the efficiency of individual psychological activities.
2. **Memories as complex economic dynamics:** Memories are complex economic dynamics that must be consciously shaped as they form identity and influence behavior. Consciously deciding on the meaning of memories is necessary in order to utilize resources effectively and resolve psychological complexes.
3. **Economic cognitive therapy:** Economic cognitive therapy, which is based on the conscious use of mental resources, aims to modify individual narratives and promote more efficient use of memories and cognitions, which can lead to improved emotional stability and increased well-being. And insights, which can lead to improved emotional stability and increased well-being.

---

422 Cf. also Bude (1991), p. 67f, p. 137ff.
423 See also Schubert (2012), p. 218ff.
424 Cf. ibid.
425 See also the appendix in this context.

THREE: The Three Key Messages in Brief

1. **Narration and imagination as fundamental tools:** Narration and imagination are fundamental tools in the human cognitive domain and shape retrospective experience through the construction of narrative structures and the re-evaluation of the past.
2. **An extended framework:** A framework extends the key components of narration and imagination with specific concepts such as IR, TN, and HS. These provide a comprehensive framework for the exploration and application of narrative and imaginative processes in an economic context and enable a targeted economic orientation of the transaction processes of the mind system.
3. **More effective use of mental resources:** The application of IR, TN, and HS contributes to deepening self-understanding, self-acceptance, and personal growth. These processes provide important economic resources for the mind system and enable more effective utilization of mental resources.

CHAPTER 4

METHODS AND TECHNIQUES OF ECONOMIC COGNITIVE THERAPY

The man of knowledge must not only love his enemies but also be able to hate his friends.[426]

Cognitive therapy is a therapeutic approach based on the findings and conclusions of the mental economy and aims to examine and, if necessary, change individual thinking and aims to examine and, if necessary, change individual thinking, perception, and memory in order to improve emotional well-being and mental health. The methods and techniques of insight therapy are varied and depend heavily on the needs and goals of the individual. The following chapter explains some of the central methods and techniques of this form of therapy, which is part of cognitive psychology.

In the previous chapters, the role of mental resources and their importance for our inner economy has been emphasized time and again. In this and the next chapter, the focus is more on the practical, individual psychological effects.

An Initial Overview

- **Cognitive restructuring:** This is a central technique in cognitive behavioral therapy, which is also used in insight therapy. It aims to identify negative thought patterns and replace them with rational, more realistic beliefs.

(*Continued*)

---

426 Nietzsche (1968), p. 357.

- **Mindfulness:** Mindfulness-based techniques, such as analytical meditation, are often used in insight therapy to help individuals focus more consciously on the present moment and better regulate their thoughts and emotions. Through regular practice, mindfulness can help to interrupt negative thought patterns and increase awareness of positive thoughts and feelings.
- **Metacognitive strategies:** Metacognitive approaches focus on how people can reflect on and regulate their own thought processes. Techniques such as recognizing and challenging irrational beliefs, examining thinking errors, and developing strategies for self-reflection can be used in cognitive therapy to increase the individual's awareness of their thinking patterns and promote adaptive cognitive processing.
- **Imagination work:** Through targeted visualization, imagination can be used in insight therapy to develop new perspectives and solutions. This technique can help to restructure negative memories or thoughts and strengthen positive self-images. Imagination techniques can also be used to explore alternative future scenarios and promote self-confidence and self-efficacy.
- **Self-management strategies:** Insight therapy can also involve the development of self-management strategies that enable the individual to effectively regulate and control their thoughts, emotions, and behaviors. This includes techniques such as time management, stress management, problem-solving skills, and the development of self-care practices.

These methods and techniques can be customized and combined to meet the specific needs and goals of the individual. They offer a variety of tools and strategies to improve individual thinking, feeling, and acting and to promote emotional well-being.

Basic Features of an Economic Cognitive Therapy Based on an Economized Mental System

Fate is that which is as it is, without one being able to say why, and that which all the wisdom and deliberation of human actions cannot change.[427]

---

427 Lü Bu We (1928), p. 378.

The techniques of the inner cognitive structure, the mental transaction processes, and overarching mindfulness have generally proven to be effective approaches in psychological therapy to support individual healing and growth processes.[428] Based on many years of work experience and numerous theoretical constructs, the following therapy concept has been developed, which builds on these theoretical approaches and aims to help individuals gain deeper insights into themselves and a deeper understanding of their inner processes as well as an economical way of dealing with them. This presentation is intended to provide an overview of the aims of economic insight therapy.

- **Promotion of inner mindfulness and awareness:**
  The promotion of inner mindfulness and awareness aims to encourage individuals to consciously focus on their thoughts, emotions, and physical sensations.[429] Through concrete, easy-to-learn, and easy-to-train mindfulness practices,[430] people at every stage of their own consciousness can learn to grasp the present moment as fully as possible and consciously direct their attention as fully as possible and to consciously direct their attention—both of which can be seen as the basis for engaging with the inner economic system. Numerous scientific studies have shown that mindfulness training not only improves emotional well-being but also strengthens overarching cognitive function (including attention control and stress management).[431]

- **Facilitating the identification and processing of unconscious emotions and thought concepts:**
  A central goal of economic insight therapy is to help an individual identify unconscious emotions and thought concepts and to process or implement them constructively. This can be achieved through techniques such as cognitive restructuring, psychoanalytical approaches, and emotional exposure.[432] By becoming aware of their inner conflicts and working through them, people can increase their psychological flexibility, optimize their use of mental resources, and develop a deeper understanding of themselves.[433]

---

428 Cf. Kabat-Zinn et al. (1990), p. 613ff.
429 See McKibben/Nan (2017), pp. 488–492.
430 Such as meditation, breathing exercises or body awareness.
431 Cf. Kabat-Zinn (2013), p. 203f. and Tang/Posner (2013), p. 118f.
432 See Chiesa/Serretti (2009), p. 1240ff.
433 Ibid.

- **Strengthening the ability to self-regulate and cope with stress:**
  Economic insight therapy also aims to strengthen the ability to self-regulate and cope with stress by teaching people effective coping strategies. This can include the development of stress management techniques such as relaxation exercises, time management, and problem-solving skills.[434] By strengthening these skills, individuals can learn to deal constructively with stressful situations and improve their emotional stability, both of which improve the overarching transactional structure of the mental mind system.
- **Support in the development of a positive self-concept and healthy self-acceptance:**
  A subsequent important goal of economic insight therapy is to help people build a positive self-concept and develop healthy self-acceptance. This includes fostering self-compassion, self-confidence, and self-efficacy.[435] By learning to be kind and forgiving to themselves and realistically assessing their strengths and weaknesses, people can achieve a deeper sense of well-being and satisfaction with themselves.
- **Promoting personal growth and self-realization:**
  Ultimately, insight therapy strives to promote personal growth and self-realization by helping people develop their full potential and achieve their life goals. This can be done by encouraging self-reflection, transformative goal-setting, and targeted personal development. By clarifying their values and life goals and working on their personal development, people can lead a fulfilling and meaningful life.[436]

Cognition in the sense of economic cognitive therapy thus refers to the awareness of the availability and efficient use of mental resources as well as the transaction processes and their architecture and their architecture (i.e., the expansion and process organization of the mental system) of the mental system itself. It is about understanding how your own mental system works and developing strategies to optimize the use of available resources.

---

434 See Hofmann/Asnaani/Vonk/Sawyer/Fang (2012), p. 430ff.
435 See also Chung (2012), p. 176f.
436 See Beck (2011), p. 145ff.

This approach implies (and explicitly presupposes) that the mind system must be considered similar to an (open) economic system—including the entire theoretical superstructure already mentioned—which operates with limited resources and carries out internal and external transactions in order to achieve certain goals.[437]

A central idea here is that it is precisely this mental system that can be trained and molded. Similar to physical training, targeted exercises and practices can help to improve cognitive abilities, strengthen emotional regulation, and increase resilience to stress and strain of all kinds. Through regular mental stimulation and targeted training, people can increase their cognitive performance and expand their mental capacity.

An important aspect of this economic realization is the anchoring and allocation of all individually perceived problems and complexes in the individual mental system. When people have a better understanding of their mental processes and transactions, they can recognize more concretely which problems or challenges are bothering them and work specifically on overcoming them. By mapping and understanding their mental landscape more accurately, they can develop strategies to reduce their individual mental stress and improve their mental health.

Other cornerstones of economic cognition are memories, resilience, and mental capacity. Memories play an important role in the construction of personal identity and have a significant influence on individual behavior and decision-making. By gaining a deeper understanding of their own memories and their significance, people can strengthen their resilience and expand their mental capacity. They learn to learn from past experiences, learn to remember positive experiences, and grow from negative experiences.

The overarching aim of economic knowledge is to raise awareness of mental resources and transaction processes, to train and shape the mental system, to reduce individual psychological stress, and to strengthen resilience and mental capacity. Through a holistic view of the mind system and targeted interventions, individuals can develop a deeper understanding of themselves and thus improve their mental health.[438]

---

437 Cf. Kahneman et al. (2011), p. 348ff.
438 Cf. Guttmacher (1979), p. 16f. and Chan/Sik Ying Ho/Chow (2002), 269f.

The Five Most Important Goals of Economic Cognitive Therapy

1. Promotion of inner mindfulness and awareness as a basis for realization.
2. Facilitating the identification and processing of unconscious emotions and thought concepts.
3. Optimization of internal transaction processes and the utilization of mental resources.
4. Strengthening the ability to self-regulate and cope with stress.
5. Support in the development of a positive self-concept and healthy self-acceptance, as well as the promotion of personal growth and self-realization.

To summarize, economic insight therapy aims to raise awareness of mental resources and transactional processes, to train and shape the mind system, and to strengthen resilience and overall mental capacity. Through a holistic view of the mental system and targeted interventions, people can develop a deeper understanding of themselves and improve their mental health and well-being.

Therapeutic Approaches to Economic Cognitive Therapy

The therapeutic approaches of economic cognitive therapy are specifically tailored to the economy of the mental system and aim to strengthen the awareness of mental resources, optimize the transaction processes of the mental system, and increase the capacity for cognition. A central focus is on the conscious examination of the economic principles of the mind-system, which make it possible to modify individual narratives and promote more efficient utilization of memories and insights.

An important therapeutic approach is to recognize the mind system precisely as an economic system that operates with mental resources and is accessible for economic resource utilization. This perspective allows individual thought and behavior patterns to be viewed in an economic context, enabling targeted interventions to increase the efficiency of mental resource utilization. Another approach is the training and molding of the mental system through targeted training in narration and imagination. And imagination. Techniques such as IR, TN, and HS are used to improve flexibility, improve the individual's ability to construct their own narrative structures, and create a connection between individual narration and external reality that is adapted to the individual's current challenges.

In addition, economic insight therapy places a strong focus on promoting resilience and increasing mental capacity. Through targeted work on the stability of the individual psychological system, strategies such as mindfulness, cognitive restructuring, and emotional regulation are used to strengthen the ability to cope with stressful life events and achieve improved mental health. The following five approaches are particularly relevant[439]:

- **Mindfulness-based meditation techniques:** Through guided meditation and mindfulness exercises, individuals are taught to focus on the present moment, observe their thoughts, and become aware of their bodily sensations. These practices promote self-awareness and help to achieve a state of inner calm and serenity, but also increase inner rationality and openness. Both mental states support the mental system in making self-economically rational decisions and finding a clear view of its own transaction processes.
- **Inner dialogue work and redefinition of self-narrative:**[440] This method is based on the assumption that people have complex inner systems consisting of different personality aspects, beliefs, emotions, and experiences. Therefore, it complements the economic mind system approach extremely well. By creating a dialogue framework, these aspects are activated and can relate to each other, creating a deeper objective understanding of oneself and one's own inner conflicts. This makes it possible to recognize unconscious thought patterns, identify critical process elements, and overcome negative self-beliefs.

Inner dialogue work has been used for some time in various therapeutic contexts (including cognitive behavioral therapy, Gestalt therapy, and systemic therapy). The process begins by helping individuals to become aware that different parts of the mind system are communicating with each other. This can be done through the exploration of inner voices or figures that represent different aspects of the person. An important aspect of inner dialogue is the promotion of respectful and supportive dialogue between the different parts of the spirit system. Individuals

---

439 These rather universal approaches (i.e., not specifically adapted to economic cognitive therapy) are only rudimentarily addressed; more details can be found in further literature.
440 See also Leuzinger-Bohleber,/Pfeifer (1998), p. 890ff.

need to be supported to understand the perspectives and needs of different inner aspects and to address conflicts in a constructive way. This can help to resolve inner resistance or blockages and facilitate positive change. Furthermore, inner dialogue can help promote an individual's self-reflection and self-acceptance. By learning to explore and recognize their inner experiences and conflicts, they can develop a deeper understanding of themselves and a greater capacity for self-regulation and self-leadership.[441]

- **Cognitive reframing techniques:** Cognitive restructuring is a therapeutic technique that fits very well into the framework of the economic mind system and aims to (positively) change the thought patterns and beliefs of individuals. It is based on the concept of the mental constitution of reality that our thoughts and interpretations significantly influence our emotions and behaviors. Individuals often go through situations in which their thoughts are characterized by negative beliefs or irrational assumptions that can lead to emotional distress. This is where cognitive restructuring comes in, helping individuals to identify, analyze, and re-evaluate their thoughts.[442]

The process of cognitive restructuring begins with conscious perception and recognizing one's own thoughts and thought processes. By learning to recognize their thought patterns, individuals can understand how this influences their emotions and behaviors. This step requires mindfulness and self-reflection to view one's own thought patterns objectively—in this respect, reframing techniques are more of a constructive methodology.[443] After the identification of unwanted, that is, negative or misleading thoughts, these thoughts are analyzed. Here, individuals are encouraged to collect evidence for and against their thoughts and to develop alternative interpretations of the situation in the spirit of TN. This process often involves challenging irrational beliefs and finding more realistic and constructive ways of looking at things. Ultimately, the situation is reinterpreted, and new, more positive thought patterns are developed. Individuals learn how to actively influence their thoughts in order to regulate their emotions and promote more constructive behavior. This restructured mind system helps

---

441 Ibid.
442 In this context, see also Hofmann (2023), p. 195ff. for a concretisation of applicability.
443 Ibid.

individuals to deal with challenges, strengthen their self-esteem, and improve their emotional well-being. Overall, cognitive restructuring enables individuals to develop a more conscious and flexible use of their mental resources. It enables them to actively manage their thought patterns and use constructive coping strategies—in line with a resource-optimized strategy.

- **Emotional competence:** In a safe space, individuals are guided to come to terms with their emotional experiences and express them in a constructive way. In the context of economic cognitive therapy, this can be done through creative forms of expression such as art therapy, writing therapy, or similar. The development of emotional competence is usually an accompanying technique that supports cognitive restructuring, for example.[444]
- **Integration of spiritual practices:** Spirituality, economic, and mental processes may seem like two completely different concepts at first glance. However, a closer look reveals that they are profoundly intertwined and influence each other. Modern psychology and neuroscience are increasingly exploring how this connection influences individual well-being and mental development.

Spirituality (often defined as the search for meaning and purpose beyond the material)[445] often involves practices such as meditation, prayer, and reflection. These practices can help to expand consciousness, promote inner peace, and develop a deeper understanding of oneself and the world. On the other hand, the concept of economic, mental processes refers to the way in which the individual mind system handles mental resources, makes decisions, and processes information. A central link between spirituality and economic mental processes is, therefore, the ability to self-reflect and consciously control one's own thoughts and feelings. Spiritual practices such as meditation can help to raise awareness of inner processes and improve the ability to self-regulate. This, in turn, can increase the efficiency of mental resource utilization and lead to optimized decision-making. In addition, spiritual experiences and insights can influence the individual's values and belief system, which

---

444 See also Seidel (2004), p. 31ff.
445 Spirituality can encompass various dimensions, such as the search for transcendence connection with something greater, ritual practices and the development of a personal belief system or world view. Cf. also Pargament/Exline/Jones (eds.) (2013), p. 178ff.

in turn can have an impact on economic and mental processes. For example, if someone develops a deeper understanding of compassion and connectedness through spiritual practices, this could lead them to change their decision-making structures in the mental mind system.

Another aspect is the role of spirituality in coping with stress and psychological strain. Spiritual practices such as prayer and mindfulness can help to reduce stress and strengthen resilience in the face of challenges. This strengthened resilience can, in turn, improve the efficiency of mental resource utilization and enable healthier coping with life events. For individuals who are open to spiritual approaches, elements from Eastern or Western spiritual traditions can be integrated into economic insight therapy.

All therapeutic approaches of economic cognitive therapy are about taking a holistic view of the mental system and developing targeted interventions and to develop targeted interventions aimed at promoting individual reflection on conscious thought processes as well as unconscious transactional processes. By allowing the mind system (as an ultimately impersonal entity within which the self is also located)[446] has more resources at its disposal and its efficiency increases, self-efficacy and thus self-acceptance can also be enhanced.[447] Of particular importance here is the process of integrating the abovementioned superordinate techniques into the existing individual mental system—that is, the individualization performance of a therapy that transforms the theoretical abstracts into practical, individually adapted concepts: The effect of cognition in the context of a therapeutic intervention is a central aspect of any psychological practice and is subject to a variety of complex dynamics. Cognition, defined as the acquisition of knowledge or understanding of certain aspects of the self or the environment, is an essential factor in the initiation and progression of the therapeutic process. Individuals facing and dealing with problems or complexes often seek to gain a deeper understanding of their psychological processes, behavioral patterns, and emotional responses. This is also the aim of economic insight therapy, which comprehensively integrates the experiential realities of *homo oeconomicus*. The effectiveness of therapy, in general, often depends on the

---

446 Cf. Dennett (2017), p. 163ff.
447 Ibid.

extent to which individuals can gain new insights and integrate these into their self-concept—economic insight therapy serves precisely this gain in insight. This process is made possible by the individual combination of the therapeutic approaches mentioned (such as cognitive restructuring, mindfulness practices, and narrative techniques already mentioned). By encouraging reflection and introspection, individuals can be supported in identifying cognitive distortions and activating, focusing, and using existing mental resources more effectively.[448]

Insight not only affects the cognitive level but also has profound emotional and behavioral implications. By gaining a deeper understanding of the causes of their psychological problems, individuals can better regulate their reactions and coping strategies.[449] This can lead to a reduction in individual psychological distress, as problems can be more concretely anchored and attributed—to the parallel allocation of efficiently utilized mental resources. Furthermore, gaining new insights can lead to an increased sense of self-efficacy as individuals realize that they are able to bring about positive changes in their lives; the positive use of resources evokes itself. This process can help to strengthen motivation to move forward and overcome obstacles.[450]

Overall, cognition functions act as a catalytic component of therapeutic change in economic cognitive therapy, enabling individuals to deepen their self-understanding, expand their capacity to act, and, at the same time, deepen their options for action. Through the continuous promotion of cognitive processes within the mental system, a significant contribution can be made to mental health and individually perceived happiness.

The treatment and cognition process

The treatment and cognitive process of economic cognitive therapy is aimed at optimally utilizing an individual's overall mental resources and increasing their general cognitive ability. The aim is to consciously deal with mental resources and transaction processes in order to reduce the individual's perceived psychological stress and promote an objective attitude toward the reality of the

---

448 See Newell (1994), p. 243ff.
449 See Beck (2024), pp. 24–39.
450 Ibid, p. 338ff.

outside world and its acceptance.[451] As already mentioned, various therapeutic approaches and techniques are used here, which are systematically interlinked. The process of economic insight therapy with its six phases is outlined below:

1. **Awareness of mental resources and transaction processes create**
   The first step in economic insight therapy is to sensitize the individual to their mental resources and internal transaction processes. This involves promoting awareness of how thoughts, emotions, and memories interact with each other, how these processes interact with each other, and how these processes influence behavior and perception. Through targeted reflection exercises and the application of cognitive techniques, the individual is enabled to recognize and understand their internal processes. Likewise, in a later step, thoughts and thought patterns of the individual's own mental system become more clearly recognizable. By developing these self-observation skills, an individual can learn to better understand and control their thoughts (and emotions).[452]

2. **Adaptation and optimization of the individual spirit system**
   As soon as a fundamental awareness of the functioning of the mind system and its economic dimension, economic insight therapy focuses on the adaptation and optimization of the mind system and its (transaction) processes. This is done by applying the core methodology introduced in the process (such as cognitive restructuring, in which dysfunctional thought patterns are identified and replaced by more realistic economic thoughts). In parallel, mindfulness practices support acceptance of the present experience and non-reactive observation, leading to better regulation of emotions. Advanced narrative techniques support the individual in reconstructing their life story and opening up new meanings of memories, thus further activating this crucial mental resource.[453]

3. **Internal modification of the internal narrative**
   The modification of an individual's often irrational or procedurally and economically flawed internal narrative is also closely linked to the adaptation and optimization of the mental system. By challenging and replacing these internal narrative structures with more realistic

---

451 Which, according to the current state of research, is a decisive factor for individually perceived happiness based on economic principles. Cf. Frey/Frey-Marti (2010), p. 458ff.
452 See Bishop (2004), pp. 232–234.
453 See Baumeister/Vohs/Tice (2007), pp. 356–359.

and economically balanced alternatives,[454] psychological problems and complexes can be actively drawn into reality and thus addressed and possibly resolved or at least reduced.[455]

4. **Reducing mental stress through coping strategies**
   The individual psychological burden caused by psychological problems can be significantly reduced through economic insight therapy, as problems can be anchored and assigned more concretely. Through the structured analysis and interpretation of one's own life circumstances and mental processes, psychological problems become less diffuse and, therefore, easier to cope with. This process of concretization helps to reduce anxiety and stress and increases the individual's ability to act.[456] This can also include the development of problem-solving skills, stress management techniques, and relaxation techniques.

5. **Memories, resilience, and mental capacity as cornerstones of the mental economy establish**
   Memories play a central role in economic cognitive therapy, as they form the basis for an individual's self-image and identity. Through the application of imagination, reconstruction memories can be interpreted and re-evaluated in an organized way, which helps to process traumatic experiences. Resilience is increased by strengthening positive coping strategies and promoting flexible thinking. Mental capacity is expanded through techniques to increase concentration and the effective utilization of cognitive resources.

6. **Integration and application of the findings**
   A central component of the therapeutic process is the integration of the insights gained into the individual's everyday life. This is done through practical exercises and targeted interventions aimed at translating the new insights into concrete behavior. Therapists support the individual in consolidating the new insights and applying them in various areas of life. An important part of economic insight therapy is also "homework" and self-exercises aimed at integrating the skills and strategies learned into an individual's everyday life. This promotes the practical application of the therapeutic principles and supports long-term changes.

---

454 In the sense of mental economy.
455 See also Beck (2011), pp. 145–175 and White/Epston (1990), pp. 5–19.
456 See Wells (2011), p. 74f.

Psychological insight therapy is effective in treating a variety of mental disorders, including depression, anxiety disorders, and post-traumatic stress disorder.[457] It provides a structured and evidence-based approach to changing thought patterns and beliefs in order to improve an individual's emotional well-being and, ultimately, quality of life (particularly through adjustment to and reappraisal of external reality); the therapy concept provides a holistic reference point for psychological healing and personal development.

The Therapeutic Approaches of Economic Insight Therapy Can Be Summarised in Three Core Statements

1. **Awareness for mental resources and transaction processes creates:** Economic insight therapy aims to sensitize the individual to their mental resources and internal transactional processes. Through reflection exercises and cognitive techniques, the understanding and control of one's own thoughts, emotions, and memories lead to a more conscious and efficient utilization of mental resources.
2. **Adaptation and optimization of the mind system:** A key approach is to view the mind system as an economic system that can be optimized through targeted interventions. This includes techniques such as cognitive restructuring, mindfulness practice, and narrative techniques that aim to change dysfunctional thought patterns, better regulate emotions, and open up new meanings of memories. The individual narrative becomes flexible and adapted to current challenges.
3. **Promoting resilience and mental capacity:** Economic insight therapy places great emphasis on increasing resilience and mental capacity. Through techniques such as mindfulness, cognitive restructuring, and emotional regulation, strategies for coping with stress and mental health are promoted. The integration of the insights gained into everyday life supports long-term positive changes and an increased sense of self-efficacy.

---

457 See Beck/Alford (2009), pp. 255–278.

Advanced Methods and Techniques of Economic Cognitive Therapy

If you think something is right, you should do it. And if you do it, nothing on earth can stop you. If you think something is wrong, let it go, and if you let it go, nothing on earth can force you to do it.[458]

In addition to the process of economic cognitive therapy just outlined, there is a whole set of specific economic-psychological methods and techniques that can be usefully applied within its framework—these will be presented and explained below.

At this point, I will briefly comment on methods and techniques, as I am often asked this question in practice: the difference between method and technique can be clearly distinguished in scientific contexts, even if the terms are often used interchangeably in everyday life. A method refers to a systematic approach that serves to achieve a specific goal or solve a problem. It always comprises an overarching strategy and theoretical principles on which the practical procedure is based. A technique, on the other hand, is a specific action or tool within a specific method that is used to implement and execute the methodological steps. Methods are usually broader and theoretically based. They provide a comprehensive framework within which techniques are applied.[459] The distinction between method and technique is essential as it provides clarity on how theoretical approaches are put into practice. Methods provide the structural and theoretical framework that guides practice, while techniques are concrete steps or tools that are applied within this framework.

> In summary, it can be said that methods represent the theoretical (and strategic) superstructure, while techniques comprise the practical steps and tools that are used to realize the methodological objectives. The two are inextricably linked, with the method providing the context and direction and the techniques providing the operational means to achieve the goal.

---

458 Lü Bu We (1928), p. 378.

459 For example, the method of cognitive behavioral therapy (CBT) can be used in psychological research, which describes a theoretical approach to treating mental disorders by changing thought patterns and behavior. Various techniques are used within this method, such as cognitive restructuring, exposure therapy or mindfulness exercises. Each of these techniques serves a specific purpose and contributes to the realisation of the overarching method.

See also Beck (2011), pp. 46–58 and 100–122.

FIGURE 12 Overview of the specific methods and techniques of economic cognitive therapy.[460]

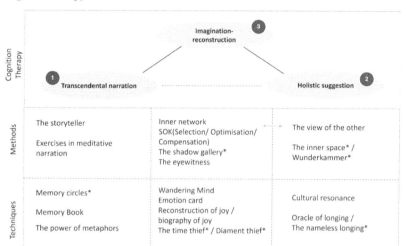

I would like to make a second comment on the following methods and techniques of economic insight therapy: in principle, they are all (like all the other topics presented) directly applicable, although some of the methods rely heavily on external dialogue and should be supported by guidance and guidance in their actual implementation. The outer dialogue reflects the inner dialogue and stimulates it. In this respect, economic insight therapy is a discursive form of counseling.

Figure 12 provides an overview of all the specific techniques and methods used in economic cognitive therapy, grouped according to the three basic methods of economic cognitive therapy.[461] The methods and techniques are also explained further in this order as follows.

Methods and techniques of IR

The methods and techniques of IR focus on analyzing and re-evaluating memories. All approaches aim to fundamentally transform the way in which individuals

---

460 Own presentation.
461 The methods or techniques marked with an asterisk (*) have been specially developed or modified for the context of economic cognitive therapy.

perceive and interpret their past experiences. The central commonality of all these methods is their focus on imagination processes, which require and promote both creativity and mental flexibility.

IR techniques use the human ability to visualize and mentally simulate to process memories analytically. These techniques enable individuals not only to think through past events cognitively but also to relive them emotionally. By re-experiencing and creatively re-organizing memories, deeply rooted emotional and cognitive patterns can be broken up and transformed.

An essential aspect of IR is the use of creativity. Creativity plays a key role as it supports the process of imagining and creating new scenarios.[462] This ability allows individuals to develop alternative perspectives on their memories and re-evaluate them. At the same time, IR requires and promotes mental flexibility. Mental flexibility refers to the ability to mentally switch back and forth between different concepts and to integrate new information and perspectives into existing cognitive structures. This flexibility is crucial to release the rigid and often maladaptive patterns that have formed around certain memories. By consciously incorporating new and varied imaginative processes, individuals learn to look at their memories from different angles and engage with new meanings and insights.

The specific techniques of IR help to better understand the cognitive and emotional functioning of one's own mental system and to change the reaction to one's own memories. By actively telling and rewriting their stories, they can develop a more coherent and positive self-perception.

Inner network

The methodology of the "inner network" in economic cognitive therapy is based on the concept that the human self (as already described)[463] consists of multiple parts and processes that interact with each other and constitute behavior and emotional experience. This therapy methodology aims to achieve a deeper understanding and comprehensive self-knowledge through the exploration and integration of these inner parts. The methodology is closely linked to concepts from systemic therapy and uses elements of self-reflection and inner dialogue.[464]

---

462 Cf. Singer (1975), pp. 45–67.
463 Cf. Chapter 3.
464 See Hermans/Gieser (2012), pp. 20–34.

The four foundations and principles of the "inner network."

1. **Multiplicity of the self:** The theory of the "inner network" assumes that the self is not monolithic but multiple. Every person has different inner parts or sub-personalities that represent different needs, desires, fears, and perspectives.[465]
2. **Inner dialogues and self-reflection:** A central component of the methodology is the promotion of inner dialogues between these different parts—or the promotion of intra-systemic exchange and transaction processes. Through targeted self-reflection and therapeutically guided inner dialogues, individuals learn to identify and name their individual inner processes and to understand their specific functions and goals.
3. **Systemic understanding:** The "inner network" is seen as a system in which the inner parts interact with each other and strive for balance. Dysfunctional patterns, such as overpowering self-criticism or suppressed emotional parts, can lead to psychological problems. The aim of the method is to create a harmonious and balanced inner system.[466]
4. **Mindfulness and acceptance:** The methodology emphasizes the importance of mindfulness and acceptance of all inner parts and processes. Instead of suppressing or ignoring certain parts, individuals should learn to recognize and accept these parts. This promotes a holistic self-image and contributes to emotional holism.[467]

At the beginning of the methodology, individuals are guided to identify their various inner parts or become aware of their underlying processes, a process that is supported by imaginative techniques, role-playing, or structured interviews. The aim is to create an inner picture or map of the inner network. In subsequent sessions, each identified part is explored in detail, with an individual entering into a conscious dialogue with these processes in order to better understand them. The overarching goal of the methodology is to achieve a harmonious integration of the various processes into a conscious part of the mind-system,

---

465 In slightly simplified terms, this view also corresponds to the actual structure of the spirit system.
466 See Schwartz/Sweezy (2019), pp. 13–40.
467 See Baer (2010), p. 168f.

which means that all parts or processes are accepted and do not exert excessive dominance. By working with the inner network, individuals develop improved self-regulation and emotional resilience by learning to recognize and resolve their inner conflicts and develop strategies to better deal with stressful situations and emotional challenges.

The methodology of the "Inner Network" is based on concepts of the inner family as developed in Internal Family Systems (IFS) Therapy.[468] Studies on the effectiveness of IFS and similar approaches show positive results in the treatment of anxiety disorders, depression, post-traumatic stress disorder (PTSD), and other mental illnesses. These studies show that working with inner parts leads to improved self-awareness, emotional balance, and mental health.[469]

As a methodology within the framework of the economic insight therapy "Inner Network," a comprehensive and integrative approach to self-knowledge and psychological healing. By exploring and integrating their inner parts, clients can develop a deeper understanding of themselves and strengthen their psychological resilience.

- The concept of the "inner network" in economic cognitive therapy is based on the multiplicity of the self, which consists of different inner parts that interact with each other and influence behavior and emotional experience.
- The aim of the methodology is to explore and integrate these parts through inner dialogue, self-reflection, systemic understanding, mindfulness, and acceptance. to achieve a harmonious inner balance and strengthen self-regulation and emotional resilience.

Modified selection, optimization, and compensation

The basic selection, optimization, and compensation (SOC) methodology is an integrative model that was developed in the context of developmental psychology.[470] This model describes adaptive mechanisms that individuals use to maintain and improve their quality of life and performance over time.[471] Economic cognitive therapy builds on its concept and utilizes its mechanisms in a broader framework tailored to the economized mind system.

---

468 See Schwartz/Sweezy (2019), p. 38f.
469 Cf. Butler et al. (2008), pp. 105–107.
470 Cf. Baltes/Baltes (1990), p. 1ff.
471 Ibid.

Selection

Selection refers to the process of choosing and prioritizing goals and activities. In the context of economic cognitive therapy, however, the momentum of selection is objectified, that is, subjected to the previously outlined decision-making logic of the transaction-based mental system. Selection takes place in the same way as in a process-based project plan[472] and can take two forms:

- Elective selection: This is the conscious decision to pursue certain goals and abandon others based on individual preferences, abilities, and resources. This form of selection enables individuals to focus their energy and resources on the most important and (potentially) most fulfilling goals.[473]
- Loss-based selection: This occurs when individuals must adapt to changing circumstances, for example, due to external restrictions or mental barriers. It involves the modification of goals and plans to fulfill the new circumstances. This can mean that certain goals are abandoned or changed to continue fulfilling activities.[474]

Optimization

Optimization refers to the investment of resources resulting from the selection to maximize the pursuit of the selected objectives. This can include various strategies[475]:

- Improvement of intrapersonal skills: Through training and (mental) practice, individuals can improve their competences in the selected areas to achieve their goals more effectively.
- More effective use of external resources: The use of support systems of all kinds can also contribute to optimization.
- Efficient use of resources: This involves the strategic planning and organization of activities to make the best possible use of available resources and support the achievement of objectives.

---

472 Ibid.
473 Ibid.
474 Cf. Baltes/Lindenberger/Staudinger (1998), p. 1055ff.
475 Ibid, p. 1034f.

Compensation

Compensation comes to the fore when events occur that jeopardize the achievement of goals. Compensation strategies enable individuals to continue to act effectively despite these events[476]:

- Alternative strategies: If the skills available to you do not lead to the achievement of your goals, you can find alternative ways to achieve the same (or comparable) goals.
- Adaptation of the goals: In some cases, it may be necessary to modify the goals themselves to adapt them to the changed abilities and situations.
- Increase in effort: Individuals can invest more time, energy, or other resources to compensate for events and still achieve their goals.

The basic fit in the framework of economic cognitive therapy lies in the process-based, relatively mechanistic flow chart of the SOC methodology—this enables a good fit for application in the therapeutic framework.

In practice, the SOC methodology is used to help individuals develop adaptive strategies and improve their quality of life despite challenges and changes. The application usually includes the following steps[477]:

1. Assessment: First, the client's current goals, abilities, and limitations are evaluated to create a basis for the selection of suitable strategies.
2. Goal setting and planning: Together, an individual selects specific, realistic, and meaningful goals (selection) and develops a plan to optimize resources.
3. Strategy development: Identification and implementation of optimization and compensation strategies to achieve the chosen goals despite possible restrictions.
4. Evaluation and adjustment: The effectiveness of the strategies applied is regularly reviewed, and if necessary, adjustments are made to further support the achievement of objectives.

By applying the SOC methodology in the context of the inner economy, individuals can learn to organize their goals and resources more efficiently,

---

476 Cf. Baltes/Baltes (1990), p. 26f.
477 Based on Baltes/Baltes (1990).

leading to an improved quality of life and a higher level of self-efficacy. This model is particularly valuable for individuals facing significant life changes.

- The methodology of selection, optimization, and compensation (SOC) in an economic context:
  ○ Selection: Selection and prioritization of goals, divided into elective selection (conscious goal setting) and loss-based selection (adaptation to changes).
  ○ Optimization: Maximizing resource investment by improving capabilities, effective use of external resources, and efficient planning.
  ○ Compensation: The application of replacement strategies, adjustment of targets, and increase in expenditure are used to ensure target achievement despite obstacles.
- Application of the SOC methodology in economic insight therapy: The SOC methodology is used in a structured, process-based framework to develop adaptive strategies that improve quality of life despite challenges and changes. The methodology includes the steps of assessment, goal setting, planning, strategy development, evaluation, and adaptation.

The shadow gallery

"The Shadow Gallery" is a psychological therapy method of economic insight therapy, which is based on the concepts and theories of Carl Gustav Jung and deals in particular with the aspect of self-knowledge and integration of the shadow into the individual mental system. This method uses various techniques to help an individual recognize and integrate unconscious parts of the self and integrate them, ultimately leading to a more holistic personality and a deeper awareness of transactional processes.[478]

The main content of the "Shadow Gallery" is based on the concept of the shadow as an integral part of the human psyche. The shadow encompasses all those aspects of the self that a person represses or does not recognize because they are seen as negative or undesirable. These aspects can include both personal characteristics and collective archetypal patterns.[479]

---

478 Cf. Jung (2001b), p. 8ff.
479 Ibid.

The Shadow Gallery methodology assumes that the integration of these repressed aspects is necessary to achieve psychological well-being and self-knowledge. The methodology involves several steps and techniques that are systematically applied to guide an individual through this six-step process:

1. **Identifying the shadow:** The first step in the "shadow gallery" is to identify the various shadow aspects of an individual. This is done using techniques such as free association, dream analysis, and projective methods. It also involves recognizing patterns and recurring themes that point to repressed or unconscious content.[480]
2. **Confrontation and recognition:** Once the shadow aspects are identified, an individual is guided to consciously confront them. This requires specific qualities (such as courage, openness, and honesty), as the confrontation with the respective shadow aspects can often be perceived as unpleasant or painful—however, the framework model of economic insight therapy supports this sub-step, as it does not include any concept of individual guilt or shame.[481] The recognition of shadow aspects is essential for the desired mental holism of insight therapy—therefore, the overview of the "shadow processes" of the mind system is an important part of that methodology.
3. **Symbolic work and creative forms of expression:** Another (optional) component of the shadow gallery methodology is working with symbols and creative expression. Through painting, writing, or visualization exercises, individuals can explore their shadow aspects in a non-verbal and often deeper way. These creative techniques help to bring unconscious content into consciousness and process it, as well as to better understand their mental processes and functions.[482]
4. **Integration and transformation:** The next step is to integrate the recognized shadow aspects into the conscious self and its mental process landscape. This can be done through narrative transformative or transcendental techniques where an individual learns to see these aspects in a positive overall context and to accept and embrace them as part of their overall mental reality.[483]

---

480 Cf. Jung et al. (1994), p. 402ff.
481 See Roesler (2006), p. 481f.
482 Cf. Jung (1994), p. 233ff.
483 Ibid, p. 168f.

5. **Working with archetypes:** In further reference to the work of C.G. Jung, archetypal images and motifs of economics and business are also used to explore deeper psychological structures. Business is also used to explore deeper psychological structures and to learn about them, to perceive the shadow aspects of mental processes as if in a gallery, and ultimately integrate them in order to gain a better understanding of all inner dynamics.[484]
6. **Reflection and self-observation:** An accompanying, ongoing process in the "shadow gallery" is self-reflection. Individuals are encouraged to document their progress and record their thoughts and feelings in diaries. This promotes mindfulness and the ability to self-observe, which supports long-term integration and inner growth.

The overarching goal of the shadow gallery methodology is ultimately "economic individuation."[485] By working with the shadow and integrating its functional significance for the spirit system, a coherent and holistic self-image can be developed, as required by economic cognitive therapy. This involves recognizing and integrating both positive and negative aspects of the mental process landscape. This awareness and integration reduce inner conflict and promote psychological wholeness. The methodology makes it possible to better recognize how the individual mental mind system works and, at the same time, increases affect regulation.[486] The acceptance and integration of the shadow aspects promote a more comprehensive sense of self-worth and an authentic, effective way of life.

The "Shadow Gallery" is a profound therapeutic method that offers a structured approach to exploring and integrating the shadow in an economic context, contributing to the wholeness and mental health of the individual. Through imaginative, creative, and analytical techniques, the "Shadow Gallery" supports the process of economic individuation—becoming what you

---

484 See also Jung (1954), pp. 211–218.
485 Individuation is a process that Jung describes as the continuous development of the self and the integration of all parts of the personality. This psychological concept establishes a link to economic cognitive therapy by demonstrating that the comprehensive integration and harmonization of an individual's inner aspects can lead to a more efficient use of mental resources. In economic terms, this means that the optimal structuring and alignment of mental processes can contribute to the promotion of a holistic and productive self-concept.
486 See Schore (2007), pp. 42–46.

already are without being able to consciously recognize it. This is the basis for an efficient mental mind system with economically working transaction processes.

- The shadow gallery is a psychological therapy method of economic insight therapy that promotes self-knowledge and the integration of repressed shadow aspects into the individual spirit system.
- The six-stage process includes identifying the shadow through techniques such as free association and dream analysis, confronting and recognizing these aspects, symbolic work and creative forms of expression, integrating and transforming the shadow aspects, working with archetypal images and motifs, and ongoing reflection and self-observation.
- The goal of the shadow gallery is economic individuation, which, by recognizing and integrating both positive and negative aspects of the mental process landscape, leads to a coherent and holistic self-image, better affect regulation, a more comprehensive sense of self-worth, and an authentic way of life.

The eyewitness

"The Eyewitness" is a method that aims to promote the understanding and processing of personal experiences through active, reflective re-enactment. This technique enables individuals to not only reconstruct their memories but also reexperience and reinterpret their memories, allowing for deeper insights and more sustainable healing.[487]

The central concept of this technique is to turn an individual into a viewer of their own experience, with the mind acting as a kind of recording device. This means that the person views their past experiences as if they were watching a film while at the same time being able to actively intervene and influence events. This distanced yet active role allows past successes to be specifically recalled and not just remembered but restaged. Through this reenactment, the events are not only relived cognitively but also emotionally.[488]

The method involves several steps. First, the experience is recalled and relived in detail, including the sensory impressions, words, and reactions that played a role at the time. It is crucial that an individual does not just remain a spectator

---

487 See Samide/Ritchey (2021), p. 849f.
488 Ibid, p. 853f.

but actively goes through the situation, reexperiences it, and, if necessary, reacts differently. This process is supported by the concept of "psychodrama," in which emotions and mental processes are mirrored and thus made conscious. An individual takes on both roles and can pause, discuss, and work out alternatives as required. This enables deep reflection and a differentiated examination of the experience.[489]

Particularly important here is the separate consideration of mental processes (thoughts) and feelings (emotions). This differentiation makes it easier to understand how certain thoughts lead to certain feelings and vice versa. Repeating this process promotes understanding and the acquisition of new insights. By reliving and actively engaging with the process, a healing process can be initiated by bringing hidden or repressed feelings to the surface and releasing them.

Another aspect of this technique is the metaphor of turning the world into a game. The rules of the game are designed in such a way that they enable ease and flexible handling of the experiences. In an individualistic culture in which there is often a collective error, such as pluralistic ignorance, this technique is particularly valuable.[490] Pluralistic ignorance describes the phenomenon in which individuals view their own inner experiences as deviating from the norm, even though many have similar feelings and thoughts but do not communicate this. This discrepancy often leads to a distorted self-perception as people feel inferior to others because they have an enormous knowledge advantage over themselves.

The "eyewitness" technique helps to bridge this inner–outer divergence. By consciously staging and reflecting on one's own experiences, the inner stream of thoughts can be interrupted and reorganized. This leads to a more concrete self-perception and self-organization. The individual learns to understand their inner world better and, at the same time, to make milder judgments, which leads to a less distorted self-perception. By interrupting the destructive effect of the continuous inner stream of thoughts, a safe space is created for narration and reflection, which enables a more authentic view of one's own mental system.

The following principles are used in the "eyewitness" methodology:

1. **Remain a mirrored observer of your own experience**
   - An individual is guided to view their experiences from a distanced perspective, like an eyewitness. This makes it possible to use one's own mental system like a recording device and to view past events without

---

489 Ibid, p. 145f.
490 Ibid, p. 153ff.

direct emotional involvement; the individual mental processes are decoupled and can be viewed in isolation.[491]
- Recalling past successes specifically: The individual not only remembers past successes but reenacts them. By actively going through the sensory impressions, words, and reactions, the experience becomes vivid and real. This involves the client reenacting the experiences and taking on the roles of various participants.
- Reexperience and react: During the reenactment, an individual can pause, discuss the events, and work out alternative reactions. This element of psychodrama reflects emotions and makes it possible to comment on and reflect on reactions and emotions. In doing so, mental processes (thoughts) and resources (emotions) separately promote a differentiated perception.
- Repetition and understanding: New insights can be gained through repeated restaging and reflection. This helps to recognize unhealed wounds or emotional scars and to promote the healing process through relief and restaging. This technique brings hidden or suppressed feelings to the surface and enables them to be integrated.

2. **Turn the world into a game**
   - A central element of this methodology is to view the outer world as a kind of game of the inner world, whereby the rules of the game are metastable.[492] This is in contrast to the often serious and rigid perception of everyday life and enables a more flexible approach to one's own experiences and emotions; an individual can take on several roles at the same time, stopping and modifying events.
   - Individualistic culture and collective error: In individualistic cultures, pluralistic ignorance often prevails, where people believe that their own thoughts and feelings are unique and deviate from the norms. This perception leads to a distorted self-perception as people feel inferior to others because they have an enormous knowledge advantage over themselves.
   - Inner–outer divergence: There is a discrepancy between inner and outer perception. While the structure of one's own inner world is known, including weaknesses and negative thoughts, this is not the case for others. This divergence leads to a dualism that distorts self-perception.

---

491 Ibid.
492 Ibid, p. 154f.

- Interrupt the inner stream of thoughts: An important aspect of the methodology is to interrupt the continuous inner stream of thoughts. This helps to experience a concrete self-perception and self-categorization that is not distorted by potentially destructive thought patterns. The "Stream of Continuous" is also fundamentally based on a destructive principle.[493]

As a multistage method, "The Eyewitness" offers a structured yet flexible framework that enables an individual to look at their past from a new perspective, gain deeper insights, and experience emotional wholeness. It encourages a holistic examination of one's own experiences and supports the process of self-discovery and self-acceptance and, thus, the transactional throughput of the mind system.

- The "eyewitness" method promotes the processing of personal experiences through reflective re-enactment, in which individuals reconstruct and reinterpret their memories. And can thus change or dissolve complexes.
- This technique allows individuals to act as distanced spectators of their own experiences, enabling them to actively intervene in the reimagined events in order to emotionally and cognitively re-experience and process past events.
- By consciously staging and reflecting on one's own experiences, the method helps to bridge the discrepancy between inner and outer perception, leading to a more authentic self-perception, which leads to a more authentic self-perception and a less and less distorted self-assessment.

---

493 The stream of continuous consciousness describes the uninterrupted flow of thoughts, perceptions, and sensations in the human mind. However, this continuous chain of mental events can also contain a destructive principle. In particular, it should be emphasized that incessant rumination or a constant flood of negative thoughts can lead to mental stress, anxiety, and depression. These negative thought loops can be destructive as they reduce cognitive and emotional resilience and impair processes in the mental system.
   Cf. Nolen-Hoeksema/Wisco/Lyubomirsky (2008), p. 402ff.

Wandering mind

The "Wandering Mind" technique initially describes a state in which the brain turns to the inner world without a specific task and involves various sensory levels, such as visual, auditory, olfactory, gustative, and somatosensory perceptions.[494] This type of free, unplanned thinking allows the mind to naturally jump from one thought to the next without being limited by external demands or tasks.[495]

One of the key characteristics of the Wandering Mind is its ability to integrate different sensory modalities. While the brain is at rest without specific tasks, visual images, sounds, smells, tastes, and physical sensations can spontaneously emerge and interact with each other. These multisensory experiences contribute to the individual creating and experiencing a rich inner world.

The Wandering Mind also encourages creative problem-solving and innovative ideas by allowing the brain to associate freely and without restrictions. Many significant scientific and artistic breakthroughs occurred during moments of mind wandering when the brain made unexpected connections between seemingly unrelated concepts.[496] This ability to generate new and original ideas is a crucial part of human creativity. In addition, the wandering mind has an important function in the processing of emotions and personal reflection. By wandering freely, individuals can explore their feelings and thoughts in a free, non-judgmental space. This can contribute to emotional regulation and a deeper understanding of one's own mental processes. Research has shown that people who regularly spend time daydreaming or mind-wandering often have higher levels of emotional resilience and psychological well-being.

The wandering mind is also important for planning and looking ahead to future events. By allowing the brain to associate freely without a specific task, scenarios and plans can be designed and mentally played through. This forward-looking way of thinking helps individuals to prepare for upcoming challenges and clarify their goals and wishes.

---

494 See Smallwood/Schooler (2015), pp. 490–492.
495 The concept of the wandering mind has been identified as a key human ability that plays an important role in mental utilisation. In the Wandering Mind state, the brain is particularly active and utilizes a variety of neural networks, including the Default Mode Network (DMN), which is involved in introspective thoughts, self-reflection, and memory retrieval. retrieval of memories.
    See Christoff/Gordon/Smallwood/Smith/Schooler (2009), pp. 8721–8723.
496 See Smallwood/Schooler (2015), p. 502ff.

- The Wandering Mind technique is an essential component of human cognition.
- This trainable ability enables the brain to work freely on all sensory levels and makes a significant contribution to active living.
- By allowing and encouraging mind wandering, individuals can develop a deeper understanding of themselves and their environment.

Emotion card

The emotion map technique (also known as "emotion mapping" or "emotion map") is an innovative psychological tool that aims to analyze individual emotional experiences or the emotional evaluation of memories, spatially and visually.[497] This technique helps to gain a better understanding of one's own emotional world and to identify emotional patterns and their triggers.

When creating an emotion map, an individual is asked to draw a map or diagram depicting different emotional states and their intensities in relation to specific life events or situations. This visual representation can be done in different ways, for example, using colors, symbols, or images that represent different emotions. The technique requires an individual to become aware of their feelings, perceive them clearly, and relate them to the triggers and contexts in which these emotions occur.

A central aspect of the emotion map is the identification of patterns and connections between emotions and certain experiences or contexts. Visual mapping often makes unconscious emotional reactions and their connections clearly visible, which enables a deeper insight into one's own emotional dynamics. This technique, therefore, promotes self-reflection and emotional awareness, which is crucial for emotional regulation and well-being.[498]

The emotion map can be used, for example, to identify and change dysfunctional thought patterns and their emotional effects on the spirit system or to facilitate access to deeper emotions and to process them. It supports the reconstruction and reevaluation of narratives from an emotional perspective.

---

497 See also Kokoska/Nicholson (2005), p. 388ff.
498 Cf. Greenberg/Paivio (1997).

- The emotion map is an effective technique that enables individuals to visually represent and analyze their emotional landscape.
- It promotes emotional awareness, self-reflection, and communication in therapy and offers valuable insights into the connections between emotions and memories.
- By identifying and reevaluating emotional patterns, the emotion map supports the realization of emotion as a resource. Emotion.

Reconstruction of joy / biography of joy

The psychological technique of joy reconstruction aims to analyze and reevaluate past joyful experiences to maximize their positive effect in the present moment. Maximize their positive impact in the present moment. It is based on the idea that joy is experienced not only in the moment but also through consciously remembering and reflecting on these moments. And reflection on these moments can have a profound effect on the individual.

Joy reconstruction begins with the memory of joyful events, considering both the aspects of joy and the associated difficulties. Joy is often described as an emotional state in which expectations are exceeded, leading to a sense of empathy with the world and one's situation.[499] This state creates emotional heights and expanses that even evoke a conditional suggestion of the transcendental.[500]

A central aspect of joy reconstruction is the development of a so-called "joy biography." This biographical reflection traces the changes and developments in joy over the course of a lifetime and helps to identify patterns and key events that have led to special moments of joy. This analysis can show how joy has shaped life and which factors were particularly favorable.[501]

Joy has the special ability to open up ego boundaries and promote trust and naivety,[502] but this can also lead to increased vulnerability. Nevertheless, experiencing and remembering joy is a central resource of the self. Joy is a universal emotion that can be evoked by a variety of triggers, such as achievement, relationships, consumption, growth, beauty, and even the absence

---

499 Cf. Kast (2010), p. 79f.
500 Cf. Csikszentmihalyi (2002), p. 124ff.
501 Cf. Kast (2010), p. 80f.
502 A personality trait characterised by credulity, ignorance, and a simple view of the world. Naive people tend to trust others without sufficient skepticism and to simplify complex situations. See also Peterson/Seligman (2004), p. 549f.

of pain.[503] An essential part of joy reconstruction is creating a precise framework for imagination. This involves identifying the triggers for joy, consciously experiencing the associated feelings, and reflecting on their impact on mood and behavior. Anticipation, which is characterized by imagination, curiosity, and uncertainty, also plays a role. By imagining joyful events in detail and reliving them, these positive feelings can be brought into the present and even expanded.[504]

Emotional contagion is another phenomenon that is utilized in joy reconstruction. Joy can not only be taken over by other people but can also be reinforced by one's own recourse to joyful memories. This "self-contagion" of joy helps to create a stronger connection to oneself and to better recognize and appreciate the quality of one's own joy. Gratitude plays an important role here, as it helps to consciously reflect on and appreciate joyful experiences. This can be supported by melancholy, which makes it possible to relive past joys and bring them into the present. This philosophy of joy, as also described by Epicurus, emphasizes the importance of both moving and still joys and their scope and pervasiveness in life.[505]

In this context, it should be emphasized that joy is also sometimes the most significant, richest emotion in an (internal and external) economic sense,[506] as it represents a cornerstone of the mental system as its *telos*. This teleological perspective implies that pleasure is not just an incidental or secondary emotion but the main goal toward which human life and its various activities

---

503 This aspect is closely linked to humor. Cf. ibid. p. 584ff.
504 Cf. Fredrickson (2001), p. 223f.
505 Cf. Kast (2010), p. 86.
506 Joy not only plays an important role on an individual and emotional level, but also has significant implications in a macroeconomic context. From an economic perspective, joy is a fundamental and extremely rich emotion that can also be seen as a constant of the human economic system. Its importance lies in its ability to promote motivation, productivity, and social capital.

Joy as a motivator and driver of productivity: Joy and positive emotions in general are powerful motivators. They not only promote individual performance, but also collective productivity in organizations and societies. According to the broaden-and-build theory, positive emotions such as joy expand the scope of thought and action of individuals, which leads to more creative problem-solving, better decision-making, and increased flexibility. This expanded mindset is crucial for innovation and increased efficiency, which are of great importance in economic systems (Cf. Fredrickson (2001), pp. 219–222).

Joy as a component of social capital: Joy contributes significantly to building and maintaining social networks and relationships. Positive social interactions that generate

are directed. Aristotle's concept of *eudaimonia* (often translated as happiness or well-being) emphasizes that the pursuit of joy and fulfillment is the ultimate goal of human life:

> The good, the highest goal, is eudaimonia. And the definition of eudaimonia is the activity of the soul according to virtue, namely according to the best and most perfect virtue in a perfect life.[507]

- Joy reconstruction is a structured technique for analyzing and evaluating past joyful experiences, which can lead to greater emotional resilience and a deeper understanding of the self.
- This technique emphasizes the diversity of sources of joy and the importance of conscious reflection and appreciation in order to maximize the positive effects of this emotion and integrate it sustainably into one's own life.

The time thief/diamond thief

The psychological technique of "time thief/diamond thief" is an integrated approach that aims to analyze and transform individual perceptions of time and personal resources in an economic context. This technique is based on the metaphorical idea that certain thought patterns and behaviors can act as either "time thieves" or "diamond thieves." While time thieves refer to activities and thoughts that steal valuable time and use it ineffectively, diamond thieves

---

joy strengthen social capital—a network of relationships based on trust, co-operation, and reciprocity. This social capital is invaluable in economic contexts as it fosters collaboration and knowledge sharing, which are essential for economic growth and development.

Pleasure and consumer behavior: From an economic perspective, pleasure is also a key driver of consumer behavior. Consumer goods and services that give pleasure are in particularly high demand. The ability of a product to generate pleasure can significantly increase its market value. This can be seen in the experience economy, where the value of products and services is increasingly determined by the experiences and emotions they generate (Cf. Pine/Gilmore (1999), p. 1ff).

Joy and life satisfaction: Life satisfaction and well-being, which are strongly dependent on the ability to experience joy, also have direct economic consequences. Happy and satisfied individuals are healthier, more productive and have lower absenteeism, which has a positive impact on the economy. Studies have shown that countries with higher subjective well-being also have higher economic performance (see Diener/Seligman (2004), p. 3ff).

507 Aristotle (1956), p. 12.

focus on those internal and external influences that undermine the potential and valuable aspects of one's life and self-image. Both factors play a role in the individual's approach to imagination and IR as a vital function of the mind system, as they are exercised (or can be inhibited) in direct correlation to these.[508]

1. **Time thieves**

    Time thieves represent all those activities and thought processes that waste an individual's available time and prevent them from completing productive and fulfilling tasks. These can be everyday distractions such as excessive use of social media, unnecessary procrastination, or inefficient time management.[509]

    The first step in the "time thief/diamond thief" technique is to identify the time thieves. To do this, the individual can keep a detailed record of their daily activities to find out which tasks and thoughts steal time. Analyzing these records makes it possible to recognize patterns and identify specific time thieves. Identification is followed by intervention. This involves developing and implementing strategies to minimize or eliminate the identified time thieves. The aim is to promote a more efficient use of time and to focus on productive and fulfilling activities.

2. **Diamond thieves**

    Diamond thieves, on the other hand, symbolize the internal and external forces that impair or undermine an individual's potential and valuable qualities. These can be negative self-beliefs, destructive criticism from outside, or self-sabotaging behavior patterns that reduce self-esteem and quality of life.[510]

    The process begins with identifying these diamond thieves through self-reflection and external support. Methods such as keeping a diary, therapeutic conversations, or self-reflection exercises can be used for this purpose. The aim is to develop a deep understanding of the sources and effects of these diamond thieves. The next step is to transform these negative influences. This can be done through cognitive behavioral therapy, positive affirmations, and the development of new, positive

---

508 Cf. Seligman (2002), p. 53ff.
509 See Steel (2007), p. 67ff. and Kuss/Griffiths (2011), p. 3528ff. and Claessens/van Eerde/Rutte/Roe (2007), pp. 258–269.
510 Cf. also Seligman (2002).

self-beliefs. By learning to recognize and neutralize their diamond thieves, individuals strengthen their self-confidence and promote their imaginative development and resilience.

The techniques of time thieves and diamond thieves are complementary and should be applied integratively. An awareness of time thieves promotes more efficient use of time while recognizing and overcoming diamond thieves boosts self-esteem and mental system efficiency across the board.[511] This dual strategy can help individuals make their lives more effective and fulfilling by addressing both external distractions and internal barriers.

- The "time thief/diamond thief" technique offers a holistic approach to improving quality of life by consciously and purposefully changing time management and self-perception.
- Time thieves are activities and mental processes that waste time. Diamond thieves are internal and external influences that undermine an individual's potential and valuable qualities.
- The "time thief/diamond thief" techniques are used integratively to address both external distractions and internal barriers. This dual strategy promotes a more effective and fulfilling life by strengthening self-esteem and the efficiency of the mental system.

Methods and techniques of TN

The methodology of TN was introduced in detail in Chapter 3. Here, I would like to go into some more general aspects and background before explaining some methods and techniques in the context of economic cognitive therapy in more detail.

Psychological narration deals with the way in which stories and narratives reflect, influence, and shape psychological processes.[512] These principles can be summarized in several core elements that encompass both cognitive and emotional dimensions.

First, all forms of narration aim at the cognitive realization (i.e., "processing") of stories. Internal narrative strands structure information in a way that optimally appeals to human cognition. All narrative structures begin

---

511 Cf. Steel (2007), p. 80f.
512 Cf. Bartlett (1932), p. 191ff.

with schema formation. A schema is a cognitive construct that individuals use to organize and interpret information.[513] The analysis of individual narrative schemas is, therefore, at the beginning of the psychological study of narrative methods and techniques.

Another important aspect is the coherence of narrative structures.[514] Psychologically speaking, all individual mental systems look for coherent stories, as these are easier to understand, process, and remember. Coherent stories also facilitate cognitive mapping in self-narratives so that events can be linked in an understandable and meaningful way.[515] Emotional involvement plays an important role here. The narrative transport theory is also related to this, which states that individuals who immerse themselves deeply in a self-told story experience a strong emotional and mental involvement.[516] This can be supported by individual psychology through various narrative techniques. A high degree of emotional involvement means that the story is not only processed cognitively but is also experienced effectively and can be reconstructed more effectively. This is also demonstrated by the concept of the emotional arc.[517] Such an emotional arc comprises clear progressions of emotions in the self-narration and clearly differentiates them from one another. The transitions are moments of conscious experience that define the value of memories in self-narration. In principle, the individual narrative influences empathy as an additional mental resource.

In the context of economic cognitive therapy, the individual (self-)narrative of the mind system activates primarily through two concrete psychological mechanisms:

- One of these is cognitive dissonance reduction. Narratives that question existing beliefs and values can initially create cognitive dissonance, but the narrative structure and the emotional arc of self-narrative (memory

---

513 Stories use familiar patterns, such as the structure of beginning, middle, and end, to facilitate understanding and memory.Cf. ibid., pp. 201–203.
514 Coherence refers to the internal logic and consistency of a narrative.
515 Ibid.
516 Narrative transport theory (NTT) assumes that when people read, watch or listen to a story, they can experience a "state of transport," which means that they feel emotionally involved, mentally focused and imaginatively transported into the world of the story. The more integrated they are into the narrative, the more likely they are to accept its messages, empathize with the characters and change their own beliefs or actions in line with the story.
 Cf. Green/Brock (2002), p. 323ff.
517 Stories that have a clear emotional progression are more effective in their narrative effects.

reconstruction) can initially absorb or reduce this dissonance and finally integrate it.[518] The narrative must, therefore, be designed in such a way that it promotes a mental process structure that is as resilient as possible and can react flexibly to dissonance.
- The other mechanism is perspective-taking. This refers to the individual psychological ability to empathize with a broad spectrum of different (also contradictory) self-narrative structures.[519]

> To summarize, the general principles of psychological narration provide a comprehensive framework for understanding how self-narration works on a cognitive-emotional (and ultimately also intersocial, i.e., collectively intersubjectively constitutive) level. They illustrate the complexity of the interactions between the various processes and transactional mechanisms of the mind system and emphasize the power of narratives to influence individual thinking, feeling, and behavior.

The Storyteller

The methodology of the "storyteller" is based on the profound effect of stories and fairy tales on human thinking, feeling, and behavior.[520] This methodology integrates cultural and traditional elements of storytelling, utilizes basic motifs of fairy tales, and employs guided narration techniques to identify the essential points of connection in an individual's life and then work on them in a targeted manner. The aim is to develop a comprehensive picture of life as a fairy tale, to promote magical thinking and imagination, and thus support inner realization and personal lines of development.

This methodology considers the deeply rooted traditions of storytelling in different cultures. Fairy tales are always stories that convey universal human experiences and values and delve deep into the collective unconscious. By incorporating these sociocultural elements, the "storyteller" methodology establishes a connection to an individual's cultural roots and traditions. This connection promotes a sense of personal identity and thus offers an optimal introduction to one's own narratives.

---

518 See Pennebaker/Smyth (2016), p. 65ff.
519 See Apperly (2012), pp. 826–829.
520 Cf. Lüthi (1976), pp. 112–118.

Fairy tales contain basic motifs such as heroic journeys, trials, transformations, and redemption, which are deeply rooted in the individual and collective psyche. In this method, these basic motifs are used to reflect an individual's inner conflicts and challenges.[521] This enables deeper reflection and a better understanding of one's own life circumstances. As a guided narration technique, this method uses the individual's ego as a "storyteller" who constructs the self-narration process (guided by their therapeutic counterpart) as a structured narrative. This takes place in several phases:

1. Storytelling phase: The presentation of one (or more) selected fairy tales, the content of which is tailored to the specific issues and challenges of an individual.
2. Reflection phase: Joint reflection on the meaning of the fairy tale motifs and their parallels to the experience and memory of one's own mental system.
3. Creation phase: An individual is encouraged to tell their own life story in the form of a fairy tale, using the basic motifs and structures of the fairy tale (or fairy tales).

This method places a strong focus on the identification and processing of connecting nodes in the client's life. These are key experiences or turning points that have had a lasting impact on an individual's life. Through the narrative structure of the fairy tale, these points are worked out and placed in a coherent context. An individual's mental system learns to understand the self-narrative as a coherent, more complex narrative structure, which leads to self-integration and increased acceptance of past memories.

Another aim of the "storyteller" is to develop a comprehensive overall picture of an individual life and the often tangled strands of events behind it. Through storytelling, life is presented as a coherent, meaningful story that includes both highs and lows. It also encourages magical thinking[522] and the imagination of the mental system. Magical thinking, which is omnipresent in fairy tales, can be utilized in economic insight therapy to develop new perspectives and solutions for existing, open, or interrupted transaction processes. It enables the mental

---

521 For example, the story of a hero who has to pass a series of tests to achieve a goal can serve as a metaphor for personal struggles and successes.
 Cf. ibid.
522 Cf. von Franz (1971), p. IV ff.

system to increasingly go beyond conventional thought processes and find creative ways of overcoming problems by finding, recognizing, and ultimately integrating holistic patterns.

> The methodology of the "storyteller" utilizes essential psychological principles of narration to support therapeutic processes. By integrating cultural and traditional storytelling techniques, universal human motives and personal life stories are linked together. The guided narration technique, the focus on life events, and the building of an overall picture promote individual magical thinking and the general imagination. This methodology makes it possible to view life as a meaningful, coherent, and holistic story, which contributes to a holistic experience and the dissolution of complexes.

Exercises in meditative narration

The therapeutic methodology of the "Exercises of Meditative Narration" integrates principles of narrative therapy and meditative practices to promote the mental suppleness of self-narration. This method assumes that stories and narratives are powerful tools for self-reflection and emotional processing, while meditative techniques help to achieve a state of inner calm and clarity. By combining these approaches, individuals can gain deeper insights into their life stories while achieving improved emotional regulation and mental balance, which facilitates narrative processes in the mind system.

The meditative narration exercises utilize the cognitive principles of schema formation and coherence as well as emotional involvement.[523] The narrative components help to integrate memories into an understandable and coherent story, while meditative practices support emotional engagement and regulation. This combination promotes narrative coherence by creating a safe and relaxed environment in which clients can reflect on and reorganize their stories. The aim of the methodology is to revise and reorganize individual narrative identities by processing and reinterpreting past experiences. This can lead to a reduction in symptoms such as anxiety, depression, and post-traumatic stress. The meditative component is also intended to increase the client's mindfulness and self-acceptance.

---

523 See Cozolino (2010), pp. 160–180.

The methodology is basically divided into six steps:

1. Introduction and setting: Each session begins with a brief introduction explaining the goals and process of the exercise. A calm and safe atmosphere is created that allows you to relax and focus.
2. Guided narrative meditation: The session begins with a guided meditation aimed at bringing an individual into a state of calm and mindfulness. This phase may include breathing exercises, progressive muscle relaxation, and visualization techniques to calm the mind and promote concentration.

   Narrative meditation utilizes the power of storytelling to direct a loving and mindful focus on an object or theme. A central element of this technique is embedding the object in its historical and shared meaning. A typical example is a meditation on a personal object, such as an heirloom. An individual is guided to connect intensely with the object, feeling its physical nature while reflecting on its history and meaning. Through this process, a deeper connection and understanding of the symbolic and emotional meaning of the object in one's life and shared history is created. Another technique of narrative meditation is finding "knots and strands." Here, an individual is encouraged to identify and link the various connections and relationships that the object represents. This exercise helps to weave a mental network that recognizes the complexity and interconnectivity of experiences and memories. This supports the integration of fragmented or repressed memories and promotes a coherent self-understanding.[524]
3. Narrative exploration. After meditation, an individual is invited to reflect on and recount a specific life story or experience. The therapist may ask questions that encourage an individual to delve deeper into their memories and feelings, helping to develop coherent and meaningful narratives.
4. Narrative restructuring: Individuals then rework and reconstruct their narratives, discovering new perspectives and developing alternative interpretations that can reduce emotional distress and promote positive narrative change. It can promote positive changes in the narrative.
5. Imaginative meditation and meditative integration: The narrative exploration is followed by a further phase of meditation aimed at

---

[524] See Brown/Creswell/Ryan (2015), pp. 90–117.

integrating the insights and changes gained. This phase can include silent meditation, mindful breathing, or the visualization of (positive) future scenarios. Imaginative meditation focuses on the creative and future-orientated examination of an object or situation. One exercise consists of looking at an object as if seeing it for the first time. An individual is guided to recognize and imagine the potential and possibilities that this object offers. This imaginative process brings the future of the object into the present and enables the participant to discover new perspectives and paths.

Another aspect of imaginative meditation is the exploration of the duality of the future. This involves splitting a future event into two possible outcomes. An individual is invited to imagine both scenarios in detail and to grasp their implications. This exercise helps to accept the uncertainties of the future and to consciously think through different possibilities and their implications. This can reduce anxiety about the future and strengthen a sense of control and preparedness.[525]

6. Conclusion and reflection: The session ends with a short round of reflection. This provides an opportunity to consolidate the findings and plan the next steps.

The effectiveness of the meditative narration methodology is based on several psychological mechanisms:

- Cognitive dissonance reduction: Through narrative restructuring, contradictory thoughts and feelings are addressed and harmonized, which contributes to the reduction of cognitive dissonance.[526]
- Emotional regulation: The meditative techniques promote relaxation and the ability to recognize and accept emotions, which contributes to general emotional stability.[527]
- Perspective-taking and empathy: By telling and reflecting on stories, an individual develops a deeper understanding of themselves and others, which strengthens their empathic abilities.
- Narrative coherence: The structuring and integration of life stories promote a coherent self-image, which is crucial for mental health and the effectiveness of the mental system.

---

525 Ibid.
526 See Pennebaker/Smyth (2016), p. 68ff.
527 Cf. Greenberg/Paivio (1997).

The methodology of meditative narration combines narrative and imagination in a meditative practice. This combination promotes a holistic approach that both integrates the past and anticipates the future. Meditative narration as a therapeutic method thus offers a framework in which individuals can systematically and mindfully explore their inner narratives and imaginations. This leads to increased self-awareness, deeper emotional processing, and an enhanced creative problem-solving ability. The exercises support the individual mental mind system to construct a coherent and meaningful narrative that both honors the past and shapes the future without undermining the present experience.[528]

- The exercises of meditative narration offer a holistic approach that combines narration with the calming and centering effects of meditation.
- This methodology has the potential to promote profound insights and change by integrating cognitive and emotional processes and strengthening an individual's narrative coherence and emotional regulation.
- The method of meditative narration in psychological therapy combines elements of narration and imagination with meditative techniques. This integrative approach aims to promote self-reflection, process emotional stress, and increase the ability to solve problems creatively.

Memory circles

The "memory circles" technique utilizes the basic principles of narration and memory research and aims to support individuals in structuring and reflecting on their memories and gaining new perspectives.

The technique of memory circles is based on the organization and structuring of episodic memory. The episodic memory comprises personal experiences and events that are localized in time and space. Memory circles serve as an organizational technique for grouping and sorting these memories by visualizing and conceptualizing them.[529]

In the practical application, individuals are asked to visualize their memories in the form of circles on a sheet of paper or digital medium. Each

---

528 Cf. Cozolino (2010), p. 173ff.
529 Cf. Conway/Pleydell-Pearce (2000), pp. 261–270.

circle represents a specific theme, event, or phase of life. These circles can vary in size, color, and position to represent different meanings and relationships. Concentrating on individual circles enables a targeted focus on specific topics within the episodic memory. The visual and structured representation supports the cognitive processing of memories, as the patient has the opportunity to view and reflect on individual experiences in isolation. This facilitates the identification and analysis of patterns and connections that may be overlooked in the less structured form of free recollection.

The technique of memory circles promotes cognitive mapping, a process in which memories are systematically organized and linked. This can help to increase the coherence of one's own narrative by integrating disparate memories into an understandable and coherent context. Visual organization also facilitates the reduction of cognitive dissonance by allowing contradictory memories to be viewed and reinterpreted within a structured framework.[530]

Emotional involvement also plays a key role. By focusing on individual circles, individuals can experience and process their emotional reactions to specific events more intensively. This deepened emotional reflection promotes emotional coherence and can support therapeutic processes such as processing trauma or coping with loss. The technique of memory circles also makes it possible to recognize additional perspectives and new connections. Through the visual and thematic grouping of memories, individuals can discover connections and relationships that they were previously unaware of. These new insights can have transformative effects on self-understanding and the development of the mind system.

Perspective-taking is also encouraged, as the visual presentation makes it easier to view memories from different angles. Memories can be viewed more easily from different angles. This can be done by reflecting on the perspectives of other people involved or by viewing the same memory from different emotional and cognitive perspectives. This multiperspectivity supports the development of empathy and a deeper understanding of one's own and others' experiences.[531]

The technique of memory circles is particularly useful in economic cognitive therapy, as it enables the systematic organization and reflection of one's own memories. The individual narrative can be integrated more coherently and positively, which leads to improved self-esteem and stronger emotional resilience.

---

530 See McAdams (1993), pp. 11–30.
531 Cf. Tulving (2002), p. 10ff.

- The technique of memory circles is a structured and focused method for organizing and processing personal memories.
- She uses the principles of narrative psychology to support cognitive and emotional processes, open up new perspectives, and make progress in dealing with one's own mental system.

Memory book

The "memory book" technique, also known as a memory book, is an established psychological intervention method. This technique is based on the principles of psychological narration and utilizes the cognitive, emotional, and social dimensions of stories to achieve effects in terms of the efficiency of the individual's mental system.[532]

The memory book serves as a structured medium in which individuals record their own narratives in the form of texts, photos, and other memorabilia. This method utilizes schema formation and coherence in the psychological narrative. Organizing life events in a chronological and meaningful structure makes it easier for those affected to organize and process their memories.

Emotional involvement is another key aspect of the memory book technique. Creating a memory book can evoke intense emotional reactions, ranging from joy at positive memories to sadness when reflecting on losses. This technique utilizes the emotional arc of stories to address and process deeply rooted emotions. Reflecting on past experiences and telling one's own life story promotes emotional processing and can help reduce symptoms such as anxiety and depression.

The technique enables an individual to find a narrative structure that helps them to integrate past traumas into their life story and thus reduce cognitive dissonance. This happens through repeated storytelling and finding new meanings in their own experiences, which is known as narrative integration.[533]

The memory book also fulfills important social functions in that it can serve as a medium of communication between individuals. It enables social exchange and can strengthen the bond and empathy between those involved. By sharing their stories, individuals can develop a collective identity and a sense of belonging, which is particularly important in social or family contexts.

---

532 See Leu (2019), pp. 13–25.
533 Cf. Kast (2010), p. 37ff.

The technique activates various psychological mechanisms that contribute to the therapeutic effect. One of these mechanisms is perspective-taking. By looking at and telling their life story from different points of view, patients can develop a deeper understanding of their own experiences and the perspectives of others. And the perspectives of others; this promotes self-reflection and self-acceptance.

- The "memory book" technique is an effective psychological intervention method that utilizes the principles of psychological narrative to promote cognitive, emotional, and social improvements.
- The structured recording and reflection of one's own narration provide a framework in which individuals can organize their memories, process their emotions, and strengthen their social relationships.

The power of metaphors

The technique "The Power of Metaphors" in psychological therapy uses the transformative power of metaphors to help individuals understand and change their thoughts, feelings, and behaviors. Metaphors are linguistic images that translate abstract concepts into concrete, tangible representations. In psychological practice, they serve as bridges between the conscious and unconscious mind, promoting understanding and supporting the therapeutic process.[534]

Metaphors work by translating complex and often abstract psychological states into tangible, everyday images. This utilizes the cognitive theory of metaphor, which states that people understand new and complex information through already-known and familiar concepts.[535] Metaphors have a strong emotional resonance. They can address and influence deeply rooted emotional states. This is closely linked to the theory of narrative transport, which states that metaphors draw an individual into a story and allow them to view their emotions from a safe distance.[536] This distanced perspective often allows individuals to view their feelings and problems more objectively.

---

534 See Lawley/Tompkins (2012), p. 54ff.
535 Ibid, p. 198ff.
536 Cf. White/Epston (1990), pp. 28–41.

In the practice of the "Power of Metaphors" technique, the aim is to find and use suitable metaphors that correspond to the client's individual experiences and challenges. And challenges of the client. The technique is applied in four steps:

1. Identification and exploration: Joint identification of current challenges; this can be done through open dialogue, reflective listening, and targeted questions. Spontaneous metaphors are particularly relevant, as they often offer insights into unconscious processes and beliefs.
2. Introduction and adaptation of metaphors: Based on the themes and patterns identified, suitable metaphors are introduced and applied to the specific situation.
3. Working with the metaphor: Working together on the metaphor to gain deeper insights. This can be done through narrative techniques such as storytelling and expanding the metaphor. The individual is encouraged to expand the metaphor further and explore how it represents different aspects of their experience.
4. Integration and transformation: Finally, the individual works to translate the metaphorical insights into concrete action strategies and behavioral changes. This may involve developing new metaphors that symbolize positive change and coping strategies. For example, the labyrinth, which initially serves as a symbol of confusion, can become a symbol of growth and discovery through work in the therapeutic process.

Metaphors are decidedly culturally embedded and help to respect and integrate an individual's social and cultural identities.[537] One must be aware of individual cultural backgrounds in order to choose metaphors that are meaningful and resonant in a specific cultural context.

The effectiveness of using metaphors in therapy is well documented.[538] Studies show that metaphors can help to accelerate the therapeutic process and increase the depth of understanding and emotional processing. They are particularly effective in the treatment of anxiety, depression, and post-traumatic stress disorder, where abstract emotional states are often difficult to put into words.

---

537 See Lawley/Tompkins (2012), p. 120f.
538 Ibid.

- The technique "The Power of Metaphors" is an effective approach in economic cognitive therapy that integrates cognitive, emotional, and cultural dimensions.
- Through the creative and targeted use of metaphors, individuals can better understand and specifically transform complex psychological states, which ultimately leads to deeper insight and lasting change.

Methods and techniques of HS

HS is an integrative approach to economic cognitive therapy that aims to harmonize an individual's entire mental system of an individual with the external, tangible reality, whereby the interface between the individual narrative and the external reality determines the field of tension of the methods and techniques. HS is also based on the belief that changes in the mental system have a direct effect on physical states and vice versa. Since narration and imagination are fundamental tools in the human cognitive domain, these methods and techniques all emphasize the intersubjective, cultural, interactive aspect—that is, suggestion—of narration and imagination and thus complete the set of methods of economic cognitive therapy.

The gaze of the other

"The Other's Gaze" is a specialized methodology that draws heavily on principles of existentialism and aims to gain deeper self-knowledge and understanding through the perspective of others. This method integrates epistemology and existentialist approaches to help individuals recognize their existence and identity in relation to social relationships. In constellation with social relationships and to reflect and understand them in a targeted way.

The methodology is based on existentialist philosophy, in particular the ideas of Jean-Paul Sartre and Martin Buber. Sartre's concept of the "gaze" plays a central role, as it describes how consciousness and the identity of an individual are influenced by the perception and the judgment of others. According to Sartre, the awareness of one's own existence and individual freedom often arises through the contrast with other people.[539] Similarly, Buber's philosophical

---

539 The awareness of one's own existence and its freedom only arise through the contrast and relationship with other people. This concerns the concept of the "gaze" (le regard), through which the awareness of one's own subjectivity and freedom arises in the face of another, who also perceives one as a subject. See Sartre (1952), p. 370ff.

approach emphasizes the importance of dialogue, in particular the "I-Thou" principle, for the emergence of authentic encounters and relationships in which the self is recognized and defined in the face of the other.[540]

It is precisely this approach that is decidedly reflected in the economized mental system of an individual since here, too, mental exchange or transaction processes (as with external reality) are a central (as with external reality) is a central component of the cognitive process. Therefore, "the view of the other" can be an effective method to better understand and comprehend this aspect individually.

The application of "The gaze of the other" in economic insight therapy takes place in several structured steps:

1. Introduction and contextualization: First, the theoretical foundations of the technique are explained. This includes an introduction to existentialist concepts such as freedom, responsibility, authenticity, and the importance of the "other" in self-perception.[541]
2. Change of perspective: The individual is encouraged to look at everyday situations from the perspective of other people. This exercise helps to develop empathy and to reflect on one's own actions and decisions from an external perspective. For example, the individual could be asked to describe a conflict from the perspective of the other person involved.
3. Dialogical reflection: Based on Buber's principle of the dialogical relationship, conversations are held in which the individual explores the perceptions and feelings of others in relation to themselves. This fosters a deeper understanding of how one's own identity and actions are shaped by social interactions.
4. Existential reflection: In this step, the individual reflects on existential questions. Techniques are used to encourage the individual to think about their existence, the role played by other people, and the individual's network of relationships. A special focus can be placed on the transactional level of this network of relationships.
5. Integration and action: The final step focuses on integrating the insights gained into everyday life. The individual develops strategies to act more consciously and authentically in social relationships and to incorporate their insights into their personal development via the "view of the other."

---

540 Cf. Buber (2023), p. 212ff.
541 Cf. Kast (2010), p. 161ff.

The methodology "The gaze of the other" works on several psychological levels:

- Self-knowledge: Through reflection and a change of perspective, an individual is encouraged to delve deeper into their own self-image and existence. This promotes self-awareness and the understanding of one's own identity in the context of social and mental interactions.
- Empathy and social intelligence: Taking the perspective of others strengthens the ability to empathize and improves social intelligence. An individual learns to better understand the feelings and thoughts of others, which improves the quality of interpersonal relationships.
- Authenticity and freedom: The existentialist component of the methodology supports an individual to live more authentically and to recognize and use their freedom. By becoming aware of their responsibilities and choices, they can make decisions that correspond to their true values and beliefs (which, in turn, are the product of mental transactional processes).
- Reduction of anxiety and isolation: Existential reflection and the dialogue process can help to reduce existential anxiety and the feeling of isolation. The individual recognizes that his or her existence and value are anchored in a complex, multidimensional, and temporally extended network of relationships.

"The gaze of the other" is a rather complex and transformative method of HS that particularly addresses the transactional principles of the mind system to better integrate them. Through the systematic use of changing perspectives, dialog-based reflection, and existential-philosophical discussion, this method offers the opportunity to deepen individual self-understanding of one's own mind system and to develop a better basis for transactional relationships.

- "The Other's View" encourages individuals to look at situations from the perspective of others to develop empathy and reflect on their own actions from an external point of view. It includes steps such as an introduction to existentialist concepts, changing perspectives, dialog-based reflection, and existential confrontation, followed by the integration of the insights gained into everyday life.

(Continued)

- The method promotes self-knowledge, empathy, social intelligence, authenticity, and an understanding of one's own spirit system. It helps to reduce existential fears and feelings of isolation by helping the individual recognize their existence and value in a network of relationships.

The inner room / wonder chamber

The therapy methodology "The Inner Space/Wonder Chamber" focuses on the rather playful exploration of an individual's inner world and places this decidedly in a context with the collective unconscious, which operates in the sociocultural context of intersubjective construction.[542] This methodology utilizes metaphorical and real objects in order to provide deeper psychological insights into the individual mind system and to promote the integration of the inner and outer world. At its center is the idea that an individual's inner space is constructed like a cabinet of curiosities in which different objects symbolize different aspects of the self and one's experiences.

In modern society, consumerism is omnipresent and has a profound influence on people's self-image and identity. The "Wunderkammer" methodology addresses this influence by encouraging an individual to critically examine the objects that populate their inner world. Consumerism often leads to an over-identification with material goods and an external focus that neglects the inner self. Economic insight therapy, therefore, also examines how consumer and luxury goods shape personal identity and possibly interfere negatively with self-perception.[543] In this respect, the "Wunderkammer" combines inner and

---

542 The term "inner cabinet of curiosities" of the psyche refers metaphorically to an inner space in which individual memories, emotions, dreams, and thoughts are collected and stored. This psychic space is not just an archive of past experiences, but a dynamic place where creative and emotional processing takes place. It can be actively used to work with the individual spirit system—mostly through associative and imaginative processes.
Cf. Varela/Thompson/Rosch (1991), pp. 145–168.

543 In a consumer-orientated society, the self (external and internal) is often defined by material possessions. Due to its focus on transactional processes, economic cognitive therapy invites us to reflect on and critically scrutinize this influence. The objects in the Wunderkammer are not products of consumption, but symbolic representations of individual mental processes or mental resources. This creates a distinction between external, material values and internal, immaterial values. This reflection can lead individuals to recognise how much their inner Wunderkammer is influenced by external consumer goods and how they can achieve an authentic self-perception of their own mental system.

outer transaction processes in a reciprocal exchange process and assigns them mental correspondences; the processes of the spirit system thus become more transparent and also more individually tangible.[544]

The objects in the Wunderkammer are not only mental and physical objects but also carry a charged cultural symbolic meaning. This charging takes place through an examination of the personal narratives, emotions, and experiences associated with the objects. The inner space created by these objects serves as a reflection of an individual's inner world and offers a tangible manifestation of abstract psychic reality. The physical reality of the objects serves as a contrast to the elusive nature of the inner world and spirit system for many; as an individual contemplates these physical objects and reflects on their meaning, a bridge is created between the outer and inner worlds. This facilitates access to the basic spirit system and promotes a holistic integration of the different processes of the self. In this respect, the "Wunderkammer" is a very basic introductory methodology.[545]

The therapeutic and epistemological process of the "Wunderkammer" methodology comprises four basic steps:

1. Exploration: An individual begins to explore their inner cabinet of curiosities under guidance and discover the various objects that can be found there.
2. Reflection: Each object is examined, and its significance in relation to the personal narrative and identity is reflected upon.
3. Integration: The insights gained through reflection are integrated into an individual's self-image, paying particular attention to systemic congruence and the resulting transactional processes between the inner and outer world.
4. Transformation: Through symbolic work with the objects, one's own spiritual system is better understood and can be system is better understood and can be opened up bit by bit; deep-rooted, previously unconscious patterns and processes can also be transformed, leading to deeper self-acceptance and inner growth.

The "Inner Space/Wonder Chamber" method offers a well-structured approach to self-knowledge and individual discovery of the mental system that

---

544 Cf. Johnson-Laird (1995), pp. 23–61.
545 Ibid.

can be used at different levels of cognition—a basis for all other approaches to economic cognitive therapy. By working with mental objects in an imagined inner space, individuals can explore both inner values and the meanings of individual mental processes. Explore the interconnectivity of the outer world (and consumerism) to their inner structure and the resulting constructed identity, and understand the transactional nature of the relationship between inner and outer reality.[546]

- The therapy methodology "The Inner Space/Wonder Chamber" uses metaphorical and real objects to playfully explore an individual's inner world, promoting deeper psychological insights and the integration of inner and outer world. It places this individual exploration in the context of the collective unconscious and sociocultural construction.
- The method addresses the influence of consumerism on identity and self-perception by encouraging individuals to critically engage with the objects in their inner world. The therapeutic process involves exploration, reflection, integration, and transformation to better understand and transform one's own mind system.

Oracle of longing / The nameless longing

The "longing oracle" technique or "the nameless longing" aims to identify and work on dysfunctional processes within the mind system and to work on them. This technique integrates elements of narrative therapy, depth psychological approaches of narrative structuring, and imaginative procedures (focusing on identity constructions) to gain access to these mostly unconscious processes. The starting point of the technique is the fact that the dysfunctional transactional processes of the mental system are reflected in a particularly significant way, which enables indirect access to them.

The central element of the longing oracle is narrative reframing. After an individual has explored their inner images and the symbols of inner longings, they are encouraged to construct an integrated overall narrative around these images. This narrative helps to bring the unconscious wishes and desires into a narrative form that is more tangible and understandable for the individual. By telling and reflecting on this story, the individual can gain new perspectives

---

546 Cf. Walsh/Vaughan (1993), p. 48ff.

on their inner, conflictual processes and find possible ways to translate their longings.[547]

Another important aspect of this is emotional regulation. By learning to recognize and concretize the causes of the dysfunctional orientation of (previously) unconscious processes, the individual can better deal with and regulate emerging emotions. By consciously confronting their own desires, individuals can learn to integrate them into their lives and find a way to fulfill or transcend them in a constructive way. Overall, it is a relieving process for the spirit system to address these types of inner dysfunctionalities and transform them into a constructive medium.[548]

The "longing oracle" technique is comparatively new and has not yet been extensively researched empirically. However, initial qualitative studies and case reports indicate that this method leads to a significant improvement in subjective well-being for many individuals through the comprehensive integration of longings.[549] Further research is required to systematically evaluate the long-term effects and effectiveness of this technique.

- The technique "Longing oracle" / "The nameless longing" is aimed at analyzing dysfunctional processes in the mind system through narrative reframing and imaginative procedures by bringing unconscious wishes and longings into tangible narrative forms.
- Recognizing and concretizing dysfunctional processes and their causes, as well as the conscious confrontation with one's own desires, enables better emotional regulation and integration of these desires into an individual's life, which can lead to a significant improvement in the efficiency of the spirit system.

---

547 Cf. White/Epston, (1990), p. 26ff.
548 See McAdams, Dan P. (1993), pp. 34–58.
549 See Scheibe/Freund/Baltes (2007), pp. 780–785.

CHAPTER 5

THE SUPPORT SYSTEMS—YOGA, MEDITATION, CULTURE, AND ESTHETICS

> He who can perceive non-action in action and recognizes how action continues when he steps back from action is the one of true reason and discernment among men.[550]

First of all, the term "auxiliary systems" deserves a comment, as I probably thought about it the longest when writing the book and, at the same time, was the most unhappy with it.

This term does not really do justice to any of the collections of methods and techniques mentioned in the following chapter—rather, we are dealing with meta-psychological and spiritual schools that are difficult to grasp, which themselves fill far more books and have different orientations than could be presented here. Nevertheless, I would only like to engage with them to the extent that they are conducive to effective mental work with memory and imagination—anything else would be presumptuous and not very useful for this book. I would like to emphasize at this point that meditation (as well as yoga and related spiritual systems) has its own, sometimes contradictory perspectives on memories, experiences, and mental processes in general, which are more focused on spiritual development than I would like to consider in my concepts of economic psychology.

But the basics are very similar for both purposes—all approaches have in common that they deal with valuable inner resources in a structured way and want to optimize their use[551]—which is why it makes a lot of sense to also

---

550 Bhagavadgita (1998), 4.18.
551 Cf. Gunturu (2020), pp. 7–10.

deal with these techniques in a basic, subordinate form, hence the (somewhat disrespectful-sounding) title of "support systems."

The term "support systems" may initially appear technical and mechanistic, but it aptly describes the support systems that can elaborate and stabilize mental processes in the context of economic cognitive therapy. In this context, support systems initially refer (regardless of their design) to external sources and structures that stabilize our imagination, narration, and suggestion, as well as stimulate and enrich our imagination, narration, and suggestion. These systems serve as a continuous source of inspiration that reconstructs and expands an individual's inner world. A particularly relevant aspect is the cultural dimension of some support systems[552]; on the other hand, there are the meta-psychological support systems of yoga, tantra, and meditation.

It is important to emphasize at this point that the techniques of meditation (and all potential meta-psychological support systems), on the one hand, and cultural immersion, on the other, are both at the end of a continuum that is not free of tension. On the one hand, cultural immersion, on the other, is at the end of a continuum that is not free of tension. It is important to keep this in mind as the book progresses—because, strictly speaking, the two systems are quite mutually exclusive. Figure 13 shows the schematic subdivision of the two types of auxiliary systems.

Central to all help systems is the **knowledge** that is acquired through them—this directly influences the individual psychological handling of the spirit system and its processes.

FIGURE 13 Auxiliary systems at a glance.[553]

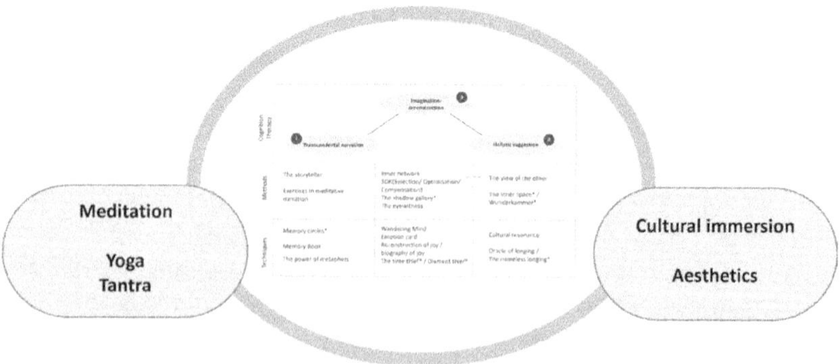

---

552 On the role of culture see also Chapters 1 and 2.
553 Own presentation.

In scientific psychology, knowledge is not only a static reservoir of information but rather a dynamic process that shapes and recursively changes the mental system.[554] This perspective emphasizes what the mind does with the content rather than the other way around. This implies that knowledge is not just passively absorbed but must be actively processed and integrated to enable growth and development. It is, therefore, helpful to be aware of the mechanisms of knowledge—these are universal for engaging with one's own mind system.

The **mechanism of knowledge building** in the human mind is complex and multilayered. First, content must be presented in a form that is meaningful and relevant to the learner. From a psychological point of view, active engagement with the learning material plays a decisive role. This engagement can take various forms, such as reflection, meditation, and contemplation on what has been learned.[555]

There are basically three levels of knowledge:

- The psychological process of knowledge building: The cognitive processes involved in the formation of knowledge include perception, attention, memory, thinking, and learning. These processes are interactive and influence each other. Perception and attention determine what information is taken in from the environment, while memory stores and retrieves this information. Thinking and learning are processes through which new information is integrated and existing knowledge structures are adapted.[556]
- The philosophical integration of knowledge into existing knowledge structures: The philosophy of knowledge (epistemology) examines the nature, sources, and limits of knowledge. Philosophical approaches emphasize the importance of critical reflection and discourse. By engaging with philosophical questions, knowledge is not only expanded but also deepened and scrutinized. This leads to a deeper understanding and the development of wisdom.[557]
- Esthetics and the imaginative creation of applied knowledge: Esthetics and creativity play an important role in the process of knowledge creation. The esthetic realization makes it possible to translate abstract

---

554 Cf. Hutchins (1995), pp. 8–35 and Varela/Thompson/Rosch (1991), pp. 239–278.
555 Ibid.
556 See Thompson (2007), pp. 389–428.
557 See Audi (2011), p. 286ff.

and complex ideas into visual, auditory, or other sensual, application-oriented forms. This promotes imaginative thinking and opens new perspectives and insights. Creative work is, therefore, an important mechanism through which knowledge is not only stored but also transformed and expanded.[558]

This also means that knowledge always has an intrinsic individual component alongside the objective, fact-based domain, namely that of integration into a specific mental system. This individuality of knowledge means that every person processes and applies knowledge in a unique way. This also depends on personal experience, previous knowledge, cognitive abilities, and emotional states. The knowledge process is supported by three mental processes: reflection, meditation,[559] and contemplation.

Reflection is the conscious act of thinking about experiences and information. It goes beyond the mere assimilation of information and involves critical evaluation and integration into the personal context. Through reflection, connections can be made between new and existing knowledge structures, leading to a deeper understanding and better application of knowledge. Reflective practices promote learning and cognitive flexibility by improving the ability to solve problems and adapt to new situations.[560]

Meditation is a technique that is often used to calm the mind and focus attention. In the context of knowledge, meditation can help to release cognitive and emotional blockages that hinder the absorption and processing of information. Meditation also promotes self-awareness and the awareness of inner processes, which supports the integration and anchoring of knowledge. Meditation improves the ability to concentrate and the working memory, which in turn facilitates learning.[561]

Contemplation goes beyond mere reflection and involves an intense and sustained engagement with a topic or idea. It promotes a deeper understanding and transformation of knowledge into wisdom.[562] Through contemplative practices, complex and abstract ideas can be internalized and integrated into

---

558 See Sawyer (2012), pp. 150–178.
559 In particular, analytical meditation, see the excursus in this chapter.
560 Cf. Moon (2004), p. 37ff. and p. 75ff.
561 See Lutz/Slagter/Dunne/Davidson (2008), p. 163ff. and Zeidan/Johnson/Diamond/David/Goolkasian (2010), p. 600f.
562 Cf. Baltes/Staudinger (2000), p. 128f. and Glück et al. (2013).

one's own world view. Contemplation makes it possible to strategically link and expand knowledge and create a lasting connection to the content learned.[563]

Knowledge is not static; it grows and develops precisely through intrapersonal interaction with the content. This growth process is, therefore, cyclical and self-reinforcing. New information expands existing knowledge structures, while existing knowledge facilitates the absorption and integration of new content. This process of growth in the content is supported and promoted by constant reflection, meditation, and contemplation. By applying these practices concomitantly, they can continuously expand and improve the depth and breadth of the individual's knowledge.[564] Overall, when considering the knowledge process that accompanies the individual's interaction with the support systems of the spirit system, it becomes clear that knowledge consists not only of the factual content that an individual absorbs but, above all, of the processes through which they process and integrate this content. The human mind grows through active engagement and creative processing; reflection, meditation, and contemplation are essential practices that support and deepen this growth process.[565]

An Initial Overview

- Both external support systems, especially cultural immersion, and internal support systems, such as internal mental techniques like meditation and yoga, can make a significant contribution to supporting the economical handling of one's own mental system. While immersion supports mental transaction processes as well as imagination, narration, and suggestion from the outside, meditation, yoga, and tantra provide an inner basis for strengthening concentration and mindfulness, which can lead to a more resilient structure of the mind system and a better in-depth understanding of it.
- Meditation plays a special dual role—a method and a technique—and will be a particularly effective tool in dealing with the inner world.
- What all support systems have in common is that they can make the use of mental resources more efficient and demonstrate new ways of dealing with one's own mental system, which is also emphasized by the process of knowledge building.

---

563 Cf. Hadot (2002), p. 111ff. and Walsh/Shapiro (2006), pp. 229–234.
564 Cf. Mezirow (1991).
565 Ibid.

Immersion Through Sociocultural-Modulated Esthetics

Will does not belong to morality, but to aesthetics, the unfounded phenomena.[566]

Culture, this colorful collective term for socially modulated esthetics,[567] plays a central role in providing external stimuli for the mental system; art, literature, music, films, and other cultural forms of expression offer rich sources of individual imagination and narration. They provide stories, images, and ideas that can influence our inner world. These cultural artifacts act as permanent and contextually adapted stimuli that are tailored to individual needs and interests. By receiving and reflecting on cultural content, our mental transaction processes are stimulated and supported in the mind system, which can lead to a deeper and richer inner world.

The integration of culture as a support system shows how external resources can enhance our cognitive and emotional abilities. Culture not only provides entertainment but also actual meaningful experiences that shape the way we think and feel. These external stimuli promote the ability to imagine by opening new perspectives and possibilities. They support narration by providing multiple stories and narrative structures that an individual can integrate into their own life story. Finally, they reinforce suggestions by using symbolic and metaphorical content to stimulate deeper levels of individual consciousness or a more far-reaching integration of the collective unconscious.[568]

The concept of immersion is a concept of scientism. This refers (in the broadest sense) to the belief that scientific knowledge and methodological approaches are the only or primary means of gaining valid knowledge about the world. Within psychological research, scientism is a philosophical basis as it emphasizes the importance of knowledge in discovering the inner world. Knowledge, understood

---

566 Musil (2000), p. 1520.
567 Culture can be understood as socially modulated esthetics because it reflects the way in which aesthetic preferences and value judgments are shaped and modified by social interactions and community norms. Esthetics refers to the perception and evaluation of beauty and art, while culture encompasses the totality of a group's social practices, beliefs, values, and material expressions. In this context, cultural norms and traditions influence the esthetic standards of a society by favoring and promoting certain forms of art, architecture, music, and fashion. These esthetic preferences are learnt and passed on within society, making them an integral part of collective identity and social cohesion. The esthetic preferences of a culture are therefore not static, but are subject to constant change, influenced by social interactions, historical events and exchanges with other cultures.
See Carroll (1998), pp. 181–189.
568 Cf. Vygotsky (1978), pp. 52–57 and 79–91 and Bruner (1991), pp. 4–15.

as systematically acquired and verifiable information, is the key to recognizing inner psychological mechanisms and the dynamics of the mental system.[569]

Immersion through esthetics builds on this understanding; esthetics plays a central role in creating immersion. Esthetically pleasing or contrasting environments, whether through visual artwork, music, or architecture, can evoke strong emotional responses and engage viewers in deep, focused attention. There are different types and degrees of immersion, ranging from simple focused exercises to complex visual environments. The degree of immersion affects the depth of the experience and the ability to reach deeper psychological and emotional levels. Through immersion, individuals can gain new perspectives and discover previously unrecognized aspects of their inner world.

The combination of scientistic and cultural immersion opens a broader spectrum of interpretation and expands the individual (inner and outer) transaction possibilities of the ego. Cultural elements integrated into immersive experiences allow individuals to explore their inner worlds through the lens of cultural symbols and narratives. This leads to a richer and more diverse understanding of one's identity and the underlying psychological processes.[570]

Knowledge alone can open many inner potentials for development and realization, but without being embedded in cultural contexts, it often remains abstract and incomplete. Cultural immersion enables knowledge to be placed in a lively and meaningful context, allowing the inner world to be experienced in all its complexity and diversity. Often, other support systems, such as purely traditional or spiritual approaches, are very hostile to knowledge. They reject scientific knowledge or regard it as irrelevant.[571] This leads to a restriction of development opportunities and the acquisition of knowledge. To counteract this problem, combination methods are required to integrate scientific knowledge and cultural immersion.

One's own individual interpretation of knowledge in relation to the inner world is crucial. A person's inner world is full of cultural peculiarities and

---

569 Many psychological insights fail due to a lack of knowledge about basic psychological processes and principles. Without a deep understanding of the underlying mechanisms, many inner-psychological phenomena remain undiscovered or misunderstood. In this context, knowledge acts as a catalyzer of insight and is therefore the most important psycho-economic resource. Knowledge not only makes it possible to recognise and understand psychological processes, but also to influence and change them in a targeted manner.
570 In this context, transgressive experiences, such as trance or intoxication experiences are also important and can be part of an immersive experience. See also Saldanha (2008), p. 174ff. and Csikszentmihalyi (2002).
571 Cf. Shweder (1991), p. 96ff. and Brooke (1991), pp. 82–112 and p. 321ff.

symbolic orders. Only in a broad cultural and scientific context can it fully reveal itself. This perspective is consistent with the theory that the world dwells within one, that is, that the individual carries within himself or herself a multitude of worlds and experiences that are made accessible through knowledge and cultural immersion can be made accessible.[572]

- The combination of scientific and cultural immersion represents a powerful approach to exploring the inner world. Knowledge, as one of the most important psycho-economic resources, enables fundamentally more comprehensive insights and promotes personal development.
- Embedding this knowledge in cultural contexts enriches the experience and interpretation of one's own inner world. Combination methods that integrate these approaches, therefore, offer a comprehensive and effective means of self-discovery and psychological healing.

The role of esthetics in the mental economy of the psyche is of central importance, especially against the background of cultural and scientific immersion. Esthetics influence not only our perception and our emotional well-being but also our cognitive processes and social and social interactions. This influence is further amplified by the complex interactions between culture and science.

The mental economy of the psyche refers primarily to the efficient management of cognitive, emotional, and energetic resources. Esthetics play an essential role in this context, as they influence the way we process information, experience emotions, and utilize energy. Aesthetic experiences can conserve

---

572 The idea that the world dwells within you is found in various philosophical and spiritual traditions. One well-known theory that takes up this idea is the theory of holism especially in the form of psychological or metaphysical holism. This states that parts of a system can only be fully understood in relation to the whole and that the whole is more than the sum of its parts. In this context, one could say that the world resides within you, in that the individual and the universe are inextricably linked. Another related theory is pantheism, particularly in its Spinozist form. Baruch de Spinoza argued that God and nature are identical, and that each person carries a part of the divine or universal essence within them. In Spinoza's view, the world, or God, is present in every individual, which is a form of immanence. (Spinoza's pantheism departs from the Christian concept of a God who stands opposite the world as another being and with whom the individual can establish a relationship. Spinoza sees God and the world as identical with each other: All things are in God).

Cf. Spinoza (1677), pp. 224–233 and Lloyd (1996), pp. 45–58.

In psychology, too, there have long been approaches that support this idea, particularly in Gestalt therapy and transpersonal psychology.

Cf. Köhler (1947), pp. 29–48.

cognitive resources by facilitating learning and remembering. They promote positive emotions and contribute to psychological resilience.[573]

Culture shapes an individual's esthetic norms and preferences and influences how esthetic objects and experiences are perceived and evaluated. In a cultural immersion, individuals are constantly confronted with esthetic elements that are embedded in the social context. This continuous exposure promotes the adaptation and integration of cultural values and aesthetic standards into one's own mental economy.[574]

Esthetics in cultural contexts can be seen as a means of identity formation and social coherence. Culturally characterized esthetic preferences and forms of expression enable individuals to feel part of a community and strengthen their social identity. This process supports the mental economy by creating a sense of belonging and security, which in turn frees up cognitive and emotional resources that would otherwise be spent on coping with uncertainty and social tensions.

Scientific immersion refers to the deep immersion in scientific paradigms and ways of thinking. Scientific esthetics, often characterized by clarity, precision, and elegance, also influence the mental economy of the psyche. In scientific practice, esthetic criteria are used to evaluate hypotheses, theories, and empirical findings. An esthetically pleasing theory is often perceived as more intuitive and convincing, which facilitates cognitive processing and promotes acceptance in the scientific community. Scientific esthetics can optimize cognitive processes by increasing the clarity and comprehensibility of information. This reduces cognitive load and promotes more efficient learning and problem solving. In addition, the esthetic dimension of science contributes to emotional motivation and engagement by arousing curiosity and fascination.

The interaction between cultural and scientistic immersion creates a complex network of esthetic experiences that influence the mental economy of the psyche; cultural contexts can shape scientific esthetics and vice versa.[575]

Esthetic experiences that integrate both cultural and scientific elements can be particularly powerful. They offer rich, multidimensional experiences that promote cognitive flexibility and creativity. These experiences support the mental economy by enabling a harmonious integration of different areas of knowledge and experience, promoting a holistic and coherent perception of the world.[576]

Overall, esthetics play a crucial role in the mental economy of the psyche of the psyche by influencing the way in which cognitive, emotional, and energetic

---

573 See Vessel/Starr/Rubin (2012), p. 255ff. and Seligman/Csikszentmihalyi (2000), pp. 12–14.
574 Cf. Shweder (1991), p. 174ff.
575 See Sweller/Ayres/Kalyuga (2011), pp. 3–14 and 17–38.
576 Ibid.

resources are managed. Against the backdrop of cultural and scientistic immersion, the importance of esthetics becomes even clearer, as it serves as a link between different worlds of experience and contributes to the holistic development and well-being of the individual. The complex interactions between cultural and scientific esthetics emphasize the need for an interdisciplinary approach to fully understand the profound impact of aesthetic experiences on the human psyche.

The Three Key Messages

1. **The role of culture and esthetics in the mental economy:** Culture, in the form of art, literature, music, and other forms of expression, offers rich sources for individual imagination and narration that enrich a person's inner world. Esthetic experiences influence our perception, emotions, and cognitive processes and are crucial for identity formation and social coherence.
2. **Scientistic and cultural immersion as a catalyst:** The combination of scientific and cultural immersion offers a comprehensive approach to exploring the inner world. Scientific methods and cultural contexts complement each other and enable deeper insights and personal development. The combination of these approaches promotes a harmonious integration of knowledge and cultural experiences, leading to a holistic understanding of one's identity and psychological processes.
3. **Supporting the mental economy through esthetics:** Esthetics play a central role in the efficient management of cognitive, emotional, and energetic resources. Esthetic experiences facilitate learning, promote positive emotions, and contribute to psychological resilience. The interaction between cultural and scientific aesthetic experiences supports the mental economy by promoting cognitive flexibility and creativity and enabling a coherent perception of the world.

The Meta-Psychological Support Systems of Yoga, Tantra, and Meditation

Knowledge is better than the mere performance of rituals. Meditation is better than knowledge. Renouncing the fruits of one's deeds (tyaga) is better than meditation. Why? Because giving up expectations is immediately followed by peace.[577]

---

577 Bhagavadgita (1998), 20.12.

The support of inner cognitive processes through mental techniques such as meditation or yoga is another important aspect of promoting mental economy and its performance. These techniques offer systematic approaches to developing concentration and mindfulness, which can be regarded as trainable skills, such as muscles.[578]

Meditation and yoga are practices that have been used for thousands of years in various cultures to promote mental and physical health as well as for overarching spiritual purposes. They aim to calm the mind and achieve a deep inner peace that enables cognitive processes to be clarified and restructured on an individual basis. To clarify and restructure cognitive processes on an individual basis. Through regular practice, these techniques can significantly increase the ability to concentrate and be mindful.[579] Concentration, understood as the ability to direct and maintain focus on a specific task or direction of thought, is strengthened through meditative practices. Mindfulness, the conscious perception of the present moment without judgment, is also promoted through such practices.

The effectiveness of these techniques can be explained by the metaphorical idea of a muscle that becomes stronger and more resilient through regular training. Meditation and yoga train the mental "muscle memory" by providing regular exercises for focusing and inner observation. This practice leads to improved self-regulation and emotional stability, which enables the individual to better cope with situational reality and achieve a higher level of overall mental stability (thanks to focused, resilient transactional processes).[580]

Numerous empirical studies have shown the positive effects of meditation and yoga on cognitive functions (especially the executive functions of the mental system[581]) and emotional health. Regular practice is associated with improvements in areas such as attention, memory, and the executive functions of the mental system.[582]

---

578 See McKibben/Nan (2017), p. 490f. and Kornfield (2008), pp. 140–159.
579 Ibid.
580 For example, Goyal et al. (2014), pp. 360–362 and Streeter et al. (2012), pp. 573–576.
581 See Gothe (2013), pp. 492–494.
582 In addition, research results impressively show that these techniques can reduce stress, alleviate anxiety and depression and increase overall life satisfaction. See Goyal et al. (2014) and Streeter et al. (2012).

Yoga and Tantra—the integration of control and acceptance in the mind system

Yoga is the practice of physical, mental, and spiritual disciplines to promote systemic unity of the mind system, while Tantra is a spiritual tradition that utilizes techniques for integrating inner acceptance to achieve holistic unity in the mind system. to create holistic unity[583] in the mind system. The methods of yoga are designed to bring control over the mind through control of the body,[584] while the methods of tantra work through acceptance of what is, connecting mental capacities and resources by eliminating contradictions and inefficient distortions.[585]

Both schools look back on a long history; both schools were (and are) often alienated, distorted, and misused for individual purposes.[586] The concepts of Tantra, in particular, have (quite wrongly) a diffuse to frowned upon reputation and are only a blurred term for most people in a Western sexualized context. In fact, tantra is actually the older, conceptually more complex school and stands for a principle of cognition that is, to a certain extent, the opposite of yoga.

---

583 The difference between systemic unity and holistic unity lies in the underlying conceptual approach and the way in which they view the relationship between the parts and the whole. Systemic unity views a system as a network of interconnected and interacting parts, focussing on the relationships and interactions between these parts. This view emphasizes that the behavior of the whole system emerges from the properties and dynamics of its components, with the structure and connections within the system being central. In contrast, holistic unity views the whole as more than the sum of its parts and emphasizes that the whole has its own identity and properties that cannot be explained by analyzing its individual parts alone. This perspective emphasises that the whole has independent characteristics and qualities that can only be understood by looking at the whole in its entirety. Both approaches are important for understanding complex systems but differ in their emphasis on the importance of the relationships between the parts as opposed to the importance of the whole as an entity in its own right.

584 The word "yoke" is derived from the word "yoga" and originally meant concentration and connection. For the etymology, see Gunturu (2020), pp. 7–10.

585 The word "tantra" comes from Sanskrit and is composed of the root's "tan" (to expand, weave) and "tra" (instrument, method). It literally means "fabric" or "continuum" and refers to the linking of different aspects of life and existence through spiritual practices.

Tantra emphasizes the unity of body and mind and often also the inclusion of different energies as a means of spiritual transformation. See Feuerstein (1998), pp. 3–5.

586 See Mallinson/Singleton (2017), pp. 24–40 and pp. 447–465 and Urban (2003), pp. 10–24 and 191–214.

However, I do not want to go into this any further here—the concept of the inner economy of the psyche has nothing to do with the New Age, and I don't want to go into the (undoubtedly very extensive) spiritual aspects of yoga and tantra—that would probably be a book in its own right that has yet to be written. At this point, it is exclusively about the instrumentalization of their methods and techniques in the service of the economy of the spirit system.

Another important point is the fact that the techniques of meditation (and yoga), in contrast to cultural immersion, are at the end of a continuum that is not free of tension—this is important to bear in mind because, strictly speaking, the two systems are quite mutually exclusive. Meditation in the tradition of the technical setting known as tantra excludes the structured forms of culture as something unreal and therefore also irrelevant, even confusing and distracting,[587] while the forms of immersion cast doubt on the reality of mental transcendence processes within a scientifically verifiable context. In other words, the two worlds speak different languages.

For the purposes of this book, however, this fact is rather in the background—I want to use both worlds to strengthen and refine mental thought processes, which will ultimately lead to higher penetration of narrative and imagination processes. This is what this chapter will also focus on; I want to emphasize the importance of integrating control and acceptance in the mind system. I will not explain these extensive schools in detail to the full extent.

It starts with breathing. Especially in the traditions of yoga and tantra, breathing is the starting point for everything. In these spiritual and philosophical systems, the breath is seen as a bridge between body and mind and serves as a universal tool.

In yoga practice, pranayama, the art of breath control, is one of the essential disciplines.[588] Pranayama literally means "expansion of the life principle" and aims to regulate the life energy known as prana. Targeted breathing techniques are used to gain control over the breath, which has a direct effect on the mind. The breath is consciously lengthened, deepened, and slowed down, which leads to a reduction in stress and anxiety. This control over the breath enables the practitioner to influence the physiological reactions of the body and achieve a deeper meditative experience.[589]

---

587 See Mallinson/Singleton (2017), p. 341ff.
588 See Gunturu (2020), pp. 25–28 and 97–109.
589 Cf. Brown/Gerbarg (2005), p. 189f. and Jerath/Edry/Barnes/Jerath (2006), p. 566ff.

Control through breathing techniques means not only the physical regulation of the breathing rate but also the cultivation of a conscious approach to one's own thoughts and emotions. By controlling the breath, attention is also trained, and the mind is focused. This practice promotes greater mindfulness and makes it possible to recognize and break through thought patterns that lead to stress and anxiety.[590]

At the same time, the tradition of yoga and tantra emphasizes the need for acceptance. Acceptance at a basic level means observing the present states of the body and mind without judgment. In the practice of breathing, an individual can learn to feel and accept the natural flow of the breath without forcing or suppressing it. In Tantra, the breath plays a similar but even more comprehensive role. Tantra aims to integrate all aspects of life and see the divine in every experience. The breath is a key tool for activating the energy centers (chakras) and promoting spiritual development. Through special breathing techniques, energies in the body are mobilized and channeled to release blockages and expand consciousness. Tantra teaches that by consciously working with the breath, a deeper connection to the self and to universal energy can be established. And to the universal energy.[591]

The integration of control and acceptance through the breath in yoga and tantra not only promotes physical well-being but also mental and emotional health. Scientific studies support these traditional views by demonstrating the positive effects of breathing techniques on the nervous system and stress management.[592]

But the breath also serves as a bridge to the outside world; it has a transitional function.

The techniques of yoga consist of physical exercises (asanas), breathing techniques (pranayama), and meditation (dhyana). These practices aim to calm the mind and strengthen the body, leading to improved perception and a clearer transition between inside and outside. Through regular yoga practice, the senses are sharpened, and the perception of the outside world can change in subtle ways. You begin to perceive the world not just superficially but also notice the fine details and inner beauty of things—both of which intensify and specify mental transaction processes. Intensified and specified.

---

590 Ibid.
591 See White (2000), pp. 3–38 and pp. 561–588.
592 Cf. Streeter et al. (2012), pp. 580–587.

Tantra goes even further and primarily integrates spiritual practices based on the union of opposites. Tantra assumes universal connectivity and interconnectedness of being and that these universal connections have profound effects on the understanding of the world itself. Through tantric practices such as rituals, meditation, and conscious breathing, consciousness is expanded, and the perception of the outside world is transformed. The outer experiences become a mirror of the inner self; transactional processes thus overcome the demarcation between inside and outside.

One of the most important teachings that both yoga and tantra impart is the importance of patience. In today's hectic world, we tend to expect instant results. But mental transformation (which is what economic insight therapy strives for) requires time and dedication. Patience is crucial to navigating through the various process stages of the practice and realizing insights and the resulting changes in consciousness and perception This patience not only helps with your own mental development but also fundamentally promotes exchange processes of all kinds.[593]

Scientific studies support many of the spiritual aspects of yoga and tantra. Research has shown that regular yoga practice can reduce stress levels, improve cognitive function, and increase emotional stability.[594] Similarly, there is evidence that meditative practices used in tantra can alter brain structure and expand consciousness.[595]

Understanding and exploring the inner world requires an individual immersion in the rules and mechanisms of dualism, which determine the interplay between mind and body, inside and outside. These two aspects are inextricably linked and mirror each other. Although the utilization of both mind and body functions may seem trivial at first, it is a complex challenge. The interdependence of mind and body means that changes in one area often have an impact on the other, emphasizing the need for a holistic approach.

The support systems presented here are often necessary and useful for gaining deep insights into the inner world. These support systems can take many forms, from structured methods such as yoga and meditation to less formal approaches such as mindfulness and self-reflection. However, it is important to avoid extremes in any form. Extreme practices and beliefs tend to take on a (pseudo-) religious character and can disrupt balance and objectivity in self-exploration.

---

593 See Guntutu (2020), p. 53ff.
594 Cf. Streeter et al. (2012), p. 588f.
595 Cf. Lazar et al. (2005), p. 1895f.

Many extreme systems and lifestyles often present themselves in a pushy way and promise quick results, but skepticism is appropriate here—the model of the economized spirit system also sets itself apart in a very practical way.

Cognition is ultimately exclusively a monologue with oneself; nothing can really be integrated into the inner world without one's own active intervention.

Gurus and teachers, who often act as guides on the path to self-knowledge, can be supportive but are not always necessary or helpful.[596] External insecurity and excessive dependence on external authorities can be a hindrance. In fact, powerful external stimuli are not necessary to explore and sharpen the inner world and its processes. Often, such external influences can create additional barriers and obstacles that hinder progress. Yoga and meditation are proven methods that can facilitate access to the inner world.[597] However, the helpful elements of these practices must, in fact, be found out for yourself, and the path to self-knowledge must be individualized.[598]

Although Buddhism is often regarded as a religion, it contains many elements of faith that focus on extreme, transcendental goals. These goals, such as the achievement of inner emptiness or the dissolution of the ego, are not always beneficial in a psychological context and can even negate one's inner world. While these goals may be interesting and desirable for some, they often offer no practical help for self-knowledge and improving mental health. It is often the basic mechanisms that move the mind forward the most. The application and iteration of techniques such as meditation increases the control and depth

---

[596] And are even viewed critically by them. Cf. Osho (2009), pp. 1101–1105.

[597] Although Buddhism is not considered a religion, it contains many elements of faith that focus on extreme, transcendental goals. These goals, such as the achievement of inner emptiness or the dissolution of the ego, are not always beneficial in a psychological context and can even negate one's inner world. While these goals may be interesting and desirable for some, they often do not provide practical help for economic self-knowledge and improving mental health. The economy of the psyche therefore focuses on the transactional and transformative view of the mind.

Cf. Fromm (1971), p. 123ff.

[598] One problematic practice that can be observed in both yoga and tantra is "meditating away" problems and psychological complexes. Practitioners use meditation techniques to suppress or repress unpleasant emotions and inner conflicts instead of actively dealing with them. This can bring short-term relief, but in the long term it can lead to emotional blunting and a loss of the ability to self-reflect. Avoiding inner conflicts through meditation can lead to deep-rooted psychological problems remaining unresolved, which impairs personal development and psychological well-being.

See Lomas/Cartwright/Edginton/Ridge (2014), pp. 167–170.

of the inner world. Meditation must be self-taught, as only the practitioner has control over their own mind. Disciplined self-training is, therefore, the key to exploring the inner world. An important effect of this practice is better access to one's own mental processes, which increases the quality and precision of the imagination and individual narrative abilities. Individual narrative abilities thus also strengthen the mind system as a whole, in its entirety.

> **The Three Key Messages**
>
> 1. **Integration and differences between yoga and tantra:** Yoga aims to control the mind through physical discipline, while tantra works through acceptance and integration of inner states. Both systems have a long history and have often been misunderstood and misused.
> 2. **Instrumentalization and mental economy:** The techniques of both systems are used in the context of mental economy to improve cognitive and emotional efficiency. This includes breath control (pranayama) in yoga and energetic techniques in tantra, which expand awareness and improve perception. Consciousness and change the perception of the outside world.
> 3. **Patience and transformation:** Patience is essential for spiritual and mental development in both systems. Scientific studies confirm the positive effects of yoga and tantra on stress management, cognitive function, and emotional stability.

Meditation as a universal tool of the economized mind system

In the following, I would like to discuss the role of meditation in working with one's own mind system in the context of economic insight therapy; here, too, the presentation remains focused on its role in a transactional and transformative context. A major problem in this context is that the idea of meditation in society at large is completely wrong.

You only have to look at any film that comes into contact with this topic: mediation is portrayed by default as a reservoir of supernatural power, as a mental retreat and bastion for the protagonist.[599] Meanwhile, all the

---

599 See Russell (2013), pp. 142–165.

visualizations I know of completely miss the silent, externally nonexistent truth of meditation—how could it be otherwise? Because meditation is, first and foremost, the absence of something (and this is difficult to visualize).

In my personal experience and my theoretical research, practically all meditation instructions and techniques miss the point and work with distractions and illusions—the very mental things that meditation wants to dissolve. For example, you can start with a mantra[600], but it will be difficult to get rid of it again.

The biggest basic problem here is the fact that there can be no instructions for good meditation in terms of its conceptual nature; it is something that everyone has to find for themselves—through thinking and feeling. Guidance is disruptive here, as no one will meditate straight away. Meditation is ideally the end of the inner dialogue—so it really doesn't need any additional outer dialogue to be effective.[601]

In contrast to classical forms of narration (which even require an external counterpart), meditation is not an active activity in the true sense of the word; it is the absence of all activity.[602] And something that can hardly be accessed without a certain lightness and joy in the self. It can hardly be tapped into.

If you want to engage in meditation, you can easily do this on your own. The following four points are particularly relevant and helpful:

- **Initial approach through mental analysis:** Prior mental analysis is of central importance to the initial approach to the practice of meditation. This preparation enables a deeper understanding of the theoretical foundations and creates a conscious attitude toward the subsequent meditative exercises.[603]
- **Thinking before every meditative action:** Every meditative action or nonaction should be preceded by a thought process. This conscious

---

600 A mantra is a sound, word or phrase that is repeated in spiritual and meditative practices to focus the mind, promote inner peace and achieve spiritual realization. Mantras are often written in ancient languages such as Sanskrit and serve as tools for concentration and transcendence of everyday consciousness. Their repetition can produce neurophysiological effects that contribute to stress reduction and improved emotional regulation.
    Cf. Álvarez-Pérez et al. (2022).
601 Cf. Nhat Hanh (1999), p. 56f.
602 Cf. Dalai Lama (2002), p. 110ff.
603 Cf. Kabat-Zinn (2003), p. 150ff.

reflection promotes mindfulness and helps to clearly define the goals and intentions of the practice, which can increase the effectiveness and depth of meditation.[604]

- **Become more aware while doing:** During the practical application of meditation, it is advisable to concentrate more on feeling. This explorative approach requires you to let go of active thinking and instead encourages joyful inner exploration. As a result, deeper emotional and intuitive insights can be gained.[605]
- **Set individual goals for meditation:** Meditation should be purposeful in its inner emptiness. Meditation, despite its nature often described as "inner emptiness," should be purposeful to unfold its full effect. The apparent paradox between inner emptiness and purposefulness is resolved when meditative practice's different levels and intentions are understood. Purposefulness in meditation can encompass several dimensions[606]:
  - Clearly defined intentions: Purposeful meditation begins with clear intentions. These intentions can aim to reduce stress, improve emotional regulation, promote mindfulness, or develop compassion. Studies show that clearly formulated goals increase the effectiveness of meditation as they focus the mind and strengthen motivation to practice.
  - Structured approaches: Purposeful meditation utilizes structured approaches and techniques, such as mindfulness meditation, analytical meditation, or concentration meditation. These techniques offer specific instructions and exercises that guide the practitioner through the meditative processes and thus enable a focused experience.
  - Measurable results: Being purposeful in meditation also allows you to track measurable results. Scientific studies show that meditators who pursue specific goals experience significant improvements in these areas.

Meditation, as a practice of inner reflection and mindfulness, fundamentally opens the mind to intuitive realizations about the interconnectedness of all things, which is the basis for the transactional nature of our existence and the

---

604 Cf. Shapiro et al. (2006), pp. 375–380.
605 See Vago/Silbersweig (2012).
606 See Lutz/Slagter/Dunne/Davidson (2008), pp. 165–169.

business itself. This practice helps to dissolve the illusion of separateness created by the ego.[607]

Meditation is also seen as the art of living fully consciously. The beauty and meaning of life lie not in the judgment of historical events or values but in the quality of conscious experiences anchored at the moment. To understand the true nature of these experiences, we must know and understand the raw material—our sensations, thoughts, and emotions. These experiences shape our personal reality. Through intellectual and intuitive understanding of the mind system, we can intentionally and purposefully shape our personal reality—one of the main functions of the economized mind.[608]

In human life, painful and pleasant experiences are inevitable, but suffering and happiness are optional—the self (or, at a higher level, the processes of the mental spirit system) has the choice. Love and compassion enable us to change things in a positive way and, at the same time, maintain the serenity of acceptance, both cornerstones of a rational, economic view of the inner and outer world.

Meditation is a practice in which conscious intentions are set and maintained. Everything we do and achieve is based on our intentions. The will to turn these intentions into reality creates the basis for stable attention and mindfulness, provided that the intentions are correctly formulated and consistently pursued. These intentions lead to mental "actions" and habits of mind. Therefore, the actual "doing" in meditation consists of patiently and persistently maintaining these intentions.[609]

Inherent in the concept of meditation, in its economic aspect, is the *model of conscious experience*: the conscious experience of the mind can be seen as a topographical map that is detailed through meditation methods and other

---

[607] In Buddhist practice, the concept of awakening is often mentioned as the climax of meditation. Awakening, often also referred to as enlightenment or liberation, is a cognitive event in which every form of inner ignorance is replaced by concrete experience. It involves a deep and lasting freedom from suffering, independent of external circumstances. This happens through the direct realisation of the true nature of reality and the spirit. In this state, life—including birth and death—is seen as an adventure, with the ultimate goal being to develop and live love and compassion. This climax is not directly relevant to the goals of economic epistemology, but rather the concepts in the process of getting there. However, the goals of this—namely love and compassion—are also highly economic, that is, valuable and worthwhile goals.
[608] Cf. Dalai Lama/Cutler (1998), pp. 295ff. and Nhat Hanh (1999), pp. 28–36.
[609] Ibid. p. 80ff.

avenues of exploration. These models offer different depths and precision in mapping the mental landscape. A central goal of meditation is to achieve stable attention and mindfulness. And mindfulness. This involves consciously directing and continuously maintaining the focus of attention.[610]

Consciousness can, therefore, also be described as a process of mutual exchange of information that takes place in the individual spirit system. It encompasses all experiences that the self perceives at a given moment. This field of conscious awareness is similar to a visual field in which sensory impressions, thoughts, feelings, and memories appear and disappear. Conscious experience manifests itself in two forms: *Attention* and *peripheral awareness*.[611]

Attention can be focused and dominate the momentary experience, while peripheral awareness remains more vague and generalized in the background. These two ways of perceiving the world correspond to two different networks in the brain: an intention-driven network and an autonomous network.[612] Attention extracts specific elements from the field of conscious awareness to analyze and interpret them. Peripheral awareness, on the other hand, provides the overall context for the conscious experience and shows the relationships of objects and phenomena to each other and to the whole.[613]

The first goal of meditation is to develop *stable attention* that is focused, sustained, and selective. This ability involves consciously directing and maintaining focus as well as controlling the scope of attention. It is about deciding exactly which object to focus attention on and with what intensity and maintaining this continuously.

Attention is the most valuable tool for exploring and understanding your own spirit system.

In a normal state, attention moves spontaneously. It scans the external world or its own mental contents for interesting things, is absorbed by suddenly occurring phenomena, or subtly switches between different perceptions. In reality, multitasking is an extremely rapid switching of attention between the main focus and peripheral objects, which leads to a certain degree of distraction if this is not consciously intended.[614]

---

610 See Yates (2015).
611 Ibid., p. 52ff.
612 Attention and peripheral awareness are associated with two different systems within the mental system that process information in fundamentally different ways. Cf. in detail Austin (2011), pp. 29–43 and pp. 53–64.
613 See also the excursus after Chapter 2.
614 See Yates (2015), p. 43ff.

During meditation, the intentional movement of attention replaces spontaneous movement. Consciously directed attention means directing and maintaining focus on a specific object or phenomenon, which corresponds to a concentrated effort. This process is partly unconscious and cannot be directly controlled by the will. However, conscious intention can influence and train the unconscious evaluation process, enabling continuous focusing.

Overcoming shifting attention leads to *exclusive (single-pointed) attention*. Conscious intention can transform the mind and completely restructure the self. Directing and maintaining attention is a matter of controlling the scope of attention. A wide scope is similar to shifting attention, as several things are involved at once, resulting in a form of multitasking. Control through a narrow focus is crucial for stable attention, while consciously switching between narrow and wide focus is also trained. Focusing on the entire field of conscious awareness can be understood as an extended "non-focus," which nevertheless contributes to the stability of attention.[615]

The second goal of meditation is the generation of attention and the reciprocal functions and interactions with peripheral awareness—this leads to *mindfulness* (defined as effective conscious awareness), which in turn is a central component of many meditative and spiritual practices. It refers to the conscious perception and interaction with the outer world and the individual's inner self. Two key components play an essential role here: attention and peripheral awareness.[616]

Attention is the process by which consciousness identifies, analyses, and interprets specific objects and phenomena. To be effective, attention transforms these objects and phenomena into concepts or abstract ideas that can be better processed. This occurs through a mental process that oscillates between intellect and intuition and is often semi-conscious.[617]

On the other hand, peripheral awareness encompasses everything that the senses perceive and works only slightly conceptually. New phenomena first appear in peripheral awareness and are then selected by attention. Peripheral awareness is inclusive and holistic, organizes the relationships between objects, phenomena, and the self, and creates the situational context by comparing it with our experiences.[618] The interaction between attention and peripheral

---

615 See Lutz/Slagter/Dunne/Davidson (2008), p. 164f. and Tang/Hölzel/Posner (2015), pp. 217–222.
616 See Yates (2015), p. 53ff.
617 Ibid.
618 Ibid.

awareness is crucial for an effective response to present situations.[619] While attention analyses objects, peripheral awareness provides the necessary context. This co-operation enables us to make precise and objective decisions and react to the environment.

The practice of mindfulness creates a correct overall picture in the field of conscious awareness. This includes the ability to recognize options and take control of them and the power to change conditioned reactions from the past. An alert awareness of the right, important objects and phenomena is essential. Mindfulness means using attention precisely, economically, and objectively and, at the same time, developing a strong peripheral awareness. This ensures that all relevant information is captured and processed.[620]

The co-operation of attention and peripheral awareness enables a more objective evaluation of objects and phenomena: Attention alone tends toward egocentric tendencies and evaluates objects and phenomena in terms of personal well-being, which is distorted by desire, fear, aversion, and emotion. Peripheral awareness, on the other hand, perceives objects and phenomena less egocentrically and integrates them as part of the overall picture, which mitigates egocentric tendencies and objectifies conscious awareness.

Both attention and peripheral awareness can be extrospective (focused on external objects) or introspective (focused on internal processes). Peripheral awareness has the whole picture of the mind in view and can observe its activities simultaneously, which is referred to as metacognitive introspective awareness. Attention, on the other hand, cannot observe its own activity; this meta-activity can only occur through peripheral awareness.[621]

The quality of reactions, whether through words, actions, emotions, or thoughts, depends strongly on the quality of the information provided by attention and peripheral awareness. Mindfulness is the best possible interaction between the two, which generates the best possible information and thus improves the quality of reactions.

---

[619] Peripheral awareness processes less important things independently and is responsible for reflexes, which makes it faster than attention, as it processes things less accurately (parallel processing vs. serial processing). If peripheral awareness is weak, attention cannot react quickly enough to all objects and phenomena, which leads to inappropriate or automatic (i.e., thoughtless) reactions.
[620] See Bishop, Scott R. et al. (2004), pp. 232 and 234f.
[621] See Brown, K. W./Ryan, R. M. (2003), p. 824ff. and Goyal, Madhav et al. (2014), p. 359ff.

The integration of attention and peripheral awareness through mindfulness promotes a deeper and more precise perception and response to the environment and one's own inner self. This leads to a higher level of insight, self-control, and mental clarity, which is supported by numerous scientific studies.

Maintaining mindfulness and conscious awareness draws their energy from the same source, which creates an interdependent exchange relationship. This relationship is clearly evident in the way attention and awareness interact and influence each other: When attention is intensely focused, the field of conscious awareness shrinks. This leads to the peripheral awareness, which normally serves as an orientation and categorization aid, dwindling. The result is a loss of the ability of awareness to focus attention on the most important objects or processes, which leads to an insufficient power of consciousness.

Another aspect is the depletion of the power of consciousness through multitasking. When attention is divided between many different objects or processes or processes, mindfulness is reduced accordingly. Accordingly, this leads to a state in which interaction with peripheral awareness is no longer possible, a phenomenon known as "tunnel vision."

The opposite phenomenon occurs in a relaxed state, when attention fades and awareness takes control. This can lead to dullness, loss of mindfulness, and drowsiness. This shows that an overall increase in the power of consciousness is necessary to achieve strong mindfulness. Only in this way can attention be used purposefully and without subjective judgments and projections.

To train this, situations should be created in which both focused attention and peripheral awareness are required. The aim is to achieve a hyperaware state in which all important details are perceived from the field of conscious awareness.[622] This leads to an improved quality of mindfulness and attention.[623] In stressful situations, this enables greater objectification and contextualization through awareness, which promotes calmness and presence.

---

622 See Yates (2015), pp. 59–61.
623 Cf. ibid., p. 61f.

1. **Misconceptions about meditation:** The general perception of *meditation* is often flawed, as it is misrepresented as a supernatural force or mental retreat when it emphasizes the absence of activity.
2. **Individual practice and inner experience:** Good meditation cannot be standardized or instructed; it is an individual experience that must be discovered through personal thinking and feeling. It aims to end the inner dialogue and promote a conscious, joyful confrontation with oneself.
3. **Essential aspects of meditation:** Meditation includes mental preparation, mindful reflection before every action, immersion in feeling, and setting individual goals. This leads to stable attention and effective conscious awareness, which improves the quality of reactions and the understanding of one's own mental processes.

Excursus: Analytical meditation

Analytical meditation is a highly structured type of intensive reflection that involves the systematic investigation of a topic with stable, clear, and focused attention and a high degree of continuous awareness. It can be used for three main categories: deepening understanding of a topic,[624] the process of problem-solving and insight in analytical meditation follows certain mental principles in four phases.[625]

The first phase, *preparation*, concentrates attention on relevant ideas and information and puts everything irrelevant on the back burner. This is a conscious process of collecting and distinguishing between the important and the unimportant, known as selective encoding.

In the second phase, *incubation*, a permanent recombination of all available ideas and information to solve the problem, takes place, which is described as selective combining[626]. At the same time, the current problem is compared with potential solutions and similar problems from the past, a process known as selective comparison.

These two processes, selective combining and comparing, take place both consciously and unconsciously. The conscious part includes logical-analytical

---

624 See Yates (2015), p. 427f.
625 Ibid.
626 Also known as the trial-and-error principle.

thought processes and intellectual problem-solving through logic (i.e., through non-insight),[627] while the unconscious part leads to problem-solving through intuition and insight.

The conscious mind is particularly effective at solving simple problems through logical applications to information. The unconscious mind, on the other hand, which works on many mental processes simultaneously, primarily solves complex problems with unusual components. Since the conscious mind works sequentially, it is less effective at solving complex problems than the unconscious, which enables parallel processing and is free from limitations.[628]

The third phase, the **solution to** a problem, can be achieved through logical thinking or through spontaneous, intuitive insight, but usually through a combination of both processes. This recursive process, in which the solution of smaller problems leads to the solution of higher-level problems, ends with the fourth phase, **verification**. Here, the solution is checked to see whether it is practically applicable. Solutions by insight must be checked and evaluated by logic to ensure their effectiveness. This verification always takes place in awareness and should take into account situational and social backgrounds such as societal, legal, and moral aspects.

The formal method of analytical meditation maximizes the benefits of conscious, logical, and unconscious intuitive mental processes. The first phase of preparation and approach begins with a normal meditation introduction that includes focused attention. The subject of the analytical meditation is brought into consciousness; sensations of breathing recede into the background and remain present in the peripheral awareness. The subject is held in consciousness and listened to without actively analyzing it in order to await the outcome of unconscious mental processes.

In the incubation and analysis phase (also known as contemplation), the thoughts and ideas from the first phase serve as a starting point for further

---

627 The distinction between logic and insight in problem solving and cognition can be seen as a contrast between two types of thinking and understanding. Logic in this context is described as non-insight because it is based on a systematic, rule-based and sequential process that occurs through conscious, analytical thought. Insight, on the other hand, refers to an intuitive, often sudden and non-sequential realization (intuition) that arises from the unconscious mind. Both approaches play an important role in cognitive processing and can complement each other to enable a more comprehensive understanding and effective problem solving.

628 Cf. Dijksterhuis/Bos/Nordgren/van Baaren (2006), p. 1005f. and Kahneman (2011), p. 133ff.

reflection and analysis from different angles. The logic and relevance of the thoughts are tested, and openness to new intuitive insights is maintained. The aim is to achieve an understanding that goes beyond pure abstraction and incorporates the experiential level.

The outcome of analytical meditation includes understanding, resolution, and decision-making or deepening of insight. A natural completion of the first two stages leads to a sense of completion, although details often require deeper investigation. More complex issues are made up of a series of incomplete outcomes, and sometimes, it is recognized that more information is needed to reach a final conclusion. The unconscious mind continues to work even after the analytical meditation is completed.

Verification and checking of results follow the path of analysis, checking for logical and intuitive errors. New insights are consolidated and integrated into the mental system, creating points of reference that can lead back to the state of realization and insight. The result of analytical meditation can also be used as an object of non-analytical meditation to better anchor thoughts and insights in the mind and easily bring them back into the focus of attention.[629]

Excursus: The Three Core Statements of Analytical Meditation in Brief

1. **Structured problem solving:** Analytical meditation is a methodical practice that combines systematic analysis, focused attention, continuous awareness to deepen understanding of issues, solve problems, and gain insights.
2. **Four-phase process:** It comprises four phases—preparation (selective encoding of relevant information), incubation (selective combining and comparing), solution (through logical thinking or intuitive insight), and verification (checking and validating the solutions).
3. **Integration of results:** The process maximizes the use of both conscious and unconscious mental processes maximizing the use of both conscious and unconscious mental processes, whereby new insights are reviewed, consolidated, and integrated into the mental system for use in future meditations and practical applications.

---

629 For a more detailed description, see Yates (2015), pp. 427–436.

CHAPTER 6

REMEMBERING IS THE VALUE OF LIFE—OR CAPITALISM IN OURSELVES

> The existence of the soul is also necessary because there must be a governor (adhiṣṭhâtṛ). As the unspiritual chariot is governed by the intelligent driver, so all unspiritual matter must be governed by a spiritual principle.[630]

This concluding chapter is intended to serve as a large bracket around the importance of the inner economy and that of individual mental resources—and, at the same time, point to overarching themes that are linked to the presented psychosocial perspective on memory and the psyche.

To categorize and look back:

The concept of inner economy refers (as explained in detail) to the way in which individuals manage their cognitive, emotional, and energetic resources within their mind system. This management is critical to psychological well-being and effectiveness in dealing with the challenges of daily life. Similar to an external economy, where resources such as time and money need to be allocated wisely, the internal economy also requires a conscious and balanced utilization of one's own mental capacities.

Mental resources include aspects such as memory (as a primary resource),[631] attention and mindfulness memory, emotional resilience, and cognitive flexibility or suppleness. These resources are not unlimited and must, therefore, be utilized in an economic context. Memories play a central role in the inner economy. They are not just passive records of past events but active constructions that influence the self-image and perception of the present. The psychosocial perspective on

---

630 Garbe (1894), p. 292.
631 See also Chapter 1.

memory emphasizes how social interactions and cultural contexts shape the way in which memories are constructed and remembered situationally.

The internal economy approach recognizes that memories do not exist in isolation but are embedded in a network of interconnective relationships and inter- and intrasubjective meanings. They contribute to identity formation and influence how individuals perceive themselves and their environment. Memories can also release or block additional mental resources or transactional processes or block them, depending on whether they are experienced as positive or stressful experiences.[632]

Finally, the integration of knowledge and momentary experience into the spirit system is an important topic. This refers to the ability to integrate new information and experiences into existing knowledge and memory structures and mental mapping processes. This integration is crucial for the personal growth of the ego and the continuous adaptation to changing situational circumstances.

An Initial Overview

- **Importance of inner economy and mental resources:** The concept of inner economy emphasizes the management of cognitive, emotional, and energetic resources that are crucial for mental well-being and coping with daily challenges.
- **The role of memories:** Memories are central, active constructions in the inner economy, which are shaped by social interactions and cultural contexts and influence the self-image and the perception of the present.
- **Integration of knowledge and experience:** The ability to integrate new information and experiences into existing knowledge and memory structures is essential for personal growth and adaptation to changing circumstances.

The Integration of the Mind System or a New Perspective on the Economy of the Psyche

We want to change the world—economically, socially, but it seems to me that significant external change will not be possible unless there is a radical psychological revolution, a transformation. transformation.[633]

---

632 See ibid.
633 Jiddu Krishnamurti, quoted from: Blau (1995), p. 155.

In recent decades, economic research has made considerable progress in analyzing the interactions between individuals and resources.[634] Nevertheless, the psychological dimension of human behavior and decision-making processes often remains underrepresented in many traditional economic approaches.

In this respect, in particular, the concept of an "economy of the psyche" is becoming increasingly important, which aims to place the intraindividual factors that influence economic activity at the center of economic considerations, is becoming increasingly important. This academic paper has initially focused on the "economy of the psyche" (i.e., the mental system itself) in order to show that economic approaches are ubiquitous and can offer new approaches to dealing with mental resources. At the same time, however, the question naturally arises as to what extent these new aspects and perspectives can contribute to a broader understanding of external economic activities.

Essentially, this concerns the following four points, which can have extrapsychic effects on an economic view of the mind system:

1. **Behavioral economics and (micro- and macroeconomic) decision-making:** As a branch of economics, behavioral economics is essentially concerned with researching the psychological factors that influence individual decision-making processes.[635] Many research findings show that human behavior is often not purely rational, as assumed by conventional economic models.[636] Instead, emotions, heuristics, and cognitive biases play a decisive role in decision-making.[637] The economics of the psyche strives to integrate these non-rational elements into economic models in order to paint a more realistic picture of human behavior.

2. **Well-being and life satisfaction:** Another novel approach to the economic integration of the mental system is the consideration of well-being and life satisfaction as key indicators of economic success. Traditional economic measures such as gross domestic product (GDP) focus primarily on material production and consumption but neglect intangible factors such as psychological well-being and quality of life. By integrating measures of life satisfaction and psychological well-being,

---

634 See also Aghion et al. (1998), p. 11ff. and Becker (2013), p. 253ff.
635 Cf. Camerer/Loewenstein (2004), pp. 3–53.
636 See also Kahnemann et al. (2011), p. 44ff. and p. 187ff. as well as Thaler et al. (2015), p. 32ff. and Thaler,/Sunstein (2008), p. 83ff.
637 Ibid.

the economy of the psyche could provide a more balanced picture of economic progress and make political decision-making more effective.[638]
3. **Psychological costs and psychological benefits:** In conventional economic analyses, costs and benefits are often measured exclusively in monetary terms. The economics of the psyche, however, is in favor of taking greater account of the effects of external factors on mental resources. By including these psychological dimensions, mental transaction processes of consciousness can contribute to a more precise evaluation of the actual cost and benefit considerations of economic activities.[639]
4. **Psychological resilience and adaptability:** In times of increasing economic uncertainty and change, psychological resilience and adaptability are becoming increasingly important factors for individual and social welfare.[640] The economy of the psyche focuses, among other things, on the effective use of mental resources, which becomes a comprehensive economic factor (both within individuals and in their external systems). Through an improved understanding of these processes, methods can be developed to strengthen an individual's mental health and resilience.[641]

The economization of the mental system offers a promising perspective for expanding and deepening conventional psychological and economic analyses by taking greater account of intrapsychic transaction processes, the functioning of the mind system and mental resources. By integrating these concepts, there is the potential to shift or evolve external economic mechanisms to better correspond to the internal economy, which has a number of positive effects and would lead to a whole series of positive internal and external effects.

However, the economization of the mental system also has far-reaching effects on the individual perception of consciousness and mental cognitive processes; the economization of the psyche leads to an inner economic approach to transcendence.[642]

Transcendence is often misunderstood and associated with a mystical context when, in fact, it is an essential component of any cognitive process.[643]

---

638 Ibid, p. 231ff.
639 See also Moser/Soucek (2007), pp. 404–414.
640 Ibid.
641 Cf. Cyrulnik (2009), p. 25f.
642 On the connection between economy and transcendence see for example Renesch (2008) and Sugden (2008), p. 483ff.
643 Cf. the fundamentally different approaches in Satre (1964) and Yates (2015), p. 399ff.

But at its core, transcendence simply refers to crossing a boundary or transcending an existing (inner) reality. In the psychology of cognition, transcendence is essential because any form of cognition requires the crossing of existing mental boundaries.

The mechanisms that underlie the concept of transcendence are reflected in the individual cognitive process. One of the central mechanisms is cognitive flexibility (also known as suppleness as a mental meta-resource),[644] which enables an individual to adopt new perspectives and go beyond previous thought patterns. This process of cognitive flexibility often requires reflection on existing beliefs and an openness to new ideas and information—both part of the mental transaction processes of the mental system and clearly resource-based. Added to this are mechanisms such as creative problem-solving or emotion regulation. By learning to regulate their mental resources, influence the processes of mind system, and consciously shape their own narrative, the economization of the mental system also develops into a transcendence factor that can lead to many insights about the self.

At this point, I would like to conclude by returning to the economic system of the mind and the two bases for its development (up to enlightenment, which can certainly be understood as a trans-idealistic concept[645]).

It is important to distinguish between an individual and a systemic level of transcendental cognitive processes: On a personal level, realization (and in an extreme form, enlightenment) is without question not a gradual process but binary—especially in conscious experience; the transition is unconscious.[646] On a systemic level (which can, in fact, be instrumentalized), however, it is a slow,[647] relatively clearly structured process in a gradual overflow scheme (Figure 14 illustrates this).

The first basis (Basis I) is always the past-based narrative and imagination processes in the self and their work with the resource of memory. In a recursive process, the mind system transforms itself on the basis of its summary memory, which leads to increasing realization, intuition, and individuation.[648] In this context, intuition is a further development of thinking, whereby its inner

---

644 Ibid, p. 355ff.
645 Also in the sense of Hommes (1953), p. 130ff.
646 This is also due to the basic functioning of the spirit system, cf. the excursus in Chapter 2.
647 In the sense of requiring time.
648 Without there being any underlying automatism here; the further development of the spirit system itself is also an economic process and therefore requires the active, conscious creation of favorable framework conditions.

182 THE MIND ECONOMY

FIGURE 14 The two strands of the cognitive process.[649]

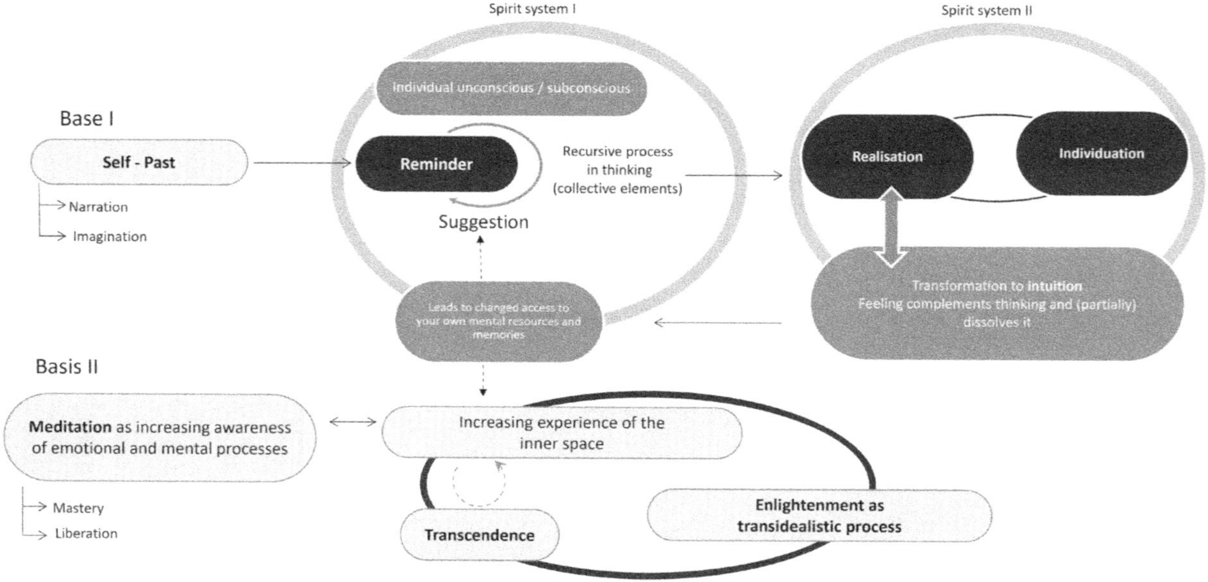

---

649 Own presentation.

processes are supplemented by feeling and thus often shortened. This basis is the process of self-realization.

The second basis (basis II) of realization is the meta-level of the individuation process itself; here, the methods of mindfulness act as a mediator for becoming aware of inner processes (which is, by definition, to be regarded as meditation). This enables an iterative exploration and expansion of the inner space, which in itself is transcendence and always carries with it the spiritual claim to enlightenment as a trans-idealistic approach.

Cognition is, therefore, of central importance for every individual in the context of the internal economy; it is the decisive transaction process in the utilization and processing of mental resources.

On the link between economy and transcendence, there is still much to theorize about the link between economics and transcendence, but the beginnings are unmistakable—going beyond existing mental boundaries and expanding our understanding of the (inner as well as outer) world is clearly part of any economic growth. Investigating the mechanisms of economic transcendence is another topic that can be derived from the mental mechanisms, processes, and systems outlined above.

The effects of the application of economics on these mental mechanisms, processes, systems, and systems are extensive—whether of an individual-psychological nature (such as through the application in the context of economic cognitive therapy)[650] or of a theoretical-psychological nature.

The Three Key Messages

1. **Interdisciplinary integration of the economy of the psyche:** The economic view of the mental system emphasizes the importance of intraindividual factors for economic action and decision-making processes by integrating psychological dimensions into traditional economic models.
2. **Broadening economic understanding:** Consideration of well-being, life satisfaction, psychological costs, and benefits, as well as resilience and adaptability, leads to a more comprehensive and realistic picture of economic activities and their impact on individual and social welfare.

(*Continued*)

---

650 See chapter 4.2.

3. **Transcendence and cognitive flexibility:** The economization of the mind system promotes cognitive flexibility and transcendence by regulating and enhancing mental resources and cognitive processes, leading to expanded individual and collective perception and cognition.

Why Capitalism Lives in All of Us—And Why That's Good News

Even a happy life cannot be without a certain amount of darkness, and the word happy would lose its meaning if it were not balanced by sadness.[651]

The rule set of the inner world and the (internal and external) costs of memory form a complex and nontrivial topic that strongly influences the individual mental economy. Memories are not simply passive records but are created through conscious experience. It is precisely this process of building memories that is an economical, value-adding process that must be consciously organized in order to be effective and sustainable for an individual and thus also more robust against mental illness.

Remembering is not an unweighted or unguided process. Rather, it is closely linked to lifestyle and actual conscious experience. Memories arise through specific experiences and their conscious processing, which requires an active and structured approach. This process can be compared to market processes in which not all memories survive; there is a market mechanism of supply and demand within our mind system.[652] Only the most meaningful and relevant memories will persist in the long term. Building memories requires the targeted use of resources. These include time, cognitive attention, and external (monetary) resources.[653] Since these resources are also limited, all memories are subject to multiple, multistage selection processes. It is not possible to retain an unlimited number or any number of different memories. There is, therefore, a need to make decisions based on an internal catalog of criteria that reflects life decisions and priorities that have already been made.

Conscious experiencing should, therefore, already be focused on remembering in its momentary essence to actively shape and consciously structure the process of remembering. This approach makes it possible to build

---

651 Jung (1975), p. 81.
652 Cf. Spitzer (1999), pp. 22–46. and Kahneman (2011), pp. 269ff.
653 Cf. Craik, Fergus/Lockhart (1972), p. 671ff. and Baddeley (1992), p. 557.

valuable and meaningful memories that can be regarded as real goods. Real goods arise from the reality of experience and cannot be replaced by a digital economy of memories.[654]

Parallel to this, hybrid strategies for memories can be presented; they can help to find a balance between the preservation of important memories and the efficient utilization of mental resources. These strategies could include the integration of conscious experiences with creative and reflective processes to optimize the quality and sustainability of stored memories.

Hybrid strategies combine integration processes of conscious experience with creative and reflexive processes to optimize the quality and sustainability of the memories experienced.

- **Integration of conscious experiences:** A central aspect of hybrid strategies is the integration of conscious experiences into memory. This means that memories are not just passively recorded but actively lived through and processed. Conscious experiences can be intensified through mindfulness techniques in which individuals are instructed to be present in the moment and to consciously register their perceptions and feelings. Such techniques not only promote the depth and detail of memories but also strengthen the emotional connection to the experiences, which supports their long-term storage.[655]
- **Creative processes:** Creative processes also play an important role in hybrid memory management strategies. Creative activities such as writing, painting, or making music can serve as tools to process and consolidate memories. Through the creative transformation of memories, they are not only anchored more deeply in but also viewed and reinterpreted from different perspectives.[656] This creative reconstruction makes it possible to make memories more flexible and resistant to decay or falsification. In addition, creative processes promote the linking of memories with positive emotions and a sense of meaning, which supports their long-term preservation.
- **Reflexive processes:** Reflective processes are another component of hybrid strategies. Reflection means that individuals consciously analyze and question their memories and place them in a larger context. Through diary writing, conversations, or therapeutic sessions, people

---

654 Ibid.
655 Cf. Kabat-Zinn (1990), p. 24f. and Shapiro (2006), p. 380f.
656 Cf. Anderson/Levy (2009), p. 189ff.

can systematically think through their experiences and recognize the underlying meanings and patterns. Reflection promotes an understanding of one's own life story and strengthens the coherence of one's self-image. It also makes it possible to process stressful memories and integrate them into a narrative structure that supports psychological well-being.[657]

In combination, these hybrid strategies aim to optimize the quality and fluidity of stored memories. In this context, quality means not only the accuracy and detail of the memories but also their emotional significance and transformative usability in everyday life. The conscious integration, creative transformation, and reflexive analysis of memories not only make them more precise and vivid but also more meaningful and useful. A high quality of memory helps individuals to learn from their experiences, better understand themselves, and target their goals and actions more effectively. Finally, the efficient utilization of mental resources is also the most important advantage of hybrid strategies. By consciously and systematically processing memories, the memory is prevented from becoming cluttered and flooded with irrelevant or stressful memories, and the resources of the mental system are being used ineffectively, or its transaction processes are being disrupted. Creative and reflective processes promote selective and adaptive memory management,[658] in which central memories are strengthened and irrelevant or stressful memories are weakened. This contributes to a better cognitive and emotional balance and prevents an overload of mental resources.

Hybrid strategies for the organization of memory processes thus offer a comprehensive and flexible method for optimizing the quality and sustainability of stored experiences while at the same time making efficient use of mental resources. By combining conscious experiences, creative processes, and reflective practices, individuals can not only preserve their memories but also actively shape them. These strategies contribute to a deeper understanding of the self, better emotional balance, and more effective utilization of one's own cognitive and emotional resources.

> The economically effective handling of memories requires a conscious, strategic approach that considers one's own mental economy and aims to create and preserve meaningful and sustainable memories.

---

657 Cf. White/Epston (1990), pp. 20–26.
658 See LeDoux (1996), pp. 200–225.

A major challenge in the integration of the internal economy is the notion of mental continuity—indeed, continuity in general.[659] The capitalism of the outer world loves and needs continuity—because continuity is the basis of growth in the outer world. And it is predictable, which makes it good for investors and shareholder meetings. What may work in the outer economy (although here, too, the limits of growth and its necessity or meaningfulness are a constant field of lively discourse) is a potentially dangerous fallacy in the inner world.

The idea of the continuity of personality, which is often portrayed as unchanging and constant, is an illusion that can be realized both in self-perception and in the use of one's own memories can lead to misperceptions and misjudgments—which in turn has a negative effect on the transactional processes of the mental system. It is also problematic to equate personality and essence, as the two are by no means the same thing:

- Personality can be understood as the sum of continuous self-perception and self-assessment of memories. It encompasses the way in which an individual interprets and evaluates their experiences, as well as the patterns that develop over time. However, these patterns are by no means static; they are subject to constant change, influenced by new experiences and insights. Personality is, therefore, a self-reflective, highly transitive system of experience and memory organization.
- The essence core, on the other hand, lies on the border region to transcendental self-dissolution and is normally unconscious and not directly accessible. While the personality can be perceived as a visible, changeable shell, the essence core usually remains hidden and forms a deeper, more stable basis of the self, which, however, is also not immutable.[660]

The functionality and structure of the personality concept mean that the objective, observable reality is fragmented into multiple subjective, changeable realities at the moment of its creation. These partial realities are subject to a permanent change in evaluation; the mind evaluates memories depending on the current experience and the resulting realizations and even changes their composition. Individual elements are emphasized or pushed into the background, depending on their significance in the current context.

---

659 This has already been discussed in a similar context in Chapter 2.
660 See also the approach of transpersonal psychology in Wilber (1977), pp. 135–169.

These mental processes take place exclusively on a partially conscious level, and a person's personality is also constantly changing and developing. Just as the body continuously renews and replaces itself, the personality also changes. There is no unchanging part that could be regarded as a constant core.[661] These changes are part of natural development and adaptation to new life circumstances and experiences.

However, there are techniques that can be used to experience and expand the conscious process level. Just as the body is constantly renewing itself, the changeability of the personality can also be understood through conscious reflection and self-observation. Through TN and IR, it becomes possible to reassess memories from the past and reveal and change complex inner structures.[662]

It should be noted at this point that the continuity of personality is often used as a spiritual vehicle, for example, in the concept of the soul. However, neuroscientific and transformational psychological findings show that there is no fixed, unchanging core. The spiritual aspect is rather rooted in the essence of changeability itself.[663]

The role of changeability is central to the self and the psyche. The concept of world consciousness emphasizes the permanent situational dissolution and reconceptualization of personality structures as the starting point of transformational narration and IR. Through these continuous transactional processes of dissolution and remodeling, the self is constantly redefined and develops further, whereby complexes can also be revealed and subjected to change—this is the transcendental function of memory..

The loss of inner continuity has a central effect on the economy of the psyche: its growth is no longer defined by the traditional of the psyche: its growth can no longer be defined by the traditional "more"; it is rather a growth inward, a slice-by-slice transcending of the ego. No recognizable limits to growth are defined here; the changes to the self are initially valuable in themselves—growth is an end for the ego.

---

[661] Cf. Dalai Lama (2002), p. 103ff.

[662] The process of reality fragmentation in the spirit system can be observed. Through conscious, comprehensive observation skills, memories can be be interpreted and developed more consciously. This conscious examination makes it possible to better understand and control the continuous development and change of the personality.

See also Chapters 3 and 4.

[663] See Johnstone, Brick et al. (2016), p. 289ff. and Beauregard/O'Leary (2008).

This reversal of the signs results in five further relevant consequences for the internal economy and its capitalist logic:

1. **The flexibility and adaptability of the mind system gain external economic value and are a realizable resource.**
   - Cognitive flexibility: Recognizing the nonlinear nature of personality promotes cognitive flexibility, as individuals are more willing to adopt new perspectives and challenge existing beliefs. This enables more effective adaptation to changing circumstances and challenges, resulting in assessable benefits.
   - Emotional resilience: The awareness of the changeability of the self strengthens emotional resilience as individuals learn to adapt better to change and cope more flexibly with psychological stress.
2. **The expansion of self-perception catalyzes and intensifies mental transaction processes.**
   - Conscious self-reflection: The elimination of the illusion of a constant personality encourages more conscious self-reflection and the continuous re-valuation of one's own behavior and thinking by breaking down cultural and social inner inhibitions. This contributes to personal development and promotes a deeper understanding of one's own psychological transaction processes.
   - Dynamic identity formation: Recognizing internal dynamics allows for more dynamic identity formation, where individuals are open to new experiences and change and recognize their identity as a growing and developing construct.
3. **All mental resources are subject to more efficient utilization and management.**
   - Conscious resource management: The realization of the changeability of the psyche leads to a more conscious management of mental resources, as their role in the transaction processes underlying this change can be better allocated.
   - Transformation and reevaluation of memories: The ability to reevaluate and transform memories from the past makes it possible to overcome psychological blockages or complexes and develop new perspectives.
4. **The mental spirit system is enabled to make better and more precise decisions.**
   - Integration of non-rational elements: Insight into the dynamic nature of the self leads to a more realistic depiction of individual

decision-making processes, which are based not only on conscious considerations but also on the emotional and cognitive factors of the unconscious. The unconscious process elements are better accepted.
- Psychic holism: A holistic approach that incorporates complex mental dynamics into individual decisions of the mind system can lead to better and more sustainable results.[664]

5. **The value of creativity and psychodynamic innovation is increased.**
   - Creative problem-solving: The dissolution of the idea of a fixed personality promotes creative problem-solving approaches, as this inner realization makes individuals more open to new ideas and unconventional solutions.
   - Innovation potential: The increased willingness to change and adapt can increase innovation potential in both personal and professional contexts, as individuals are more courageous in breaking new ground and taking risks when the concept of the monolithic self falls away.

As a result, the elimination of inner continuity ultimately leads to a more flexible, adaptable, and creative psyche that is better able to cope with life's challenges and changes. This contributes to more efficient utilization of mental resources and improved decision-making, which ultimately increases mental well-being and individual and collective performance.

This inner capitalism is not a reflection of the outer world; rather, the outer world and liberal capitalism are the consequence of inner capitalism. Market-orientated, transaction-based action is part of human existence; it is the basis of our thinking—indeed, it is anchored in the mental system itself.

Like economic capitalism, where (among other things) capital is used efficiently to achieve optimum profit[665], the inner capitalism of the spirit

---

664 Cf. Müller, Ralph-Axel et al. (1991), p. 54ff

665 The minimum principle and the maximum principle are central concepts in economics and especially in the theory of capitalism—and are often misunderstood or misinterpreted. These principles primarily describe different approaches to the efficient use of resources and the maximization of results. Both principles are crucial for understanding economic decision-making processes and their application in different contexts.

The minimization principle aims to achieve a specific goal with the least possible use of resources. The aim is to minimize the resources used while the desired result remains constant. The minimum principle is often considered in the context of resource conservation and cost reduction. It plays an important role in the sustainable economy, where the aim is to minimize the consumption of resources while reducing the environmental impact. By applying the minimum principle, companies and individuals can increase their efficiency and competitiveness.

system strives to utilize the available mental resources in such a way that they support the spirit system as efficiently as possible. as efficiently as possible. This unusual perspective promotes the conscious and strategic utilization of mental resources—and, at the same time, relieves the burden on the relationship to one's own mind system, which is often regarded as the ego but is actually a complex system in which the conscious ego only plays a small part.[666] This fundamental change of perspective also has a whole range of other positive effects on the psychological transaction structure:

- Promoting self-efficacy and autonomy: A central aspect of inner capitalism is the emphasis on self-efficacy and individual autonomy. Individuals are encouraged to recognize, evaluate, and use their own resources to achieve personal goals. This self-determination strengthens the feeling of control over one's own life and increases the motivation to continuously work on oneself and develop further. The idea that you can improve your life circumstances through conscious effort and smart use of resources promotes a positive self-image and increases satisfaction.
- Promoting flexibility and adaptability: Internal capitalism also emphasizes the importance of flexibility and adaptability. In an ever-changing world, the ability to respond and adapt quickly to new situations is crucial. This flexibility enables individuals to deal efficiently with stress and uncertainty and to reallocate their resources to successfully overcome challenges. The continuous adaptation and optimization of one's own behavior and thinking contribute to a resilient and robust psyche.

In contrast to the minimum principle is the maximum principle. This principle aims to achieve the best possible result with given resources. The aim is to maximize output while keeping inputs constant. The maximization principle is closely linked to efficiency and productivity. It emphasizes the optimization of the use of available resources in order to achieve the greatest possible benefit.

Both the minimum principle and the maximum principle are fundamental approaches to the allocation of resources and increasing efficiency in capitalism. While the minimum principle aims to minimize the resources used in order to achieve a defined goal, the maximum principle concentrates on maximizing the yield from the available resources.

Cf. Varian (2014).
666 This aspect has already been discussed in detail in Chapter 3.

- Long-term investment in personal growth: Another positive aspect of inner capitalism is the emphasis on long-term investment in personal growth. Similar to economic investments that aim to maximize future profit, inner capitalism encourages individuals to invest in their own development. This can be done through education, self-reflection, meditation, or other forms of personal development. Such investments promote sustainable growth and long-term satisfaction by laying the foundations for a fulfilling and successful life.
- Balance between short-term and long-term goals: Inner capitalism also helps to find a balance between short-term and long-term goals. While short-term gratifications and achievements are important to maintain motivation and satisfaction, long-term goals are crucial for sustainable development and deeper well-being. The ability to balance between these two types of goals allows individuals to satisfy both immediate needs and pursue long-term visions, contributing to a harmonious and balanced lifestyle.
- Psychological resilience and growth: Finally, inner capitalism contributes to psychological resilience by promoting continuous development and self-improvement. By consciously and strategically utilizing their resources, individuals can not only better overcome current challenges but also continuously expand their skills and competencies. This leads to a sense of personal fulfillment and increases the ability to successfully overcome future obstacles.

The Three Key Messages

1. **The conscious and value-adding organization of memories:** Memories are not passive records but are created through active experience and conscious processing. This process of building memories can be seen as an economic, value-adding process that must be consciously organized in order to be effective and sustainable. As individuals consciously create and select memories, the quality and relevance of these memories are increased. This helps to reduce psychological stress and strengthen resilience to mental illness. The conscious handling of memories is comparable to a market mechanism in which only the most significant and useful memories are retained in the long term.

(*Continued*)

2. **Integration of conscious, creative, and reflective processes for memory management:** hybrid strategies that combine conscious experiences, creative processes, and reflective practices promote the quality and sustainability of memories. These strategies make it possible not only to preserve memories but also to actively shape them and integrate them into daily life. Conscious experiences intensify the emotional connection to experiences through mindfulness techniques, creative processes such as writing or painting anchor memories more deeply in the mind, and reflective practices such as diary writing or therapeutic sessions promote understanding of one's own life story. Such approaches lead to more efficient utilization of mental resources and support a better emotional balance.
3. **Flexible and dynamic identity formation by recognizing the changeability of the self:** The elimination of the illusion of a constant personality promotes cognitive flexibility and emotional resilience. By accepting the changeability of the self, individuals can adapt better to new circumstances and cope more flexibly with psychological stress. This dynamic identity formation makes it possible to continuously integrate new experiences to continuously integrate new experiences and insights into their own self-image. This strengthens the ability for conscious self-reflection and effective management of mental resources, which in turn increases individual adaptability and psychological well-being. The flexibility of the mental system thus becomes a valuable resource that enables both personal and professional challenges to be better mastered.

Six: The Three Key Messages in Brief

1. **Integration of the economy of the psyche into everyday thoughts:** Integrating the economy of the psyche into everyday thoughts and actions leads to a more comprehensive understanding of one's own individual decision-making processes and actions and offers new opportunities for development.

(Continued)

2. **Creating value from memories:** The conscious and value-adding organization of memories makes it possible to reduce psychological stress and strengthen resilience to mental illness. This is achieved through an active, conscious approach to memory, which leads to higher inner quality and relevance.
3. **Conscious memory management:** The integration of conscious, creative, and reflective processes for memory management promotes the quality and sustainability of memories, which leads to more efficient utilization of mental resources and an improved emotional balance. This supports flexible, dynamic identity formation by recognizing the mutability of the self and enables better adaptability to new challenges in life.

EPILOGUE I—WHAT REMAINS OF LIFE

He who binds to himself a joy
Does the winged life destroy;
But he who kisses the joy as it flies
Lives in eternity's sunrise.[667]

Toward the end of this book, I would like to remind you once again to marvel. We must marvel at how our mental system is structured and constructed, what mechanisms it harbors, and what resources it uses.

There are memories.

In the vast landscape of the human mind, a self-designed construct exists that outlasts time: memory. These fleeting fragments of our past carry an immense value that often goes unnoticed, especially in our unreflected everyday lives, but is deeply woven into our being. Memories are fundamental to who we are and who we think we are; they are not just mental images or sounds but also the colors, scents, and feelings that form the mosaic of our individual lives. They are the invisible fabric that holds our identity together and defines the meaning of our existence. In many ways, we are nothing but memories.

In psychology, the role of memories is not only to reconstruct past events but also to act. Our memories are not static in any way; they are dynamic and constantly reshape themselves through the lens of our current experiences and situational emotions. And situational emotions. This phenomenon (much discussed in this book) is referred to as the reconstructive nature of memory[668]

---

667 Blake (2013), p. 144.
668 See Roediger/Marsh (2007), p. 105f.

and shows how memories not only reflect past reality but also influence our current perception and interpretation.

Looking at the meaning of memory as a meta-situational construct of oneself from an existential perspective, one quickly realizes that it plays a fundamental role in the search for the much-maligned meaning of life; here, the meaning of life is often located in the fulfillment of memories. The inherent value of memory is particularly evident in extreme situations in which everything else has been taken away—this is where the value of memory becomes clear and makes the concept of an inner economy better understood.

Memories also serve as a bridge between generations by passing on the heritage and stories of ancestors to descendants. Family memories and cultural stories strengthen the sense of intersubjective belonging and identity. In modern psychology, this transgenerational transmission is seen as a means of resilience, especially in communities that have experienced traumatic events. The collective memory becomes a bulwark that strengthens communities and holds them together in times of need.[669]

The concept of "autobiographical memories" further illuminates the value of life from an introspective perspective.[670] This type of memory allows us to view our lives as a cohesive narrative, which contributes to a coherent self-image. By looking back on significant events and integrating them into our life story, we create a narrative sense that supports our identity and gives us a sense of continuity.

Ultimately, memories are the key to appreciating life in all its fullness. They give us the opportunity to honor the past, find meaning in the present, and look to the future with optimism. Memories are the treasure of our mental system, reminding us that every moment contributes to the valuable (even in an economic sense) mosaic of our lives. They are the objective proof that our existence leaves traces—in ourselves and in the spirit systems of those we encounter. A collective, transpersonal, and transcendental web of identity and linked memory is created—which defines inner and outer value, constitutes it socially, and thus makes it one of the most important mental concepts of the human psyche.

The role of actively, mindfully, and consciously living through mental concepts and insights is also important here. In contrast to knowledge, which can be imparted externally and acquired through teaching, reading, or observation,

---

669 Cf. Halbwachs (1992), p. 72ff.
670 Ibid.

realization is a process that must be developed within the individual mental system. Cognition requires a deep, personal experience and understanding that goes beyond the mere acquisition of information. It implies an inner transformation and integration, which can only be achieved through active confrontation and reflective living through experiences.

There is mindfulness.

In this context, mindfulness is important as a mental resource. Mindfulness understood as a nonjudgmental, present awareness, enables individuals to carefully observe and reflect on their inner processes, thoughts, and emotions attentively and reflect on them.[671] By mindfully experiencing mental concepts, individuals can delve deeper into their own psyche and discover unconscious aspects of their mental system. This process not only promotes awareness of one's own inner dynamics but also enables the integration of insights on a deep, personal level.

There would be realisation.

The mental economy is its concept of a mental system working according to economic principles, within which memories, feelings, and other mental constructs also (or especially) have a real, external value. The self must be optimized.[672] In this model, mental processes are seen as transactions in which memories, emotions, and thoughts act as "valuable" resources that influence the individual's psychological well-being and functional efficiency.

This economic point of view implies that the mental system endeavors to achieve a state of equilibrium in which the various mental resources are optimally utilized and integrated. Memories, in particular (as specific images of mental resources), play an essential role in this system—as demonstrated broadly and comprehensively in this book. They not only provide a basis for the self-identity of the mental system but also serve as situational reference points for evaluating current experiences and planning future actions. The concept of "mental capital" becomes relevant here, as memories (initially regardless of their actual form; the individual tends to be far too quick to categorize memories into a grid of "good" or "bad") are seen as mental assets that fuel the entire emotional ecosystem. Specific negative memories, on the other hand, can also be seen in this context as mental debts that cause stress and inner conflict.

Emotions and other mental constructs, such as beliefs and thought patterns, are also considered resources within this economic model. Emotions act as

---

671 See Bishop et al. (2004), pp. 236–241.
672 Cf. Kahneman (2011), p. 187ff.

indicators of the psychological "market situation" and influence decision-making processes as well as general mood and motivation.[673] The ability to regulate emotions can, therefore, be understood as a form of emotional intelligence that contributes to the maximization of psychological well-being. As explained above, economic cognitive therapy, therefore, focuses on promoting the regulation and integration of emotions in order to enable or support a stable and functional mental system.

The same applies to the integration of unconscious mental processes or process parts. This also contributes to an efficient mental economy by increasing the coherence of the mental system. By making repressed "shadows" conscious and integrating them, the mental mind system is optimized as it can activate unused resources and, at the same time, reduce existing inner conflicts, which in turn increases an individual's adaptive capacity in dealing with the external world.

The mental economy presented in this book thus offers a broad framework for individually understanding and optimizing the interplay of memories, emotions, and other mental constructs systematically and optimizing them. By applying economic principles to the mental system, a truly holistic view of the human psyche can be developed, considering both individual resources and their interactions in order to achieve a harmonious and efficient inner balance.

And this perspective also provides relief. For one thing, psychological processes—even if they are negative or have a negative impact on the overall system—are no longer seen as an illness to be treated (which they often are not)[674] but as a natural

---

673 Ibid.

674 From a long-term and distanced perspective on psychotherapy, it can be seen that an increasing number of people are receiving more and more psychological diagnoses. At the same time, the number of psychotherapists and psychological counsellors is increasing, and we can even speak of an ongoing "psychologisation" of society as a whole.

Two different views can be identified in psychotherapy. The first view is characterised by a rationalistic and cognitive approach that is scientifically based. This approach emphasises the individual's personal responsibility in a systemic context. Strict criteria are applied when making a diagnosis, often focusing on the principle of minimal intervention, expediency, efficiency and cost minimization. Hypotheses and diagnoses are falsified; the approach is characterised by self-criticism.

The second view focuses on a helping and supportive attitude, emphasizes the victim status of the affected individuals and accepts their perceptions of mental health problems as truth. Relationships are emphasised and unproven hypotheses are accepted as explanations.

part of a complex—never contradiction-free—system that is largely not subject to conscious control, or even to consciousness itself.

Despite the supposedly technocratic, cool view of the human psyche and its organizational and working principles, economic cognitive therapy and the theoretical models on which it is based are primarily concerned with the value of life itself.

One must not forget that the overriding goal of the inner economy is economic individuation, which not only enables you to become what you already are but also increases the efficiency of mental transaction processes.[675] Economic cognitive therapy views the mental system as a dynamic network which different parts and processes are in constant interaction. These interactions are not only functional but also significant as an absolute phenomenon, as they influence the subjective experience and perception of one's own life. By integrating repressed aspects and placing them in a positive-pragmatic overall context, this form of therapy promotes a more holistic sense of self-worth and—especially in the increasingly disintegrating postmodern world—an authentic way of life.

Furthermore, economic insight therapy makes a central contribution to self-knowledge by encouraging individuals to reflect on and understand their inner processes and dynamics. Dynamic-economic insight therapy shows that the technocratic and analytical view of the human psyche is in no way at odds with a deep appreciation of consciousness and the uniqueness of psychic assets. On the contrary, it offers a structured and systematic approach to unfolding the full potential of the human spirit system and thus experiencing life in all its fullness. Integrating the shadow and harmonizing the inner parts through the basic human concept of economic value[676] not only promotes mental health but also enables a deeper understanding and greater appreciation of one's own life.

Therapies are continued even if no changes in behavior are apparent; contradictions are ignored, and everyday phenomena that would previously have been considered conversations in the field of theology or philosophy and art are now viewed therapeutically.

In recent years, there has been a general social and professional trend towards the second view. The economic view of the spiritual system offers an alternative in terms of content alone and tends to feel more connected to the first view. The treatment of mental illness can quickly become the illness itself.

See also Helbig/Jürgen (2007), pp. 109–113.

675 Cf. Jung (1994), p. 77ff.
676 Cf. Kahneman/Tversky (2000), p. 84ff.

The very statement "the value of life" already contains the basis of the economic system of thought—individual life and experience have an intrinsic value in themselves that must be discovered, recognized, and preserved.

What remains of life—is value. Value is an absolute and, at the same time, abstract quantity within ourselves. This value lies far less in the external world, with its physical or digital goods or intersubjective concepts, but in our mental resources, such as memories and knowledge.

This inner paradigm shift is crucial for successfully dealing with your own spirit system and your own psyche. On a small scale, this can amount to a revolution.

The Three Key Messages in Brief

1. **Memories are the basis of the mental system and life values:** Memories are not just fleeting mental images but the invisible fabric that holds our identity together and defines the meaning of our existence. They influence present self-understanding and future action through their reconstructive nature by dynamically molding themselves with current experiences and shaping our perceptions.
2. **Transformative and transcendental meaning:** Memories serve as a bridge between the psyche and the external world and are the basis of all mental transactions and transformation processes. They make it possible to view life as a coherent narrative, which leads to a coherent self-image and a sense of continuity and purpose.
3. **Economic insight therapy and inner value:** Economic insight therapy emphasizes the value of life through the integration of repressed aspects of the mind system, leading to a harmonious inner balance. This method views the mental spirit system as a dynamic network in which resources such as memories, emotions, and thoughts are optimally utilized to promote mental health and holistic self-esteem. The therapy also emphasizes mindfulness processes and active living through mental processes to promote deeper self-knowledge and an authentic way of living. Integrating repressed aspects supports the development of a coherent self-image and strengthens the subjective experience and appreciation of life itself.

EPILOGUE II—WHAT GOES BEYOND THAT

The highest knowledge does away with knowledge. The highest love forgets to love. The highest virtue is not virtue.[677]

Rien n'est si insupportable à l'homme que d'être dans un plein repos, sans passions, sans affaire, sans divertissement, sans application. He then feels his néant, his abandonment, his insufficiency, his dependence, his impuissance, his vide. Incontinent, il sortira du fond de son âme l'ennui, la noirceur, la tristesse, le chagrin, le dépit, le désespoir.[678]

In the processual investigation of the human psyche and its dynamics, we come across concepts that fundamentally expand our understanding of the self and its development. And its development—the two quotes above span the field between whose extremes this realization oscillates. Oscillates between. Their concepts include acceptance, transformation, and transcendence—all concepts and terms from the supposedly spiritual realm. These terms are central not only to psychology but also to philosophy and economics as they aptly and comprehensively describe the process of inner growth and self-realization. Together, they enable us to go beyond mere existence and gain a deeper, holistic perspective on life itself.

---

677 Lü Bu We (1928), p. 296.
678 "Nothing is so unbearable for man as to be in complete rest, without passions, without business, without entertainment, without diligence. Then he feels his nothingness, his abandonment, his inadequacy, his dependence, his impotence, his emptiness. Inexorably he will bring forth from the depths of his soul boredom, darkness, sadness, sorrow, vexation, despair."
Pascal (1670), 136/139, "Divertissement," o.Sz.

At first glance, economic principles and spiritual or even transcendental aspects of individual life appear to be different areas. While economics deals with material resources, production processes, and the exchange of goods and services, spirituality is more concerned with questions about the meaning of life, personal development, and the pursuit of inner peace and fulfillment.

Acceptance is the first step in this process. It means accepting reality as it is without resistance or denial. In psychotherapy, acceptance is often described as a form of radical acceptance that allows individuals to fully recognize and accept their current experiences without judging or changing them. This attitude makes it easier to come to terms with difficult emotions, traumatic memories, and unwanted aspects of the self. Acceptance creates space for compassion and self-love, which forms the basis for profound change.

Building on the acceptance follows the *transformation*. This process goes beyond mere acceptance and involves an active change and reorganization of the self. Transformation is a dynamic process in which the individual overcomes their old patterns, beliefs, and behaviors and develops new ways of being. In practice, this often means that individuals are encouraged to face their fears and insecurities, discover their hidden potential, and move in a new direction. Transformation is a sign of growth and development that leads to a more authentic and fulfilling life. *Acceptance* is closely related to acceptance and a catalyst for transformation but goes in a slightly different direction, implying an active willingness to receive and integrate what is. Acceptance means not just passively accepting reality but actively welcoming it and integrating it into one's life. This involves recognizing and integrating all aspects of the self, both positive and negative. Ultimately, acceptance creates an inner holism and processual balance that enables the individual to live in congruence with what is.

Transcendence finally goes one step further. While transformation is a profound change of the self, transcendence means going beyond the individual self in its current being. In transpersonal psychology, transcendence is described as the state in which the individual transcends the ego and experiences a connection to something greater, often described as the divine or the universal.

At the end of this book, it is important for me to emphasize that this very transcendence is part of the fundamental economic fabric in which the human spirit operates—transcendence is not a spiritual concept but a deeply economic one. It is a natural state in which the individual recognizes that they are part of a greater whole and that their existence has a deeper meaning and shared coherence. In this respect, immersion in an economic structure within the psyche is a deeply native process that can explain a whole range of mental phenomena far better than other approaches and provides concrete and practicable implications on an individual psychological basis that can be used to solve problems, complexes, and inner conflicts. Transcendental aspects of economic behavior and human economic activity refer to those dimensions that go beyond purely material and monetary interests and have deeper meanings and implications in human societies. These reciprocal aspects include philosophical, ethical, social, and even spiritual elements that influence the understanding and practice of the external economy.

From a philosophical perspective, the design of the external economic system is not only about the efficient allocation of resources or achieving prosperity through growth but also about the question of the purpose of economic activities and their impact on individual and social well-being. Moral and ethical considerations play a central role here, as economic decisions are often linked to questions of justice, sustainability, and social responsibility.

First and foremost, the economy is an intersubjective social construct that influences coexistence and interactions within a society. It is about how economic decisions and institutions shape and structure the social fabric by distributing resources, reinforcing or weakening social hierarchies, and enabling or restricting access to opportunities and goods. The question of a "good" economy is, therefore, also always a moral and spiritual question linked to the search for meaning and the pursuit of personal fulfillment. This includes the question of how economic practices and institutions can contribute to the realization of individual and collective values that go beyond purely material goals.

Taken together, these concepts form a comprehensive framework for understanding human growth and self-realization within an economic framework that follows clear rules. Acceptance is the starting point that makes it possible to see reality as it is. Transformation is the next step that brings active change and a new self-awareness. Transcendence expands the awareness beyond the individual self and connects the individual with the greater whole. Acceptance finally integrates all aspects into a universal economic holism.

This process of going beyond oneself is, in many ways, the ultimate goal of individual human development. And also that of the economy. It enables us to realize our full potential, lead a fulfilled and authentic life, and experience a comprehensive connection to our spirit system to other entities, as well as to the outer world. Through acceptance, transformation, and transcendence in our lives, we create the foundation for a life that transcends mere existence and reveals the true value and meaning of our being.

The time of the now is characterized by an increasing alienation of the individual from the economic principles of their environment. We increasingly experience the economy as an unleashed, inhuman juggernaut that we can no longer influence and that does not care about individual dimensions.

In psychology, the process of alienation refers to a phenomenon in which individuals become increasingly distant from their own memories and experiences. This alienation can be caused by various factors, including traumatic events, chronic stress, or mental health problems. A central feature of alienation is the feeling of dissociation, in which one's own memories are perceived as alien or disconnected.[679] The situation is no different with the economic principles within, where chaotic conditions prevail; society and the individual strive apart and yet are forced ever closer together. Economic cognitive therapy offers a way out of the "reverse entropy of the soul."

This term can be applied metaphorically to the psychological dynamic in which people achieve a state of greater inner order and coherence through conscious effort. While physical entropy describes the tendency toward disorder in closed systems, the reverse entropy of the soul can be understood as a process of reorganization and integration in which psychological resources are used to create an inner holism.[680]

This also reflects human experience, in which the pursuit of knowledge and truth often leads to a confrontation with the limits of understanding. So, the more we learn about our spirit system, the more we recognize the vast, fraying spaces of what is still unknown within us. This dichotomy leads to a "possibilities of emptiness and the emptiness of possibilities," a paradox between Buddhism and materialism (or the overarching Western rationalism, especially in its strictly scientific form) that is deeply rooted in existential and psychological reflection.[681] The possibilities of emptiness refer to the potential that lies in the state of emptiness or nothingness. In many spiritual traditions and psychological theories, emptiness is not seen as complete nothingness but as a space of infinite possibilities—nothingness and everything are not opposites but coincide. The emptiness within us offers a state of potentiality from which completely new ideas, concepts, and transformations can emerge.[682]

---

679 See Van der Kolk (2014), p. 179ff.
680 See Schore (2012), pp. 122–146.
681 It is also interesting to consider Hinduism here, especially in its dualistic form as in the Vedanta system of philosophy. Although Hinduism and Buddhism share many similarities and are historically closely linked, they differ in key philosophical and metaphysical points. Hinduism, for example, accepts the concept of an eternal soul (Atman), while Buddhism advocates the doctrine of the non-self (Anatta). (Anatta), which denies the existence of an unchanging, eternal soul.
682 Cf. Chalmers (1996), p. 285ff.

On the other hand, the emptiness of possibilities describes the feeling of being overwhelmed and paralyzed in the face of unlimited options. In a world in which almost every possibility seems conceivable, individuals can experience a feeling of disorientation and inability to make decisions, similar to today's external, consumerist economy. This emptiness arises from an inability to find clear direction or meaning, which can lead to a state of existential emptiness.

Overall, these concepts are comprehensively interwoven and reflect the complex nature of human existence and reality, in which the search for meaning and realization both opens up new horizons and reveals the limits of conscious knowledge and experience. This dimension of economic cognition raises many questions that have not yet been comprehensively addressed.

I would like to explore the *economy of memory* with a brief look at one last, often decisive mental resource: *Gratitude*.

Gratitude is a complex and multilayered phenomenon that is inherently embedded in human experience and social interactions. It encompasses not only the experience of joy but also the shared joy that arises in interpersonal relationships. Joy and gratitude are inextricably linked and mutually dependent. The overflowing feeling of gratitude is consciously perceived and can be both evoked and communicated. A high threshold is required to feel and express genuine gratitude.

The formulation of gratitude plays a crucial role in the inner economy—just as growth may be the goal of its external counterpart, gratitude is its goal. Gratitude is inner growth. It enables us to accept and embrace meaningful relationships and the externality of achievements. Gratitude requires enduring and accepting one's own dependence on others and the influence of countless external factors on one's own life. This process is very different from envy, which, according to Immanuel Kant, is destructive and leads to isolation.[683] Envy often arises from the desire to surpass others and the frustration of not being able to do so. In contrast, gratitude encourages the active perception of the enrichment that people and situations bring to one's own life and thus contributes to the "expansion of the soul."[684] It is impossible to demand genuine gratitude; it only arises voluntarily and authentically.

Erich Fromm describes the transition from having to being through gratitude. This transition emphasizes the importance of emotional experiences and experiences over material possessions. Gratitude transforms the need for

---

683 Cf. Kant (1977), pp. 199–203.
684 Ibid.

possessions into an appreciation of being, allowing the individual to live a deeper, more fulfilling life.[685] Through gratitude, one experiences a shift from an emphasis on having, which is often associated with material possessions and external success, to being, which emphasizes inner well-being and the quality of relationships.

It can, therefore, be argued that gratitude is not just an emotion but a teleological resource of the human mental system and social interactions; it has an economic dimension. By feeling and expressing gratitude, one transforms one's perception and experience of life, away from having and toward being. And this is exactly what the inner economy is about in many core areas. The economy is transcendent.

---

685 Cf. Fromm (1991), pp. 109–112.

GLOSSARY

Agility: Mental agility is the ability to respond flexibly and adaptably to different situations and challenges. It enables individuals to deal effectively with complex and unexpected situations by dynamically adapting their thinking strategies, perspectives, and problem-solving approaches. This ability goes beyond mere intelligence and includes aspects such as creativity, adaptability, and openness to new experiences and ideas. A key characteristic of mental agility is the ability to move away from entrenched thought patterns and develop alternative perspectives. This involves actively questioning assumptions and recognizing connections between seemingly unrelated concepts. For example, someone with high mental agility can adopt different viewpoints in a conversation and look at complex problems from different perspectives, leading to more innovative and comprehensive solutions. Mental agility plays a crucial role in today's rapidly changing world, where technological advances and societal changes are constantly bringing new challenges and opportunities. In professional contexts, it enables professionals to adapt quickly to new working conditions and technologies, develop creative solutions, and work efficiently as part of a team. In personal lives, it encourages a positive and proactive approach to change and challenges, leading to greater life satisfaction and resilience. The development of mental suppleness can be supported through targeted exercises and practices. The practice of mindfulness and meditation can also promote mental flexibility by helping to maintain a clear and open mind that is less susceptible to stress and fixed mindsets. Psychological research is increasingly recognizing the importance of mental agility as a key skill for well-being and success in the twenty-first century. Studies show that people with high mental flexibility are better able to deal with uncertainty and ambiguity, making them more resilient to the challenges of modern life.

Archetypes: Archetypes are deeply rooted psychological patterns that are universally present in the collective unconscious and manifest themselves in symbolic form. They act as basic building blocks for the construction of myths, religious beliefs, artistic expressions, and individual dreams. Examples of archetypes are the hero, the goddess, the shadow, and many others that recur in different cultures and ages.

Awareness: Awareness is defined in scientific psychology as a state of consciousness characterized by a comprehensive, non-judgmental perception of present experiences and sensory impressions. It is a type of awareness that is characterized by openness and acceptance toward momentary experiences and inner states without immediately analyzing or evaluating them. In the context of cognitive science, awareness is often described in contrast to focused attention. While focused attention analyses certain aspects of experience in isolation and in detail, awareness is more holistic and integrative. It allows the individual to perceive many different sensory impressions simultaneously and see them in a larger context without the need for in-depth cognitive processing of each individual impression. Neurobiologically, awareness is associated with specific brain activities that involve both cortical and subcortical areas. These activities support the simultaneous processing of information from different sensory modalities and help to create a coherent picture of the current environment. Research has shown that practices such as mindfulness meditation can promote awareness and help strengthen the neural networks associated with this type of perception. Awareness also has an important role in emotional regulation. By noticing their current feelings and thoughts without immediate judgment, individuals can achieve greater emotional balance and reduce reactive behavior. This ability to remain present and accepting is central to many therapeutic approaches based on mindfulness, such as mindfulness-based cognitive therapy (MBCT) and dialectical behavioral therapy (DBT).

Collective unconscious: The concept of the collective unconscious, introduced by Carl Gustav Jung, is a fundamental pillar of depth psychology and offers an insight into the collective aspects of the human psyche. In contrast to the individual unconscious, which contains the personal experiences, traumas, and inner conflicts of an individual, the collective unconscious refers to a common foundation of psychic functions that exist across cultural and temporal boundaries. The collective unconscious thus forms a kind of psychological heritage of humanity that serves as a basis for the development of individual ego structures. It is crucial to understand the universal patterns and symbols that emerge in various cultural expressions, such as dreams, myths, fairy tales, and legends. These cultural manifestations of the collective unconscious share many common elements that can be traced back to archetypal structures. The discovery and exploration of the collective unconscious provides a deeper insight into the human psyche and its cultural manifestations. It shows how universal psychic structures shape and influence human experience. In psychotherapy, working with the collective unconscious can help to understand and resolve deep-seated psychological conflicts by enabling the individual to engage with the universal patterns and symbols of their psyche.

Complex: A (psychological) complex is a concept from depth psychology that describes a complex and structured organization of thoughts, emotions, ideas, and memories grouped around a central theme or experience. Grouped around a central theme or experience. These complexes can contain both conscious and unconscious elements and often have a strong emotional charge. They influence a person's behavior, perception behavior, perception, and reactions to certain situations by shaping their thinking and feeling in relation to the central theme. Psychic complexes can arise from traumatic events, recurring life patterns, cultural influences, or unconscious conflicts and play an important role in psychoanalytic therapy as well as in self-reflection and personal development.

Consolidation: The process by which memories are stabilized and stored in the memory.

Context-dependent memory: The idea that the memory of information is more accurate if the context during encoding matches the context during retrieval.

Core complex and archetype: The human psyche is a complex web of feelings, thoughts, perceptions, and memories that are interwoven in a multilayered constellation. These constellations, also known as complexes, are attracted by a core complex that is formed around specific contexts. These contexts can be characterized by individual experiences and archetypal structures of the collective unconscious. The core complex, which is anchored in the depths of the psyche, draws on a reservoir of archetypes that are regarded as common structural elements of the human mind. These archetypes are universal patterns and symbols deeply rooted in human culture and history. They act as the basic building blocks for constructing experiences and building meaning. It is important to note that these complexes can be both conscious and unconscious. While some can be consciously perceived, others exist in the deep layers of the unconscious. Nevertheless, the complexes anchored in the unconscious can also affect the conscious mind by appearing as "affects." These effects can influence conscious intentions and thus influence the behavior and perception The occupation of these complexes can be both positive and negative. Positive complexes can lead to a sense of well-being, fulfillment, and meaning, while negatively charged complexes can lead to neurotic symptoms and psychological disorders. These negative complexes can result from traumatic experiences, unresolved conflicts, or deep-rooted fears and affect the emotional balance of the individual. In psychoanalysis and other psychological approaches, the concepts of complexes and core complexes play an important role in the study and treatment of psychological disorders and personal growth. By understanding and working with these complexes, a profound transformation of individual consciousness and well-being can be achieved.

Culture: Culture is a multilayered and multifaceted concept that encompasses different areas of human life and exerts a significant influence on individual and collective behavior, norms, values, beliefs, traditions, art, language, religion, and institutions. In a broad sense, culture can be seen as the entire social heritage of a group or society, which develops over generations and is passed on both actively and passively. This transmission and passing on of cultural knowledge practices and artifacts enables the members of a community to orientate themselves, form social bonds, construct identity, and interpret their world. Construct identity and interpret their world. Culture not only shapes people's behavior and interactions but also influences their perception of time, space, nature, and society. Culture manifests itself in different levels and forms of expression, including tangible artifacts such as works of art, architecture, and tools, as well as intangible elements such as language, music, rituals, and customs. These different aspects of culture are interwoven and form a complex fabric that shapes the identity of a community or society and strengthens its cohesion. It is important to note that culture is inherently dynamic and subject to constant change, influenced by social, economic, political, and technological changes and developments. Through interactions between different cultures, new cultural phenomena can develop, while at the same time, traditional practices and values can be preserved or transformed.

Dullness: Dullness is a psychological condition characterized by a feeling of heaviness, sluggishness, and lack of clarity in thinking and feeling. In scientific terms, dullness describes an impairment of cognitive and emotional functioning that is often accompanied by reduced alertness and responsiveness. People suffering from dullness often report a feeling of mental fogginess, difficulty concentrating, and a general slowing down of the thought process. This condition can be caused by various factors, including lack of sleep, stress, depression, anxiety, or certain medical conditions such as hypothyroidism or chronic fatigue syndrome. In neuroscience, dullness is thought to be associated with reduced activity in certain brain regions, such as the prefrontal cortex, which is responsible for complex cognitive tasks and decision-making. Dysregulation of neurotransmitters such as serotonin and dopamine may also play a role.

Ephemeral moments: "Ephemeral moments" refers to fleeting or short-lived moments or events that only exist or are perceptible for a short period of time. These moments can be both positive and negative and can take various forms, such as moments of happiness, fleeting thoughts, unexpected encounters, or spontaneous emotions. The term "ephemeral moments" emphasizes the transience and uniqueness of these experiences that can often leave a lasting impression, even if they are only short-lived.

Episodic memory: Episodic memory refers to the memory of personal events and of personal events and experiences in a specific time and environment.

Explicit memory (declarative memory): This refers to the conscious recollection of facts and events that can be verbalized.

Immersion: Immersion in a psychological context describes the immersion of an individual in an activity or environment, whereby they are completely absorbed in the experience, and the outside world and sense of time largely fade out. This state is characterized by intense concentration, a strong sense of personal involvement, and often a high degree of emotional fulfillment. Immersion is often experienced in connection with activities such as reading and playing, as well as creative activities such as painting and writing. In this state, the individual merges with the experience, creating a sense of connection and immediate participation. The immersive state is often the result of an optimal interplay between challenge and ability, leading to a flow experience in which the person is completely absorbed in the moment. From a psychological perspective, immersion can provide a form of escape from reality while also serving as a valuable tool to promote learning, creativity, and personal growth.

Implicit memory (non-declarative memory): Implicit memory refers to the non-conscious remembering of skills and procedures, such as riding a bike or playing a musical instrument.

Individuation: In Carl Gustav Jung's theory, individuation is a lifelong process aimed at realizing a person's individual potential and achieving comprehensive mental health. This process involves consciously engaging with various aspects of the self, including conscious and unconscious content, personal and collective experiences, and archetypal patterns. And archetypal patterns. A central concept in Jung's theory of individuation is that of the self, which is seen as the central organizing principle of the psyche. The self represents the complete, harmonious integration of all psychic forces and is the goal of individuation. Through the process of individuation, a person strives to realize their self by unfolding their individual potentials and achieving a deep inner unity. Another important aspect of individuation is the confrontation with the shadow. The shadow encompasses those aspects of the self that are unconscious, repressed, or unwanted. As part of individuation, it is important to confront the shadow to integrate these hidden aspects and achieve a wholeness of self. This process can be painful and challenging as it involves confronting unpleasant or negative aspects of the personality. In addition, individuation also involves confronting archetypal content, which are universal, symbolic patterns that operate in the depths of the unconscious. These archetypal patterns, such as the hero or the goddess, can serve as role models that guide and support the individual development process.

Longing: Longing is understood as a complex emotional phenomenon characterized by an intense, often bittersweet mixture of pleasure and pain. It refers to a deep longing or nostalgic yearning for an idealized state, person, place, or time that either existed in the past, is unattainable in the present, or is hoped for in the future. Longing often involves a spectrum of feelings, including bliss, hope, sadness, and loss. These emotions are closely interwoven and create an intense inner experience; it is often both retrospective and prospective. A central aspect of longing is the feeling of lack or incompleteness. The object of longing often seems unattainable or difficult to reach, which intensifies the intensity of the desire. The objects of longing are often idealized and transcend reality, which can lead to a distortion of perception in which what is desired is perceived as more perfect than it actually was or could be. Desire also has cognitive and motivational components. Cognitively, it involves thinking about and remembering what is desired. Motivational refers to the impulses for action and striving that are triggered by the longing, whether in the form of endeavors to achieve the desired or through the search for similar experiences or states.

Long-term memory: Long-term memory is responsible for the long-term storage of information. It has a large capacity and can retain information over long periods of time.

Mental health problems: Mental health problems refer to a variety of conditions that can affect a person's thinking, feelings, behavior, or social interactions. These problems can be of a temporary nature or persist long-term and can vary in severity. Mental health problems can take various forms, including anxiety disorders, depression, eating disorders, addictions, personality disorders, PTSD, and many others. They can be caused by a variety of factors, including genetic predisposition, biochemical imbalances in the brain, traumatic events, stressful life circumstances, unhealthy lifestyle habits, or a combination of factors. Symptoms of mental health problems can vary from person to person but can include mood changes, excessive anxiety or worry, sleep disturbances, changes in eating patterns, withdrawal from social activities, problems coping with everyday tasks, irritating behavior, physical complaints with no clear cause, and other behavioral changes. It is important to emphasize that mental health problems are not a weakness and can affect anyone, regardless of age, gender, ethnicity, or social status. However, they can be treated with appropriate support, be it through psychotherapy, medication, self-help strategies, or a combination of different approaches. Early recognition and appropriate intervention are crucial to alleviate suffering and promote a better quality of life.

Mood-dependent memory: The tendency to remember information better when the emotional mood during encoding matches the mood during recall.

Narratology: Narratology is a multidisciplinary field that deals with the structure, function, and interpretation of narratives. It examines the way stories are constructed, how they are presented, and how they work on an individual and social level. Essentially, narratology involves analyzing narrative techniques, examining narrative structures, and interpreting narrative texts in different contexts. It examines how narratives serve to shape identities, convey values, establish social norms, transmit knowledge, and share experiences.

Perception: In a psychological-scientific context, perception is a complex process in which sensory information from the environment is received, organized, and interpreted by our sensory organs. This process enables us to understand and react to the world around us. Perception is not just the passive reception of stimuli but an active and constructive process in which our brain filters sensory data, structures it, and compares it with previous experiences, memories, and knowledge. This leads us to find meaning and significance in what we see, hear, smell, taste, and feel. Different cognitive processes, such as attention, learning, and memory, play a central role in perception and influence how we process and interpret information. Perception is, therefore, a fundamental component of human experience and behavior that enables us to orientate ourselves in our environment and act appropriately.

Psychosynthesis: Psychosynthesis (developed by Roberto Assagioli in the early twentieth century) is a school of psychology that emphasizes the integration of different aspects of the human being in order to promote a comprehensive understanding and holistic development of the individual. Central to psychosynthesis is the idea that the human psyche is made up of different parts that need to be integrated and harmonized in order to lead a fulfilling life.

Self: The self is an empirical concept that is of fundamental importance in both psychology and psychotherapy. It functions not only as a theoretical concept but also as a guiding principle for therapeutic practice. In its essence, the self represents the unity and wholeness of all psychological phenomena in a person, which unite to form the overall personality. This overall personality contains both conscious and unconscious parts of the individual. While conscious elements can be experienced directly, the self also includes the inexperienced and the not yet experienced, which are in the unconscious. This holistic perspective on the self emphasizes the complexity of the human psyche and its continuous development throughout life. The self serves as the starting point and goal of a lifelong individuation process that aims to bring the various aspects of the unconscious closer to the conscious. This process of convergence is often understood as a process of adaptation in which the individual integrates their personal experiences, beliefs, and values to form a coherent identity. A central component of this individual development process is the ego-self axis. This axis represents the connection between the conscious ego and the broader self. Through the exploration and integration of unconscious content, the individual can establish a deeper connection to the self and achieve a higher level of self-realization and psychological well-being. In psychotherapeutic practice, the concept of self plays a crucial role as it serves as a guide for the process of self-reflection, self-acceptance, and personal transformation. Therapeutic approaches focus on strengthening self-aim to promote individual growth and development by helping the individual to establish a deeper connection to their true self and achieve authentic living.

Semantic memory: Semantic memory refers to the knowledge of facts about facts, concepts, and linguistic information that is not tied to a specific time or place.

Sensory memory: Sensory memory refers to the short-term storage of sensory information, such as sight (iconic memory) and hearing (echoic memory).

Short-term memory (working memory): Short-term memory is responsible for the short-term storage and processing of information. It has a limited capacity and duration.

Wisdom: Wisdom is a complex construct that is viewed from different perspectives in the scientific literature. Psychologically, wisdom can be defined as the ability to possess deep knowledge and insight into human life and behavior, combined with the ability to apply this knowledge in a constructive and adaptive way. Wisdom encompasses cognitive, reflective, and affective dimensions and manifests itself in the ability to solve complex problems, make ethical decisions, and lead a balanced life. Cognitively, wisdom refers to a comprehensive knowledge of the fundamental paradoxes and uncertainties of life. It involves a deep understanding of the conditions and dynamics of human existence and the ability to apply this knowledge in different life situations. People who are considered wise can consider different perspectives and keep the bigger picture in mind. Reflective wisdom includes the ability to self-reflect and self-regulate. Wise people can view themselves and their experiences from a detached perspective, which allows them to avoid biased judgments and critically question their own beliefs and values. This ability to reflect makes it possible to learn from experience and develop personal maturity. Affective dimensions of wisdom relate to empathy, compassion, and emotional regulation. Wise individuals demonstrate a high level of emotional intelligence that enables them to understand and respond empathetically to the feelings of others. They can regulate their own emotions and act in accordance with ethical and moral principles. Wisdom is, therefore, an integrative quality that enables individuals to apply knowledge for the good of others and for their own good.

FURTHER READING

I would like to precede the actual bibliography with another list—namely that of books that I consider to be particularly helpful and productive, works that have made a particular contribution to my own work and research—in short, literature that is particularly valuable for the development of the economy of the psyche.

Please note that this selection is purely subjective—albeit subjectively justified.

Chalmers, David J. (1996): The Conscious Mind: In *Search of a Fundamental Theory*, Oxford: Oxford University Press.

The book is considered a milestone in the philosophy of mind and consciousness research and represents a detailed investigation and a sound theoretical basis for the understanding of consciousness. Chalmers' work has had a significant impact on modern consciousness research. It has revitalized the debate about the nature of consciousness and led to much further research.

Fromm, Erich (1991): *To Have or to Be. Die Seelische Grundlage für eine neue Gesellschaft*, 20th edition, Munich: Deutscher Taschenbuch Verlag.

To have or to be is an inspiring and provocative book that encourages us to question our own values and lifestyles. It calls for a radical reorientation of our society and, at the same time, offers a hopeful perspective for a more fulfilling and humane future. The book is a timeless work that offers profound insights into the human condition and encourages a fundamental change in thinking and behavior.

Gunturu, Vanamali (2020): *Yoga - History, Philosophy, Practice*, Munich: C.H. Beck.

The book is an excellent introduction to the world of yoga. It offers a balanced mix of theoretical knowledge and practical guidance, is both informative and inspiring, and is characterized by a careful and detailed treatment of the various historical and philosophical aspects of yoga.

> Jung, Carl G. (2022): *Archetypes - Urbilder und Wirkkräfte des kollektiven Unbewussten*, 6th edition, Ostfildern: Patmos.
> Jung, Carl G. (2022): *The Relationship between the Ego and the Unconscious*, 5th edition, Ostfildern: Patmos.

These two books provide a sound introduction to the central aspects of Jung's work. In my opinion, the depth of Jung's psychological branch is vital, and it offers numerous concepts in modern psychology that have not yet been fully reflected upon.

> Kahneman, Daniel (2011): *Thinking, Fast and Slow*, New York: Farrar, Straus and Giroux.

The book is a groundbreaking work that explores the duality of our thinking; Kahneman offers profound insights into the workings of the human mind. It is a must-read for anyone who wants to understand why we think and act the way we do.

> Kast, Verena (1995): *Imagination as a Space of Freedom. Dialogue between the Ego and the Unconscious*, Munich: Deutscher Taschenbuch Verlag.

This book illuminates the transformative power of imagination in the psychological process. It offers valuable perspectives on the use of inner imagery for personal development. Kast's clear language and well-founded examples make it an inspiring work on the possibilities of inner freedom.

> Lü Bu We (1928): *Spring and Autumn of Lü Bu We (Lüshi Chunqiu)*, translated by Richard Wilhelm, Jena: Eugen Diederichs.

This book (for me personally, one of the most interesting new discoveries in writing this book) brings the wisdom and philosophical insights of one of the most influential ministers of the Qin dynasty closer. The work combines historical narratives, moral teachings, and philosophical reflections that are very fresh to read today. It is a valuable work as it contains a very unique perspective on Chinese philosophy and spirituality.

> Newell, Allan (1994): *Unified Theories of Cognition*, 3rd edition, Cambridge: Harvard University Press.

The book offers a groundbreaking perspective on cognitive science by attempting to develop a comprehensive theory that integrates all aspects of human thought. Newell's approach of unifying different cognitive phenomena under a single theoretical framework represents both an intellectual challenge and an inspiring vision for the future of cognitive research.

Nhat Hanh, Thich (1999): *The Miracle of Mindfulness: An Introduction to the Practice of Meditation*, Boston: Beacon Press.

Osho (2009): *The Book of Secrets—112 Meditation Techniques for Discovering Inner Truth*, Munich: Arkana.

Yates, Culadasa J. (2015): *The Mind Illuminated*, Chicago: Dharma Treasure Press.

For me, these three books are a comprehensive presentation of what meditation is. With them, you can explore the subject of meditation and mindfulness independently and also go through completely different mental developments. The "Vigyan Bhairav Tantra," interpreted by Osho, is surprising. It was Yates' work that first introduced me to some of the mechanisms of the inner economy.

BIBLIOGRAPHY

Abraham, A. (2015): How social dynamics shape our understanding of reality, in Warnick, J., Landis, D. (eds.): *Neuroscience in Intercultural Contexts.* International and Cultural Psychology, pp. 243–256, New York: Springer.
Abraham, A. (2018): The wandering mind: Where imagination meets consciousness, *Journal of Consciousness Studies,* 25(11–12), pp. 34–52(19).
Achtziger, A. (et al.) (2014): The neural basis of belief updating and rational decision making, *Social Cognitive and Affective Neuroscience,* 9(1), pp. S. 55–62.
Aghion, P. (et al.) (1998): *Endogenous Growth Theory,* Cambridge: MIT Press.
Alberini, C. M. (2005): Mechanisms of memory stabilization: Are consolidation and reconsolidation similar or distinct processes?, *Trends in Neurosciences,* 28(1), pp. 51–56.
Álvarez-Pérez, Y. (et al.) (2022): Effectiveness of mantra-based meditation on mental health: A systematic review and meta-analysis, *International Journal of Environmental Research and Public Health,* 13; 19(6), p. 3380.
Anderson, M. C., Levy, B. J. (2009): Imagining the past: The impact of imagination on memory, in Markman, K. D., Klein, W. M. P., Suhr, J. A. (eds.): *Handbook of Imagination and Mental Simulation,* pp. 187–202, Hove: Psychology Press.
Andy, C., Chalmers, D. (1998): The extended mind, *Analysis,* 58(1), pp. 7–19.
Apperly, I. A. (2012): What is "theory of mind"? Concepts, cognitive processes, and individual differences, *Quarterly Journal of Experimental Psychology,* 65(5), pp. 825–839.
Aristotle (1956), in: *Nicomachean Ethics.* Dirlmeier, F. (trans. and ed.) Berlin: Akademie Verlag.
Aristotle (2021): *Parva naturalia – De memoria et reminiscentia,* Berlin: de Gruyter.
Assagioli, R. (1933): Dynamic psychology and psychosythesis, *Hibbert Journal,* 32, pp. 184–192.
Assagioli, R. (1937): Spiritual development and its alternative maladies, *Hibbert Journal,* 36, pp. 69–84.
Assmann, J. (1988): Collective memory and cultural identity, in: Assmann, J., Hölscher, T. (eds.): *Culture and Memory,* pp. 9–19, Frankfurt am Main: Suhrkamp.
Assmann, J. (2018): *Das kulturelle Gedächtnis Schrift, Erinnerung und politische Identität in frühen Hochkulturen,* 8th edition, Munich: C.H. Beck.
Ates, M. (2023): *Phenomenology of the Dream,* Cambridge: Felix Meiner Verlag.
Atkinson, R. C., Shiffrin, R. M. (1968): Human memory: A proposed system and its control processes, in: Spence, K. W., Spence, J. T. (eds.): *The Psychology of Learning and Motivation,* vol. 2, pp. 89–195, Cambridge: Academic Press.

Audi, R. (2011): *Epistemology: A Contemporary Introduction to the Theory of Knowledge*, 3rd edition, New York: Routledge.
Austin, J. H. (2011): *Selfless Insight. Zen and the Meditative Transformations of Consciousness*, 2nd edition, Cambridge: MIT Press.
Baars, B. J. (2002): The conscious access hypothesis: Origins and recent evidence, *Trends in Cognitive Sciences*, 6(1), pp. 47–52.
Baddeley, A. D. (1992): Working memory, *Science*, 255(5044), pp. 556–559.
Baddeley, A. D., Hitch, G., Allen, R. (2020): A multicomponent model of working memory, in: Logie, R., Camos, V., Cowan, N. (eds.): *Working Memory: The State of the Science*, pp. 10–43, New York: Oxford University Press.
Baer, R. (2010): *Assessing Mindfulness and Acceptance Processes in Clients: Illuminating the Theory and Practice of Change*, Oakland: New Harbinger Publications.
Baltes, P. B. (2008): Position paper: Outline of a life-span psychology of longing: Utopia of a perfect and perfect life, *Psychologische Rundschau*, 59(2), pp. 77–86.
Baltes, P. B., Baltes, M. M. (eds.) (1990): Psychological perspectives on successful aging: The model of selective optimization with compensation, in: *Successful Aging: Perspectives from the Behavioral Sciences*, pp. 1–34, Cambridge: Cambridge University Press.
Baltes, P. B., Lindenberger, U., Staudinger, U. M. (1998): Life span theory in developmental psychology, in: Lerner, R. M. (ed.): *Handbook of Child Psychology: Theoretical Models of Human Development*, 5th edition, Vol. 1, pp. 1029–1143, New York: Wiley.
Baltes, P. B., Staudinger, U. M. (2000): Wisdom: A Metaheuristic (Pragmatic) to orchestrate mind and virtue toward excellence, *American Psychologist*, 55(1), pp. 122–136.
Bamberg, M. (1999): Is there anything behind discourse? Narrative and the local accomplishment of identities, in: Maiers, W. (et al.) (eds.): *Challenges to Theoretical Psychology*. Selected and edited proceedings of the seventh Beannial, Conference of The International Society for Theoretical Psychology Berlin (1997), pp. 220–227, North York: Captus University Publications.
Baron von Hardenberg, G. P. F. L. (1960), in: Kluckhohn, P., Samuel, R. (eds.), *Novalis Schriften*, vol. 2, 3rd edition, Stuttgart: Kohlhammer.
Bartlett, F. C. (1932): *Remembering: A Study in Experimental and Social Psychology*, Cambridge: Cambridge University Press.
Baumann, P. (2006): *Erkenntnistheorie*, Stuttgart: Metzler.
Baumeister, R. F., Vohs, K. D., Tice, D. M. (2007): The strength model of self-control, In: Baumeister, R. F., Vohs, K. D. (eds.): *Handbook of Self-Regulation: Research, Theory, and Applications*, pp. 351–373, New York: Guilford Press.
Beauregard, M., O'Leary, D. (2008): *The Spiritual Brain. A Neuroscientist's Case for the Existence of the Soul*, New York: HarperCollins Publishers.
Beck, A. T. (et al.) (2024): *Cognitive Therapy of Depression*, 2nd edition, New York: Guilford Press.
Beck, A. T., Alford, B. A. (2009): *Depression: Causes and Treatment*, Philadelphia: University of Pennsylvania Press.
Beck, J. S. (2011): *Cognitive Behaviour Therapy – Basics and Beyond*, 2nd edition, New York: Guilford Press.
Becker, G. S. (2013): *The Economic Approach to Human Behaviour*, 2nd edition, Chicago: University of Chicago Press.
Benoit, R. (2019): *Memories of the Future*, Leipzig: Max Planck Institute for Human Cognitive and Brain Sciences.

Berger, P., Luckmann, T. (2023): The social construction of reality, in: Longhofer, W., Winchester, D. (eds.): *Social Theory Re-Wired: New Connections to Classical and Contemporary Perspectives*, 3rd edition, pp. 92–101, New York: Routledge.
Bergson, H. (1903): Introduction à la métaphysique, *Revue de métaphysique et de morale*, 11(1):1, pp. 1–36.
Bergson, H. (1948): *Thinking and Creative Becoming*. Aufsätze und Vorträge, Meisenheim am Glan: Westkulturverlag Anton Hain.
Bernard, C. (1865): *Introduction à l'étude de la médicine expérimentale*, Paris: Édition Garnier.
Berne, E. (2005): *Transactional Analysis of Intuition: A Contribution to Ego Psychology* (Vol. 45), 4th edition, Paderborn: Junfermann Verlag.
Bhagavadgita (1998): *Translation by Sri Aurobindo*, 2nd edition, Freiburg im Breisgau: Herder.
Biegoń, D., Nullmeier, F. (2014): Narratives about narratives. Status and methodology of narrative analysis, in: Gadinger, F., Jarzebski, S., Yildiz, T. (eds.): *Politische Narrative: Konzepte – Analysen – Forschungspraxis*, pp. 39–65, Wiesbaden: Springer VS.
Billhardt, F., Storck, T. (2021): *Perception and Memory – Psychoanalysis and General Psychology*, Psychoanalysis in the 21st Century, Stuttgart: W. Kohlhammer Verlag.
Bishop, S. R. (et al.) (2004): Mindfulness: A proposed operational definition. *Clinical Psychology: Science and Practice*, 11(3), pp. 230–241.
Blake, W. (2013): *Between Fire and Fire, Poetical Works, bilingual edition*, 3rd edition, Munich: Deutscher Taschenbuch Verlag.
Blau, E. (1995): *Krishnamurti 100 years*, Grafing: Aquamarine.
Blum, U., Dudley, L., Leibbrand, F., Weiske, A. (2015): *Applied Institutional Economics: Theories – Models – Evidence*, Wiesbaden: Gabler Verlag.
Bödeker, W., Friedrichs, M. (2011): Kosten der psychischen Erkrankungen und Belastungen in Deutschland, in: Kamp,L., Pickshaus, K. (eds.): *Regelungslücke psychische Belastungen schließen* (pp. 86–96). Düsseldorf: Hans-Böckler-Stiftung.
Bohleber, W. (2004): Memory, trauma and historical reality. Remembering. Freiburg discussions on literary psychology. *Yearbook for Literature and Psychoanalysis*, Königshausen & Neumann, pp. 43–53.
Bohleber, W. (2007): Memory, trauma and collective memory – the struggle for memory in psychoanalysis. *Psyche*, 61(4), pp. 293–321.
Bohleber, W. (2019): *From Orthodoxy to Plurality – Controversies over Key Concepts of Psychoanalysis*, Göttingen: Vandenhoeck & Ruprecht.
Boltanski, L., Chiapello, E. (2006) [1999]: *The New Spirit of Capitalism*, Konstanz: UKV.
Borghardt, T., Erhardt, W. (2016): *Buddhist Psychology – Fundamentals and Practice*, Munich: Arkana.
Bovensiepen, G. (2019): *Die Komplextheorie: Ihre Weiterentwicklungen und Anwendungen in der Psychotherapie*, Stuttgart: W. Kohlhammer Verlag.
Brand, G. (2013): Die Narration der Narration – Eine Kritik in drei Akten, in: Gasser, G., Schmidhuber, M. (eds.): *Personale Identität, Narrativität und Praktische Rationalität. The Unity of the Person from a Metaphysical and Practical Perspective*, pp. 181–199, Paderborn: Brill mentis.
Breyer, T., et al. (2015): *Ökonomische Utopien*, Berlin: Neofelis Verlag.

Brooke, J. H. (1991): *Science and Religion: Some Historical Perspectives*, Cambridge: Cambridge University Press.
Brown, K. W., Creswell, J. D., Ryan, R. M. (2015): *Handbook of Mindfulness: Theory, Research, and Practice*, New York: Guilford Press.
Brown, K. W., Ryan, R. M. (2003): The benefits of being present: Mindfulness and its role in psychological well-being. *Journal of Personality and Social Psychology*, 84(4), pp. 822–848.
Brown, R. P., Gerbarg, P. L. (2005): Sudarshan Kriya Yogic breathing in the treatment of stress, anxiety, and depression: Part I-neurophysiologic model, *Journal of Alternative and Complementary Medicine*, 11(1), pp. 189–201.
Brüllmann, P., Rombach, U., Wilde, C. (2014): Introduction: Imagination, transformation and the emergence of the new, in: Brüllmann, P., Rombach, U., Wilde, C. (eds.): *Imagination, Transformation and the Emergence of the New*, pp. 1–22, Berlin, Munich, Boston: De Gruyter.
Bruner, J. (1987): Life as narrative, *Social Research*, 54(1), pp. 11–32.
Bruner, J. (1991): The narrative construction of reality, *Critical Inquiry*, 18(1), pp. 1–21.
Buber, M. (2023): *The Dialogue Principle: I and You. Dialogue. The Question to the Individual. Elements of the Interpersonal. On the History of the Dialogue Principle*, Munich: Gütersloher Verlagshaus.
Bucher, A. A. (2014): *Psychologie Der Spiritualität: Handbuch*, 2nd, completely revised edition, Weinheim Basel: Beltz.
Bude, H. (1991): Die Rekonstruktion kultureller Sinnsysteme, in: von Rosenstiel, L. (et al.) (ed.): *Handbuch qualitative Forschung: Grundlagen, Konzepte, Methoden und Anwendungen*, pp. 101–112, Munich: Beltz – Psychologie Verlags Union.
Bürmann, I. (1997): *Überwindung des Dualismus von Person und Sache*, Bad Heilbrunn: Klinkhardt.
Butler, L. D. (et al.) (2008): Mediation with trauma survivors: Immediate and long-term effects of mindfulness-based stress reduction on posttraumatic stress symptoms, *Journal of Clinical Psychology*, 64(1), pp. 100–111.
Camerer, C. F., Loewenstein, G. (2004): Behavioral Economics – Past, Present, Future, in Camerer, C. F., Loewenstein, G., Rabin, M. (eds.): *Advances in Behavioral Economics* (pp. 144–161). Princeton: Princeton University Press.
Carroll, N. (1998): Art and cultural identity, *The Journal of Aesthetics and Art Criticism*, 56(2), pp. 181–194.
Casey, E. S. (2000): *Remembering: A Phenomenological Study*, 2nd edition, Bloomington, Indianapolis: Indiana University Press.
Cermak, L. S. (2014): Memory as a processing continuum, in *New Directions in Memory and Aging (PLE: Memory): Proceedings of the George A. Talland Memorial Conference*, pp. 261–278, London: Psychology Press.
Chalmers, D. J. (1996): *The Conscious Mind: In Search of a Fundamental Theory*, Oxford: Oxford University Press.
Chan, C., Sik Ying Ho, P., Chow, E. (2002): A body-mind-spirit model in health: An Eastern approach, *Social Work in Health Care*, 34(3–4), pp. 261–282.
Chiesa, A., Serretti, A. (2009): A systematic review of neurobiological and clinical features of mindfulness meditations, *Psychological Medicine*, 40(8), pp. 1239–1252.
Chlupsa, C. (2016): *The Influence of Unconscious Motives on the Decision-Making Process: How Implicit Codes Control Management Decisions*, Wiesbaden: Springer Fachmedien.

Chopra, D. (2023): *Life in Abundance. The Inner Path to Wealth*, Munich: Irisana Verlag.
Christie, T. S., Schrader, P. (2015): Cognitive cost as dynamic allocation of energetic resources. *Frontiers in Neuroscience*, 9, pp. 289–311.
Christoff, K., Gordon, A. M., Smallwood, J., Smith, R., Schooler, J. W. (2009): Experience sampling during fMRI reveals default network and executive system contributions to mind wandering, *Proceedings of the National Academy of Sciences*, 106(21), S 8719–8724.
Chrudzimski, A. (2013): *Intentionality, Time Consciousness and Intersubjectivity: Studies in Phenomenology from Brentano to Ingarden*, Vol. 3, Berlin: Walter de Gruyter.
Chung, S. J. (2012): The science of self, mind and body, *Open Journal of Philosophy*, 2, pp. 171–178.
Churchland, P. S. (1989): *Neurophilosophy: Toward a Unified Science of the Mind-Brain*, Cambridge: MIT Press.
Claessens, B. J., van Eerde, W., Rutte, C. G., Roe, R. A. (2007): A review of the time management literature, *Personnel Review*, 36(2), pp. 255–276.
Clark, A. (2008): *Supersizing the Mind: Embodiment, Action, and Cognitive Extension*, New York: Oxford University Press.
Conway, M. A., Pleydell-Pearce, C. W. (2000): The construction of autobiographical memories in the self-memory system, *Psychological Review*, 107(2), pp. 261–288.
Cozolino, L. (2010): *The Neuroscience of Psychotherapy: Healing the Social Brain*, 2nd edition, New York: W.W. Norton & Company.
Craik, F. I. M., Lockhart, R. S. (1972): Levels of processing: A framework for memory research. *Journal of Verbal Learning and Verbal Behaviour*, 11(6), pp. 671–684.
Csikszentmihalyi, M. (2002): *Flow: The Classic Work on How to Achieve Happiness*, New York: Harper & Row.
Cyrulnik, B. (2009): Résilence et adaptation, in: Nader-Grosbois, N. (ed.): *Résilience, régulation et qualité de vie*, pp. 21–29, Paris: UCL.
Cyrulnik, B. (2018): *Shame: The Many Facets of a Tabooed Feeling*, Munderfing: Fischer & Gann.
Cyrulnik, B. (2021): Narrative resilience. *Multisystemic Resilience: Adaptation and Transformation in Contexts of Change*, 100, pp. 135–147.
Dalai, L. (2002): *The Path to Happiness. Finding Meaning in Life*, 9th edition, Freiburg im Breisgau: Herder.
Dalai, L., Cutler, H. C. (1998): *The Art of Happiness: A Handbook for Living*, New York: Riverhead Books.
Damasio, A. R. (1994): *Descartes' Error: Emotion, Reason, and the Human Brain*, New York: Putnam Publishing.
Damasio, A. R. (2000): *I Feel therefore I am. The Decoding of Consciousness*, Munich: List Verlag.
Daniel, T. O., Stanton, C. M., Epstein, L. H. (2013): The future is now: Reducing impulsivity and energy intake using episodic future thinking, *Psychological Science*, 24(11), pp. 2339–2342.
De Beauvoir, S. (1947): *Pour une morale de l'ambiguïté*, Paris: Gallimard.
Deco, G., Rolls, E. T. (2005): Attention, short-term memory, and action selection: A unifying theory, *Progress in Neurobiology*, 76(4), pp. 236–256.
Dennett, D. C. (2017): *Brainstorms: Philosophical Essays on Mind and Psychology*, Cambridge: MIT Press.

DePaul, M. R., Ramsey, W. M. (1998): *Rethinking Intuition: The Psychology of Intuition and Its Role in Philosophical Inquiry*, Oxford: Rowman & Littlefield.

Dessí, R. (2008): Collective memory, cultural transmission, and investments. *The American Economic Review*, 98(1), pp. 534–560.

Dieckmann, H. (2013): *Complexes: Diagnostik und Therapie in der analytischen Psychologie*, Berlin Heidelberg: Springer.

Diemer, K., et al. (2017): Optimal resource allocation and the market, in *Resource Allocation, Competition and Environmental Economics: Economic Policy in Theory and Practice*, Berlin, Heidelberg: Springer Gabler.

Diener, E., Seligman, M. E. P. (2004): Beyond money: Toward an economy of well-being. *Psychological Science in the Public Interest*, 5(1), pp. 1–31.

Dijksterhuis, A., Bos, M. W., Nordgren, L. F., van Baaren, R. B. (2006): On making the right choice: The deliberation-without-attention effect, *Science*, 311(5763), pp. 1005–1007.

Dipper, L. (2016): Erinnerung und Stimmung: Nutzung einer Ressource und Bearbeitung einer Belastung (Doctoral dissertation, University of Ulm).

Dörner, D. (2013): Wollen im Wahrnehmungshandeln und Denken – Thinking and willing: Ein systemtheoretischer Ansatz, in: Heckhausen, H., Gollwitzer, P. M., Weinert, F. E. (eds.): *Jenseits des Rubikon: Der Wille in den Humanwissenschaften*, 2nd edition, pp. 238–250, Berlin Heidelberg: Springer.

Drobe, C. (2016): *Menschsein als Selbst- und Fremdbestimmung: Eine theologische Reflexion philosophischer, literarischer und sozialwissenschaftlicher Zugänge zur Identitätsfrage*, Berlin: De Gruyter.

Drüe, H. (1963): Edmund Husserl's system of phenomenological psychology, in Graumann, C. F., Linschroten, J. (eds.): *Phänologisch-psychologische Forschungen, Band 4* (pp. 8–34), Berlin: De Gruyter.

Ebbinghaus, H. (1885): *Über das Gedächtnis: Untersuchungen zur experimentellen Psychologie*. Leipzig: Duncker & Humblot.

Ebbinghaus, H., Dürr, E. (1913): *Grundzüge der Psychologie*, Leipzig: Veit & Companie.

Eccles, J. S., Wigfield A. (2002): Motivational beliefs, values, and goals. *Annual Review of Psychology*, 53(1), pp. 109–132.

Egger, J. W. (2015): Self-efficacy – A cognitive construct, in Integrative behavioral therapy and psychotherapeutic medicine. *Integrative Models in Psychotherapy, Supervision and Counselling*, pp. 283–311, Wiesbaden: Springer.

Eisenhardt, K. M., Graebner, M. E. (2007): Theory building from cases: Opportunities and challenges, *Academy of Management Journal*, 50(1), pp. 25–32.

Erikson, E. H. (1968): *Identity: Youth and Crisis*, New York: W.W. Norton & Company.

Erikson, E. H. (1973): *Identity and the Life Cycle*, Frankfurt am Main: Suhrkamp.

Erll, A., Rigney, A. (eds.) (2009): Introduction: Cultural memory and its dynamics, in: *Mediation, Remediation, and the Dynamics of Cultural Memory*, pp. 1–14, Berlin, New York: De Gruyter.

Erreich, A. (2016): Unconscious fantasy as a special category of mental representations, *Psyche*, 70(6), pp. 481–507.

Essen, S. (2012): Systemische Therapie und Spiritualität Von der Notwendigkeit szenischer Theologie, in: Baier, K. (ed.): *Handbuch Spiritualität: Zugänge, Traditionen, interreligiöse Zugänge*, pp. 112–126, Darmstadt: Wissenschaftliche Buchgesellschaft.

Euler, W. (2004): Consciousness – Soul – Spirit. Untersuchungen zur Transformation des Cartesischen "Cogito" in der Psychologie Christian Wolffs, in: Rudolph, O. -P., Goubet, J. -F. (eds.): *Die Psychologie Christian Wolffs: Systematische und historische Untersuchungen*, pp. 11–50, Berlin, Boston: Max Niemeyer Verlag.
Fehr, E., Schwarz, G. (eds.) (2002): *Psychologische Grundlagen der Ökonomie – Über Vernunft und Eigennutz hinaus*, Zurich: Verlag Neue Zürcher Zeitung.
Fetscher, R. (1985): The self, the Id, and the unconscious, *Psyche*, 39(3), pp. 241–275.
Feuerstein, G. (1998): *Tantra: The Path of Ecstasy*, Boulder: Shambhala Publications.
Fletcher, M. (2010): Stranger and own presence. On otherness, self and time, in: Flatscher, M., Loidolt, S.: *Das Fremde im Selbst – das Andere im Selben*. Transformations of Phenomenology, pp. 50–63, Würzburg: Königshausen & Neumann.
Fodor, J. A. (1983): *The Modularity of Mind: An Essay on Faculty Psychology*, Cambridge: MIT Press.
Fouillée, A. (1890): *La liberté et le déterminisme*, 3ème ed., Paris: Felix Alcan.
Fredrickson, B. L. (2001): The role of positive emotions in positive psychology: The broaden-and-build theory of positive emotions, *American Psychologist*, 56(3), pp. 218–226.
Freeman, M. (2006): Autobiographical memory and the narrative unconscious, in: Welzer, H., Markowitsch, H. J. (eds.): *Warum Menschen sich erinnern können*, pp. 78–94, Stuttgart: Klett-Cotta.
Freire, P. (2022): Pädagogik der Unterdrückten, in: Bauer, U., Bittlingmayer, U.H., Scherr, A. (eds.): *Handbuch Bildungs- und Erziehungssoziologie*. Education and Society, Wiesbaden: Springer VS.
Freud, S. (1946): Das Unbewusste, in: Ders., *Gesammelte Werke*, Vol. 10, Frankfurt am Main: Fischer.
Freud, S. (1988) [1915]: Das Unbewusste, in: *Gesammelte Werke*, Vol. 10, Munich: DTV.
Freud, S. (2009): *The Discomfort in Culture. Und andere kulturtheoretische Schriften*, Frankfurt am Main: Fischer Taschenbuch Verlag.
Frey, B. S., Frey-Marti, C. (2010): Happiness-The view of economics, *Wirtschaftsdienst*, 90(7), pp. 458–463.
Frey, B. S.,, Benz, M. (2001): Economics and psychology: an overview. Working paper/ Institute for Empirical Research in Economics, 92nd vol.
Frey, D. (2007): Innovation and creativity, *Encyclopaedia of Psychology*, 6, pp. 810–845.
Frey, D., Jonas, E., Maier, G. W. (2007): Psychologie des Geldes, in: Dieter, F., von Rosenstiel, L. (eds.): *Wirtschaftspsychologie: Wirtschafts- Organisations- und Arbeitspsychologie (Enzyklopädie der Psychologie)*, pp. 75–148, Göttingen: Hogrefe.
Friston, K. (2010): The free-energy principle: A unified brain theory? *Nature Reviews Neuroscience*, 11(2), pp. 127–138.
Fromm, E. (1971): Psychoanalyse und Zen-Buddhismus, in: Fromm, E., Suzuki, D. T., Martino, R. d. (eds.): *Zen-Buddhismus und Psychoanalyse* (pp. 78–92), Frankfurt am Main: Suhrkamp.
Fromm, E. (1991): *To Have or to Be. Die Seelische Grundlage für eine neue Gesellschaft*, 20th edition, Munich: Deutscher Taschenbuch Verlag.
Garbe, R. (1894): *The Sâmkhya Philosophy. Eine Darstellung des indischen Rationalismus*, Leipzig: H. Haessel.
Gazzaniga, M. S. (2005): *The Ethical Brain: The Science of Our Moral Dilemmas*, New York: Harper Perennial.

Geertz, C. (1973): *The Interpretation of Cultures*, New York: Basic Books.
Geimer, A. (2012): Bildung als Transformation von Selbst- und Weltverhältnissen und die dissoziative Aneignung von diskursiven Subjektfiguren in posttraditionellen Gesellschaften, *Zeitschrift für Bildungsforschung*, 3(2), pp. 229–242.
Gergen, K. J. (2009): *An Invitation to Social Construction*, 2nd edition, London: SAGE Publications.
Germer, C., Siegel, R. D. (eds.). (2014): Wisdom and compassion, in: *Wisdom and Compassion in Psychotherapy: Mindful Ways to Deepen Therapeutic Practice*, pp. 1–38, Freiburg: Arbor Verlag.
Glück, J. (et al.) (2013): How to measure wisdom: Content, reliability, and validity of five measures, *Frontiers in Psychology*, 4, p. 405.
Goldenberg, G. (2007): *Neuropsychologie: Grundlagen, Klinik, Rehabilitation*, 4th edition, Munich: Elsevier, Urban & Fischer.
Goldie, P. (2003): One's remembered past: Narrative thinking, emotion, and the external perspective, *Philosophical Papers*, 32(3), pp. 301–319, op. cit.
Goldie, P. (2013): Narrative thinking, emotion and planning. in: Koroliov, S. (ed.): *Emotion and Cognition*, pp. 187–203, Berlin, Boston: De Gruyter.
Gollwitzer, P. M., Bayer, U. C., Wicklund, R. A. (2002): The acting self: Symbolic self-completion as goal-directed self-development, in Frey, D. (eds.): *Central Theories of Social Psychology*, pp. 191–212, Bern: Huber.
Gothe, N. P. (2013): The acute effects of yoga on executive function, *Journal of Physical Activity and Health*, 10(4), pp. 488–495.
Goyal, M. (et al.) (2014): Meditation programs for psychological stress and well-being: A systematic review and meta-analysis, *JAMA Internal Medicine*, 174(3), pp. 357–368.
Green, M. C., Brock, T. C. (2002): In the mind's eye: Transportation-imagery model of narrative persuasion, in Green, M. C., Strange, J. J., Brock, T. C. (eds.): *Narrative Impact: Social and Cognitive Foundations*, pp. 315–341, Mahwah: Lawrence Erlbaum.
Greenberg, L. S., Paivio, S. C. (1997): *Working with Emotions in Psychotherapy*, New York: Guilford Press.
Greene, R. R., Galambos, C., Lee, Y. (2004): Resilience theory: Theoretical and professional conceptualizations. *Journal of Human Behavior in the Social Environment*, 8(4), pp. 75–91.
Gregorio, S. (et al.) (eds.) (2024): *Geist und Imagination: Zur Bedeutung der Vorstellungskraft für Denken und Handeln*, Berlin: Suhrkamp Verlag.
Groeben, N., Christmann, U. (2012): Narration in Psychology, in: Aumüller, M. (ed.): *Narrativität als Begriff. Analyses and examples of application between philological and anthropological orientation*, pp. 299–321, Berlin: de Gruyter.
Groeben, N., Scheele, B. (1977): *Argumente für eine Psychologie des Reflexiven Subjekts: Paradigmawechsel vom behavioralen zum epistemologischen Menschenbild*, Darmstadt: Dr. Dieter Steinkopff Verlag.
Gunturu, V. (2020): *Yoga – History, Philosophy, Practice*, Munich: C.H. Beck.
Guttmacher, S. (1979): Whole in body, mind & spirit: holistic health and the limits of medicine, Hastings Centre Report, pp. 15–21.
Hadot, P. (2002): *Philosophy as a Way of Life: Spiritual Exercises from Socrates to Foucault*, Oxford: Blackwell.
Halbwachs, M. (1992): *On Collective Memory*, Chicago: University of Chicago Press.

Hannover, B., Kühnen, U. (2003): Culture, self-concept and cognition, *Zeitschrift für Psychologie*, 211, pp. 212–224.
Hansch, Dieter (2013): *Psychosynergetics: The Fractal Evolution of the Psychic. Foundations of General Psychotherapy*. Germany, Opladen: Westdeutscher Verlag.
Hany, E. A., Heller, K. A. (1993): Entwicklung kreativen Denkens im kulturellen Kontext, in: Mandl, H., Dreher, M., Kornadt, H. -J. (eds.): *Entwicklung und Denken im kulturellen Kontext*, pp. 99–115, Göttingen: Hogrefe.
Hardy, J. (1987): *A Psychology with a Soul. Psychosynthesis in Evolutionary Context*, London: Routledge & Kegan Paul.
Hardy, J., Whitmore, D. (1990): Psychosynthesis – A brief introduction to the historical background and working methods, in Rowan, J., Dryden, W. (eds.): *New Developments in Psychotherapy*, pp. 221–229. Bremen: Transform Verlag.
Hartmann, D. (1998): *Philosophische Grundlagen der Psychologie*, Darmstadt: Wissenschaftliche Buchgesellschaft.
Haußer, K. (1995): *Identitätspsychologie*, Berlin Heidelberg: Springer.
Hautzinger, M., Pössel, P. (2017): *Cognitive Interventions*, Göttingen: Hogrefe Verlag.
Headey, B., Wearing, A. (1989): Personality, life events, and subjective well-being: Toward a dynamic equilibrium model. *Journal of Personality and Social Psychology*, 57(4), pp. 731–739.
Heckhausen, H. (2013): Wollen als Gegenstand alltäglicher Erfahrung: Wünsche – Wählen – Wollen, in: Heckhausen, H., Gollwitzer, P. M., Weinert, F. E. (eds.): *Jenseits des Rubikon: Der Wille in den Humanwissenschaften*, 2nd edition, pp. 1–9, Berlin Heidelberg: Springer.
Heidegger, M. (1988), in: Mörchen, H. (ed.): *Vom Wesen der Wahrheit: Zu Platons Höhlengleichnis und Theätet* (Freiburg Lecture, Winter Term 1931/1932). vol. 34, 8th edition, Frankfurt am Main: Vittorio Klostermann.
Heiner, K. (2008): Identity constructions in late modern society. Risky opportunities with precarious resources, *ZPS*, 7, pp. 291–308.
Heinz, A. (2016): *Psychische Gesundheit: Begriff und Konzepte (Horizonte der Psychiatrie und Psychotherapie)*, Stuttgart: W. Kohlhammer Verlag.
Helbig, S., Hoyer, J. (2007): Does a little help a lot? A minimal intervention for patients during the waiting period for outpatient behavioral therapy, *Verhaltenstherapie*, 17(2), pp. 109–115.
Helsper, W. (2013): *Selbstkrise und Individuationsprozeß: Subjekt- und sozialisationstheoretische Entwürfe zum imaginären Selbst der Moderne* (Vol. 17), Berlin: Springer.
Henning, C. (2016): Grenzen der Kunst, in: Kauppert, M., Eberl, H. (eds.): *Ästhetische Praxis. Art and Society*, pp. 112–120, Wiesbaden: Springer.
Henninger, M. (2016): Resilienz, in: Frey, D. (ed.): *Psychologie der Werte: Von Achtsamkeit bis Zivilcourage (Basiswissen aus Psychologie und Philosophie)*, pp. 157–165, Berlin Heidelberg: Springer.
Herles, B. (2011): *Wert im Spiegel ökonomischer Rationalität: eine kritische Betrachtung*, Siegburg: Eul Verlag.
Hermans, H. J. M., Gieser, T. (2012): *Handbook of Dialogical Self Theory*, Cambridge: Cambridge University Press.
Hermans, H. J. M. (1999): Self-narrative as meaning construction: The dynamics of self-investigation, *Journal of Clinical Psychology*, 55(10), pp. 1193–1211.

Hermans, H. J.M., Hermans-Jansen, E. (1995): *Self-Narratives: The Construction of Meaning in Psychotherapy*, New York: Guilford Press.

Herrmann, U. (2022): *Das Ende des Kapitalismus*, 3rd edition, Cologne: Kiepenheuer & Witsch.

Hoell, A., Salize, H. J. (2019): Social inequality and mental health, *Der Nervenarzt*, 90(11), pp. 1187–1206.

Hoffmann, E. T. A. (2022): *The Devil's Elixirs*, Göttingen: Literatur- und Wissenschaftsverlag.

Hoffmann, O. (2014): *Rethinking Innovation – Histocentric Analysis of Innovation Mechanisms in the Watch Industry*, Wiesbaden: Springer Gabler.

Hoffmann, O. (2020): *Vom nützlichen Luxus*, Kulmbach: Börsenbuchverlag.

Hofmann, F. (2023): *REFRAME-The Psychology of Innovation*, Regensburg: Metropolitan.

Hofmann, S. G., Asnaani, A., Vonk, I. J. J., Sawyer, A. T., Fang, A. (2012): The efficacy of cognitive behavioural therapy: A review of meta-analyses, *Cognitive Therapy and Research*, 36(5), pp. 427–440.

Hofmann, S. G., Sawyer, A. T., Witt, A. A., Oh, D. (2010): The effect of mindfulness-based therapy on anxiety and depression: A meta-analytic review, *Journal of Consulting and Clinical Psychology*, 78(2), pp. 169–183.

Hofmannsthal, H. v. (1979): *Collected Works in Ten Individual Volumes: Reden und Aufsätze III. essays on poetry and art. Reisebuch*, Frankfurt am Main: Fischer.

Hofstede, G. (1980): *Culture's Consequences: International Differences in Work-Related Values*. Beverly Hills, London: Sage Publications.

Holland, A. C., Kensinger, E. A. (2010): Emotion and autobiographical memory, *Physics of Life Reviews*, 7(1), pp. S. 88–131.

Holmes, E. A., Mathews, A. (2010): Mental imagery in emotion and emotional disorders, *Clinical Psychology Review*, 30(3), pp. 349–362.

Hommes, J. (1953): *Zwiespältiges Dasein. Die existentiale Ontologie von Hegel bis Heidegger*, Freiburg: Herder.

Huber, C. E. (1964): *Anamnesis in Plato*, Munich: Max Hueber.

Hummell, H. J. (1971): *Die Reduzierbarkeit von Soziologie auf Psychologie: Eine These, ihr Test und ihre theoretische Bedeutung*, Braunschweig: Vieweg+Teubner Verlag.

Husserl, E. (1968): *Collected Works (Critical Edition), Volume IX: Phenomenological Psychology*, 2nd edition, Berlin: Springer.

Husserl, E. (1980): Gesammelte Werke (Kritische Edition), Volume XXIII: Phantasie, Bildbewusstsein, Erinnerung. On the phenomenology of vivid visualizations. Texts from the Nachlass (1898–1925), Berlin: Springer.

Husserl, E. (2004): *Collected Works (Critical Edition), Volume XXXVIII: Perception and Attention. Texte aus dem Nachlass (1893–1912)*, Berlin: Springer.

Hutchins, E. (1995): *Cognition in the Wild*, Cambridge: MIT Press.

James, W. (1890): *Principles of Psychology*, New York: Henry Holt & Co.

Jäncke, L. (2021): *Neuroplasticity – Malleable Brain*, Zurich: Spektrum Verlag.

Jerath, R., Edry, J. W., Barnes, V. A., Jerath, V. (2006): Physiology of long pranayamic breathing: Neural respiratory elements may provide a mechanism that explains how slow deep breathing shifts the autonomic nervous system, *Medical Hypotheses*, 67(3), pp. 566–571.

Johnson-Laird, P. N. (1995): *Mental Models: Towards a Cognitive Science of Language, Inference, and Consciousness*, 6th edition, Cambridge: Harvard University Press.

Johnstone, B. (et al.) (2016): Selflessness as a foundation of spiritual transcendence: Perspectives from the neurosciences and religious studies, *The International Journal for the Psychology of Religion*, 26(4), pp. 287–303.
Jung, C. G. (1921) [1960]: Definitionen, in: Baumann, D. Jung-Merker, L. (eds.): *Ders, Gesammelte Werke VI: Psychologische Typen*, Olten Freiburg: Walter Verlag.
Jung, C. G. (1944) [1972]: Traumsymbole des Individuationsprozesses, in: Baumann, D. Jung-Merker, L. (eds.): *Ders, Gesammelte Werke XII: Psychologie und Alchemie*, Olten Freiburg: Walter Verlag.
Jung, C. G. (1954): Archetypes and the collective unconscious, in: Baumann, D. Jung-Merker, L. (eds.): *Ders, Gesammelte Werke, Vol. IX/I*, Olten Freiburg: Walter Verlag.
Jung, C. G. (1975), in: Adler, G., Jaffé, A. (eds.): *Letters, Volume 2: 1951–1961*, Princeton: Princeton University Press.
Jung, C. G. (1994): Psychologische Typen, in: Baumann, D. Jung-Merker, L. (eds.): *Ders., Gesammelte Werke, Vol. VI*, Olten Freiburg: Walter Verlag.
Jung, C. G. (2001a): *Briefe I: 1906–1945*, Olten Freiburg: Walter Verlag.
Jung, C. G. (2001b): Aion. Beiträge zur Symbolik des Selbst, in: Baumann, D. Jung-Merker, L. (eds.): *Ders, Gesammelte Werke, Vol. IX/II*, Olten Freiburg: Walter Verlag.
Jung, C. G. (2022): *Archetypes – Urbilder und Wirkkräfte des kollektiven Unbewussten*, 6th edition, Ostfildern: Patmos.
Jung, C. G. (2022): *The Relationship Between the Ego and the Unconscious*, 5th edition, Ostfildern: Patmos.
Kabat-Zinn, J. (1990): *Full Catastrophe Living: Using the Wisdom of Your Body and Mind to Face Stress, Pain, and Illness*. New York: Delta.
Kabat-Zinn, J. (2003): Mindfulness-based interventions in context: Past, present, and future. *Clinical Psychology: Science and Practice*, 10(2), pp. 144–156.
Kabat-Zinn, J. (2013): *Mindfulness for Beginners: Reclaiming the Present Moment-and Your Life*, Boulder: Sounds True.
Kahneman, D. (2011): *Thinking, Fast and Slow*, New York: Farrar, Straus and Giroux.
Kahneman, D., Tversky, A. (2000): *Choices, Values, and Frames*. Cambridge: Cambridge University Press.
Kaiser-El-Safti, M. (2001): *The Idea of Scientific Psychology: Immanuel Kant's Critical Objections and their Constructive Refutation*, Würzburg: Königshausen & Neumann.
Kanfer, F. (2013): Volition and disorders of volition in action – Self-regulation and behaviour, in: Heckhausen, H., Gollwitzer, P. M., Weinert, F. E. (eds.): *Beyond the Rubicon: The Will in the Human Sciences*, 2nd edition, pp. 286–299, Berlin Heidelberg: Springer.
Kant, E. (1787): *Critique of Pure Reason [KdrV B]*, 2nd, expanded and revised edition, Riga: Johann Friedrich Hartknoch.
Kant, I. (1977), in: Weischedel, W. (ed.)ssss: *Die Metaphysik der Sitten*, Frankfurt am Main: Suhrkamp Verlag.
Kast, V. (1995): *Imagination as a Space of Freedom. Dialogue Between the Ego and the Unconscious*, Munich: Deutscher Taschenbuch Verlag.
Kast, V. (2010): *What Really Counts Is the Life Lived. The Power of Life Review*, Freiburg im Breisgau: Kreuz Verlag.
Kast, V. (2014): *Depth Psychology According to C.G. Jung – A Practical Guide*, Ostfildern: Patmos.
Kast, V. (2017): *The Creative Leap*, Ostfildern: Patmos Verlag.

Kellermann, H. (1980): A structural model of emotion and personality: psychoanalytic and sociobiological implications, in: Plutchik, R., Kellermann, H. (eds.): *Theories of Emotion* (Vol. 1), pp. 349–384, New York: Academic Press.

Kempert, S., Schalk, L., Saalbach, H. (2019): Sprache als Werkzeug des Lernens: Ein Überblick zu den kommunikativen und kognitiven Funktionen der Sprache und deren Bedeutung für den fachfachlichen Wissenserwerb, *Psychologie in Erziehung und Unterricht*, 66(3), pp. 176–195.

Kernis, M. H., Goldman, B. M. (2006): A multicomponent conceptualization of authenticity: Theory and research, Advances in experimental social psychology, 38th vol., pp. 283–357.

Keupp, H. (1999): *Identity constructions. Das Patchwork der Identitäten in der Spätmoderne*, Reinbek bei Hamburg: Rowohlt.

Kirchgässner, G. (2013): *Homo Oeconomicus: The Economic Model of Individual Behavior and Its Application in Economics and Social Sciences*, Tübingen: Mohr Siebeck.

Klessmann, M. (2018): *Ambivalenz und Glaube: Warum sich in der Gegenwart Glaubensgewissheit zu Glaubensambivalenz wandeln muss*, Stuttgart: W. Kohlhammer Verlag.

Knoblauch, H. (2009): *Populäre Religion: auf dem Weg in eine spirituelle Gesellschaft*, Frankfurt am Main, New York: Campus Verlag.

Knoblauch, H. (2012): Soziologie der Spiritualität, in: Baier, K. (ed.): *Handbuch Spiritualität: Zugänge, Traditionen, interreligiöse Zugänge*, pp. 91–111, Darmstadt: Wissenschaftliche Buchgesellschaft.

Knoblauch, S. H. (2019): Fluidity of emotions, *Psyche*, 73(4), pp. 235–263.

Koch, S., von Rosenstiel, L. (2007): Werte, Wertewandel und Konsumverhalten, in: von Rosenstiel, L. (ed.): *Wirtschaftspsychologie: Wirtschafts- Organisations- und Arbeitspsychologie (Enzyklopädie der Psychologie)*, pp. 745–782, Göttingen: Hogrefe.

Köhler, W. (1947): *Gestalt Psychology*. New York: Liveright.

Kokoska, M. S., Nicholson, H. (2005): Mapping emotions: The image of emotion and emotion of image, *Behaviour Research Methods*, 37(3), pp. 388–399.

Kölbl, C., Straub, J. (2010): Zur Psychologie des Erinnerns, in: Gudehus, C., Eichenberg, A., Welzer, H. (eds.): *Gedächtnis und Erinnerung – Ein interdisziplinäres Handbuch*, pp. 22–44, Stuttgart: J.B. Metzler.

Komes, J., Wiese, H. (2013): Memory defects-the limits of intact memory. *Memory Disorders: Diagnostics and Rehabilitation*, 3, pp. 40–48.

Kornfield, J. (2008): *The Wise Heart. The Universal Principles of Buddhist Psychology*, 2nd edition, Munich: Goldmann Arkana.

Kosslyn, S. M., Ganis, G., Thompson, W. L. (2013): Mental imagery and the human brain. Progress in Psychological Science around the World. Volume 1 Neural, Cognitive and Developmental Issues, Psychology Press, pp. 195–209.

Kounios, J. (et al.) (2006): The origins of insight in resting-state brain activity. *Neuropsychologia*, 44(13), pp. 2811–2820.

Kraus, W. (2000): *The Narrated Self: Die narrative Konstruktion von Identität in der Spätmoderne*, Herbolzheim: Centaurus Verlag & Media.

Küchle, S. (2012): *Dilemma Structures in Business Ethics and Social Psychology: A Comparison*, Münster: Lit Verlag.

Kuhn, T. (2016): Structure and influencing factors of group-oriented meta-knowledge: Influences of social identification and its foci on transactive memory systems in teams and organizations (Doctoral dissertation, University of Duisburg-Essen).

Kuss, D. J., Griffiths, M. D. (2011): Online social networking and addiction review of the psychological literature. *International Journal of Environmental Research and Public Health*, 8(9), pp. 3528–3552.

Lagneau, J. (1925): *De l'existence de Dieu*, Paris: F. Alcan.

Lawley, J., Tompkins, P. (2000): *Metaphors in Mind: Transformation through Symbolic Modelling*, London: The Developing Company Press.

Lazar, S. W. (et al.) (2005): Meditation experience is associated with increased cortical thickness, *Neuroreport*, 16(17), pp. 1893–1897.

Lazarus, R. S., Kanner, A. D., Folkman, S. (1980): Emotions: A cognitive-phenomenological analysis, in Plutchik, R., Kellerman, H. (eds.): *Theories of Emotion* (Vol. 1), pp. 189–218, New York: Academic Press.

LeDoux, J. E. (1996): *The Emotional Brain: The Mysterious Underpinnings of Emotional Life*, New York: Simon & Schuster.

Leibbrand, F. (1998): *Theoretische Diskussion und abstrakte Handlungstheorie: Ein methodologisches Abstraktionsstufenmodell und seine Anwendung in der Handlungsökonomik, Erfahrung und Denken*, Vol. 82, Berlin: Duncker & Humblot.

Leipner, I. (2018): Digital Mindset – Hybris of the Digital Age, in Keuper, F., Schomann, M., Sikora, L., Wassef, R. (eds.): *Disruption and Transformation Management*, pp. 123–144, Wiesbaden: Springer Gabler.

Leu, B. (2019): *Fear, Loss, Grief and the Question of Meaning*, Wiesbaden: Springer.

Leutz, G. A. (1974): *Psychodrama: Theorie und Praxis*, Berlin Heidelberg: Springer.

Leuzinger-Bohleber, M.,, Pfeifer, R. (1998): Remembering in the transference-past in the present? Psychoanalysis and embodied cognitive science: An interdisciplinary dialogue on memory, *Psyche*, 52(9–10), pp. 884–918.

Lichtenberg, G. C. (2017): *Sudelbücher*, 14th edition, Frankfurt am Main: Suhrkamp.

Linden, M., Strauß, B. (2018): *Risks and Side Effects of Psychotherapy*, 2nd edition, Berlin: Medizinisch-Wissenschaftliche Verlagsgesellschaft.

Lloyd, G. (1996): *Spinoza and the Ethics*, London: Routledge.

Logie, R., Camos, V., Cowan, N. (eds.) (2020): The state of the science of Working memory – an introduction, in: *Working Memory: The State of the Science*, pp. 1–9, New York: Oxford University Press.

Lomas, T., Cartwright, T., Edginton, T., Ridge, D. (2014): A qualitative analysis of experiential challenges associated with meditation practice, *Mindfulness*, 5(2), 167–173.

Lü Bu We (1928): *Spring and Autumn of Lü Bu We (Lüshi chunqiu)*, translated by Richard Wilhelm, Jena: Eugen Diederichs.

Lucius-Hoene, G. (2000): Construction and reconstruction of narrative identity, *Forum Qualitative Social Research*, 1(2), Art. 18, o.Sz, pp. 231–239.

Luhmann, N. (1975): General theory of organised social systems, in: *Sociological Enlightenment* 2, 4th edition, Wiesbaden: Verlag für Sozialwissenschaften.

Luhmann, N. (1988): *Erkenntnis als Konstruktion*, Bern: Benteli Verlag.

Lüthi, M. (1976): Psychologie des Märchens, in: *Ders.: Märchen*, 6th edition, pp. 109–117, Stuttgart: J.B. Metzler.

Lutz, A., Greischar, L. L., Rawlings, N. B., Ricard, M., Davidson, R. J. (2004): Long-term meditators self-induce high-amplitude gamma synchrony during mental practice, *Proceedings of the National Academy of Sciences*, 101(46), pp. 16369–16373.

Lutz, A., Slagter, H. A., Dunne, J. D., Davidson, R. J. (2008): Attention regulation and monitoring in meditation, *Trends in Cognitive Sciences*, 12(4), pp. 163–169.

Mallinson, J., Singleton, M. (2017): *The Roots of Yoga*, London: Penguin Classics.
Malter, R., Rickert, H., Lask, E. (1969): Vom Primat der transzendentalen Subjektivität zum Primat des gegebenen Gegenstandes in der Konstitution der Erkenntnis, Zeitschrift für philosophische Forschung, (H. 1), pp. 86–97.
Mandler, G. (1980): The generation of emotion: A psychological theory, in: Plutchik, R., Kellerman, H. (eds.): *Theories of emotion* (Vol. 1), pp. 219–244, New York: Academic Press.
Marcia, J. E. (1966): Development and validation of ego-identity status, *Journal of Personality and Social Psychology*, 3(5), pp. 551–558.
Marcia, J. E. (1980): Identity in adolescence, in: Adelson, J. (ed.): *Handbook of Adolescent Psychology*, pp. 159–187, New York: Wiley.
Mauser, W., Pfeiffer, J. (eds.) (2004): *Erinnern, Jahrbuch für Literatur und Psychoanalyse*, Vol. 23, Würzburg: Königshausen & Neumann.
McAdams, D. P. (1993): *The Stories We Live By: Personal Myths and the Making of the Self*, New York: Guilford Press.
McDowell, I. (2023): Mental Processes and Health: The Mind-Body Connection, in: Ders, Understanding Health Determinants. Explanatory Theories for Social Epidemiology, Cham: Springer.
McKenzie, S. P. (2022): *Reality Psychology: A New Perspective on Wellbeing, Mindfulness, Resilience, and Connection*, Cham: Springer Nature.
McKibben, E. C., Nan, K. M. J. (2017): Enhancing holistic identity through yoga: Investigating body-mind-spirit interventions on mental illness stigma across culture case study. *Open Journal of Nursing*, 7, pp. 481–494.
McNally, R. J. (2005): *Remembering Trauma*, Cambridge: The Belknap Press of Harvard University Press.
Merleau-Ponty, M. (1974): *Phenomenology of Perception*. Berlin: de Gruyter.
Mezirow, J. (1991): *Transformative Dimensions of Adult Learning*, San Francisco: Jossey-Bass.
Minsky, M. (1985): *The Society of Mind*, New York: Simon & Schuster.
Moon, J. A. (2004): *A Handbook of Reflective and Experiential Learning: Theory and Practice*, New York: Routledge.
Moser, K., Soucek, R. (2007): Wirtschaftspsychologie und die Natur des Menschen, in: Moser, K. (ed.): *Wirtschaftspsychologie*, pp. 401–415, Berlin Heidelberg: Springer.
Moulton, S. T., Kosslyn, S. M. (2009): Imagining predictions: Mental imagery as mental emulation, *Philosophical Transactions of the Royal Society B: Biological Sciences*, 364(1521), pp. 1273–1280.
Mühling, M. (2020): *Narration and Contingency, Post-Systematic Theology I*, Leiden: Brill Fink.
Müller, R. -A. (1991): *The (Un) divisible Mind: Modularism and Holism in Cognitive Research*, Berlin: Walter de Gruyter.
Mummendey, H. D. (2006): *Psychologie des 'Selbst' – Theorien, Methoden und Ergebnisse der Selbstkonzeptforschung*, Göttingen: Hogrefe.
Münster, G. (2022): What is time? – Gedanken eines Physikers, the German version of a contribution to the "Symposium on Time" of the European Psychoanalytical Federation (EPF), Brussels, April 2022.
Musil, R. (2000), in: Frisé, A.(eds.): *Der Mann ohne Eigenschaften, II. from the estate*, Reinbek bei Hamburg: Rowohlt.

Neisser, U. (1994): Self-narratives: True or false, in: Neisser, U., Fivush, R. (eds.): *The Remembering Self: Construction and Accuracy in the Self-Narrative*, no. 6, pp. 1–18, Cambridge: Cambridge University Press.

Neumann, B. (2005): *Erinnerung – Identität – Narration: Gattungstypologie und Funktionen der "Fictions of Memory,"* Berlin: De Gruyter.

Newell, A. (1994): *Unified Theories of Cognition*, 3rd edition, Cambridge: Harvard University Press.

Nhat Hanh, T. (1999): *The Miracle of Mindfulness: An Introduction to the Practice of Meditation*, Boston: Beacon Press.

Nietzsche, F. (1968): Also sprach Zarathustra, in Colli, G., Montinari, M. (eds.): *Nietzsche Werke, Kritische Gesamtausgabe*, vol. 6, pp 73–98. Berlin: Walter de Gruyter.

Nolen-Hoeksema, S., Wisco, B. E., Lyubomirsky, S. (2008): Rethinking rumination, *Perspectives on Psychological Science*, 3(5), pp. 400–424.

Norretranders, T. (1997): *Spüre die Welt – Die Wissenschaft des Bewusstseins*, Berlin: Rowohlt Verlag.

OECD (2005): *How Does the Brain Work? On the Way to a New Learning Science*, Stuttgart: Schattauer.

Ong, A. D., Bergeman, C. S., Bisconti, T. L., Wallace, K. A. (2006): Psychological resilience, positive emotions, and successful adaptation to stress in later life, *Journal of Personality and Social Psychology*, 91(4), pp. 730–749.

Osho (2009): *The Book of Secrets – 112 Meditation Techniques for Discovering Inner Truth*, Munich: Arkana.

Osranek, R. (2017): *Sustainability in Companies. Review of a Hypothetical Model for Initiating and Stabilizing Sustainable Behavior*, Wiesbaden: Springer Fachmedien.

Pargament, K. I., Exline, J. J., Jones, J. W. (eds.) (2013): *APA Handbook of Psychology, Religion, and Spirituality (Vol. 1): Context, Theory, and Research*, Washington: American Psychological Association.

Pascal, B. (1670): *Les Pensées*, Paris: Les Pensées de M. Pascal sur la religion et sur quelques autres sujets, qui ont été trouvées après sa mort parmy ses papiers, Paris: Guillaume Desprez.

Pearson, D. G., Deeprose, C., Wallace-Hadrill, S. M. A., Burnett Heyes, S., Holmes, E. A. (2013): Assessing mental imagery in clinical psychology: A review of imagery measures and a guiding framework, *Clinical Psychology Review*, 33(1), pp. 1–23.

Pennebaker, J. W., Smyth, J. M. (2016): *Opening Up by Writing It Down: How Expressive Writing Improves Health and Eases Emotional Pain*, New York: Guilford Press.

Pessoa, F. (2008): *Das Buch der Unruhe*, 3rd edition, Frankfurt am Main: Fischer Taschenbuch Verlag.

Peterson, C., Seligman, M. E. P. (2004): *Character Strengths and Virtues: A Handbook and Classification*, New York: Oxford University Press.

Pfister, H. -R., Jungermann, H., Fischer, K. (2010): *Die Psychologie der Entscheidung*, Vol. 3, Heidelberg: Spektrum Akademischer Verlag.

Pietsch, D. (2020): *Principles of Modern Economics: Ecological, Ethical, Digital*, Wiesbaden: Springer.

Pilard, N. (2018): C.G. Jung and intuition: From the mindscape of the paranormal to the heart of psychology, *Journal of Analytical Psychology*, 63(1), pp. 65–84.

Pine, B. J., Gilmore, J. H. (1999): *The Experience Economy: Work Is Theatre & Every Business a Stage*, Boston: Harvard Business School Press.
Plutchik, R. (1980): A general psychoevolutionary Theory of Emotion, in: Plutchik, R., Kellerman, H. (eds.): *Theories of Emotion* (Vol. 1), pp. 3–34, New York: Academic Press.
Poe, E. A. (1849): Marginalia, The Southern Literary Messenger, Vol. 29.
Pohl, R. (2007): *Das autobiographische Gedächtnis: Die Psychologie unserer Lebensgeschichte*, Stuttgart: W. Kohlhammer Verlag.
Polkinghorne, D. E. (1988): *Narrative Knowing and the Human Sciences*, Albany: State University of New York Press.
Polkinghorne, D. E. (1991): Narrative and self-concept, *Journal of Narrative and Life History*, 1(2–3), pp. 135–153.
Polkinghorne, D. E. (1996): Explorations of narrative identity, *Psychological Inquiry*, 7, pp. 363–367.
Polkinghorne, D. E. (1998): Narrative psychology and historical consciousness. Relationships and perspectives, in: Straub, J. (ed.): *Erzählung, Identität und historisches Bewußtsein. The Psychological Construction of Time and History*. Memory, History, Identity I, pp. 12–45, Frankfurt am Main: Suhrkamp.
Potter, J. (2005): Thoughts on post-cognitive psychology, *Psychology, and Social Criticism*, 29(3/4), pp. 59–73.
Priddat, B. P. (2017): Creative destruction as the 'agens movens' of the economy? (No. 2017-44). Wittener Diskussionspapiere zu alten und neuen Fragen der Wirtschaftswissenschaft, Vienna: o.Verl.
Pritzel, M., Markowitsch, H. J. (2017): *Why We Forget: Psychological, Natural and Cultural Science Findings*, Berlin: Springer.
Proust, M. (2000): *In Search of Lost Time, Volumes 1–3, Vol. 3: Die wiedergefundene Zeit*, Frankfurt am Main: Suhrkamp.
Quante, M. (1993): Mental causation: The crisis of non-reductive physicalism. *Zeitschrift Für Philosophische Forschung*, 47(4), pp. 615–629.
Raab, Thomas (2023): Phantasy, displacement and motivation in an ecological model of memory, in: Wieners, O. (ed.): *Theorie des Denkens: Gespräche und Essays zu Grundfragen der Kognitionswissenschaft*, pp. 297–339, Berlin: de Gruyter.
Reckwitz, A. (2012): *Die Erfindung der Kreativität: Zum Prozess gesellschaftlicher Ästhetisierung*, Berlin: Suhrkamp.
Renesch, J. (2008): Humanising capitalism: the vision of hope; a challenge for transcendence, *Journal of Human Values*, 14(1), pp. 1–9.
Richins, M. L., Dawson, S. (1992): A consumer values orientation for materialism and its measurement: Scale development and validation, *Journal of Consumer Research*, 19(3), pp. 303–316.
Ricoeur, P. (2014): *La mémoire, l'histoire, l'oubli*, Paris: Le Seuil.
Rinofner-Kreidl, S. (2009): Shame and guilt. On the phenomenology of self-referential feelings, *Phänomenologische Forschungen*, 1, pp. 137–173.
Roediger III, H. L., Dudai, Y., Fitzpatrick, S. M. (2007): *Science of Memory: Concepts*, New York: Oxford University Press.
Roediger III, H. L., Marsh, E. J. (2007): The positive and negative consequences of false memories: Remembering words not presented in lists, in: Nairne, J. S. (ed.), *The Foundations of Remembering: Essays in Honor of Henry L. Roediger, III*, pp. 105–116, New York: Psychology Press.

Roesler, C. (2006): A narratological methodology for identifying archetypal story patterns in autobiographical narratives, *The Journal of Analytical Psychology*, 51(4), pp. 574–596.

Rosa, H. (2018): Resonance, in: Kölbl, C., Sieben, A. (eds.): *Stichwörter zur Kulturpsychologie*, pp. 347–354, Gießen: Psychosozial-Verlag.

Rosenberg, G. H. (1999): On the intrinsic nature of the Physical, in: Kaszniak, A. W., Chalmers, D., Hameroff, S. R. (eds.): *Toward a Science of Consciousness III: The Third Tucson Discussions and Debates*, pp. 33–48, Cambridge: MIT Press.

Rosenberg, G. H. (2004): *A Place for Consciousness. Probing the Deep Structure of the Natural World*, New York: Oxford University Press.

Roth, G. (2010): *How Unique Is the Human Being? Die lange Evolution der Gehirne und des Geistes*, Heidelberg: Spektrum Akademischer Verlag.

Rüegg-Stürm, J. (1998): Newer systems theory and entrepreneurial change – Outline of a systemic-constructivist "Theory of the Firm," *Die Unternehmung*, 52(2), pp. 3–17.

Rüegg-Stürm, J. (2001): *Organisation und organisationaler Wandel: Eine theoretische Erkundung aus konstruktivistischer Sicht*, Opladen/ Wiesbaden: Westdeutscher Verlag.

Rugg, M. D., Vilberg, K. L. (2013): Brain networks underlying episodic memory retrieval, *Current Opinion in Neurobiology*, 23(2), pp. 255–260.

Russell, C. A. (2013): *The Meditative Mind in Popular Film*, New York: Routledge.

Ryan, R. M., Sheldon, K. M., Kasser, T., Deci, E. L. (1996): All goals are not created equal: An organismic perspective on the nature of goals and their regulation, in: Gollwitzer, P. M., Bargh, J. A. (eds.): *The Psychology of Action: Linking Cognition and Motivation to Behavior*, pp. 7–26, New York: The Guilford Press.

Ryba, A. (2018): *The Role of Unconscious and Preconscious-Intuitive Processes in Coaching with Special Consideration of the Client's Personality Development*. Göttingen: Vandenhoeck & Ruprecht.

Sachs, S., Hauser, A. (2002): *Das ABC der betriebswissenschaftlichen Forschung – Anleitung zum wissenschaftlichen Arbeiten*, Zurich: Versus.

Saldanha, A. (2008): *Psychedelic White: Goa Trance and the Viscosity of Race*, Minneapolis: University of Minnesota Press.

Samide, R., Ritchey, M. (2021): Reframing the past: Role of memory processes in emotion regulation, *Cognitive Therapy and Research*, 45, pp. 848–857.

Sartre, J. -P. (1952): *Das Sein und das Nichts*, Reinbek bei Hamburg: Rowohlt Verlag.

Sartre, J. -P. (1964) [1939]: *The Transcendence of the Ego: Philosophical Essays 1931–1939*, Reinbek bei Hamburg: Rowohlt Verlag.

Sawyer, R. K. (2012): *Explaining Creativity: The Science of Human Innovation*, New York: Oxford University Press.

Schacter, D. L., Benoit, R. G., Szpunar, K. K. (2017): Episodic future thinking: Mechanisms and functions, *Current Opinion in Behavioural Sciences*, 17, pp. 41–50.

Schacter, D. L. (1996): *Searching for Memory: The Brain, the Mind, and the Past*, New York: Basic Books.

Schacter, D. L. (2002): *The Seven Sins of Memory: How the Mind Forgets and Remembers*, Bosten: Houghton Mifflin Company.

Schacter, D.. L. (et al.) (1995): *Memory Distortion: How Minds, Brains, and Societies Reconstruct the Past*, Cambridge: Harvard University Press.

Schaeffler, R. (2019): *Themes of Individual and Social Anthropology in Philosophical Anthropology. The Image of Man and the Order of Society*, Wiesbaden: Springer VS.

Schäfer, C. S. (2012): *Extraordinary Experiences: Constructing identity and change in autobiographical narratives* (Vol. 1.), Münster: LIT Verlag.
Scheibe, S., Freund, A. M., Baltes, P. B. (2007): Toward a developmental psychology of Sehnsucht (life longings): The optimal (utopian) life, *Developmental Psychology*, 43(3), pp. 778–795.
Scheibe, S., Freund, A. M. (2008): Approaching Sehnsucht (life longings) from a life-span perspective: The role of personal utopias in development, *Research in Human Development* 5 (2), pp. 121–133.
Scheidt, C. E. (et al.) (2015): *Narrative Coping with Trauma and Loss*, Stuttgart: Schattauer.
Schein, E. H. (1985): *Organisational Culture and Leadership*, San Francisco: Jossey-Bass.
Schiller, F. (1903): Über die ästhetische Erziehung des Menschen in einer Reihe von Briefen, in: Petersen, J. (ed.): *Schillers Werke, Nationalausgabe*, Vol. 7, Berlin: G. Grote'sche Verlagsbuchhandlung.
Schlager, S. (2020): Theoretische Fundierung des Konstrukts "Oberflächlichkeit," in: *Zur Erforschung des Zusammenhangs zwischen Sprachkompetenz und Mathematikleistung (Essener Beiträge zur Mathematikdidaktik)*, pp. 81–119, Wiesbaden: Springer Spektrum.
Schlegel, L. (1995): *Transactional Analysis: Psychotherapy that Creatively Combines Cognitive and Depth-Psychological Aspects*, Stuttgart: Schäffer-Poeschel.
Schlicht, E. (2007): Psychologie in der Wirtschaftslehre, in: Dieter, F., von Rosenstiel, L. (eds.): *Wirtschaftspsychologie: Wirtschafts- Organisations- und Arbeitspsychologie (Enzyklopädie der Psychologie)*, pp. 1–6, Göttingen: Hogrefe.
Schmid, H. B. (2000): *Subject, System, Discourse: Edmund Husserl's Concept of Transcendental Subjectivity in Social Theory (Vol. 158)*, Dordrecht: Kluwer Academic Publishers.
Schmidt, J. B. (2019): *Das Transzendente in der Psychotherapie: Über Spiritualität und Präsenz im therapeutischen Wirken*, Munich: Kösel-Verlag.
Schmidt, M. G. (2003): Staging, remembering, narrating – On the sequence of therapeutic change, *Psyche*, 57(9–10), pp. 889–903.
Schönhammer, R. (2013): *Einführung in die Wahrnehmungspsychologie*, 2nd edition, Stuttgart: UTB.
Schöpf, A. (2014): *Philosophische Grundlagen der Psychoanalyse (Psychoanalysis in the 21st Century – Disciplines, Concepts, Applications)*, Stuttgart: Kohlhammer Verlag.
Schore, A. N. (2007): *Affektregulation und die Reorganisation des Selbst*, Stuttgart: Klett-Cotta.
Schore, A. N. (2012): *The Science of the Art of Psychotherapy*, New York: W. W. Norton & Company.
Schubert, F. -C. (2012): Psychische Ressourcen – Zentrale Konstrukte in der Ressourcendiskussion, in: Knecht, A., Schubert, F. -C. (eds.): *Ressourcen im Sozialstaat und in der Sozialen Arbeit: Zuteilung-Förderung-Aktivierung*, pp. 205–223, Stuttgart: Kohlhammer.
Schwartz, R. C., Sweezy, M. (2019): *Internal Family Systems Therapy*, 2nd edition, New York: Guilford Press.
Seidel, W. (2004): *Emotional Competence. Brain Research and the Art of Living*, Munich: Elsevier, Spektrum Akademischer Verlag.
Seifert, C. M. (et al.) (1995): Demystification of cognitive insight: Opportunistic assimilation and the prepared-mind perspective. *Cognitive Psychology*, 27(2), 181–238.
Seligman, M. E. P. (2002): *Authentic Happiness: Using the New Positive Psychology to Realise Your Potential for Lasting Fulfillment*, New York: Free Press.

Seligman, M. E. P., Csikszentmihalyi, M. (2000): Positive psychology: An introduction, *American Psychologist*, 55(1), pp. 5–14.
Shapiro, S. L. (et al.) (2006): Mechanisms of mindfulness, *Journal of Clinical Psychology*, 62(3), pp. 373–386.
Shweder, R. A. (1991): *Thinking Through Cultures. Expeditions in Cultural Psychology*, Cambridge: Harvard University Press.
Singer, J. L. (1975): *The Inner World of Daydreaming*, New York: Harper & Row.
Smallwood, J., Schooler, J. W. (2015): The science of mind wandering: Empirically navigating the stream of consciousness, *Annual Review of Psychology*, 66, pp. 487–518.
Soucek, R. (et al.) (2018): Mindfulness in an organizational context: the influence of individual and organizational mindfulness on resilient behavior, mental health, and work engagement, Group. Interaction. Organization. *Journal of Applied Organisational Psychology (GIO)*, 49.2 (2018), pp. 129–138.
Southwick, S. M. (et al.) (2014): Resilience definitions, theory, and challenges: interdisciplinary perspectives. *European Journal of Psychotraumatology*, 5(1), pp. 25338–25355.
Spinoza, B. d. (1677) [1994]: Ethics, in: Curley, E. (ed.): *A Spinoza Reader: The Ethics and Other Works*, pp. 256–275, Princeton: Princeton University Press.
Spitzer, M. (1999): *The Mind within the Net: Models of Learning, Thinking, and Acting*, Cambridge: MIT Press.
Squire, L. R.,, Zola-Morgan, S. (1991): The medial temporal lobe memory system, *Science*, 253(5026), pp. 1380–1386.
Steel, P. (2007): The nature of procrastination: A meta-analytic and theoretical review of quintessential self-regulatory failure, *Psychological Bulletin*, 133(1), pp. 65–94.
Stein, A. H. (1996): The self-organizing psyche: Nonlinear and neurobiological contributions to psychoanalysis, in: *Nonlinear Dynamics in Human Behavior*, vol. 4, pp. 256–275, Berlin, Heidelberg: Springer.
Storck, T. (2022): *Ich und Selbst (Basic Elements of Psychodynamic Thinking)*, Stuttgart: Kohlhammer Verlag.
Storp, C. (2009): Zur Entstehung der individuellen Wirklichkeit und ihrer Bedeutung in der Medizin, (Doctoral dissertation, LMU Munich).
Straus, E. (2013): *Vom Sinn der Sinne: ein Beitrag zur Grundlegung der Psychologie*, Berlin: Springer.
Streeter, C. C. (et al.) (2012): Effects of yoga on the autonomic nervous system, gamma-aminobutyric-acid, and allostasis in epilepsy, depression, and post-traumatic stress disorder, *Medical Hypotheses*, 78(5), pp. 571–579.
Sugden, R. (2008): Credible worlds: The status of theoretical models in economics, in: Hausman, D. M. (ed.): *The Philosophy of Economics. An Anthology*, 3rd edition, pp. 476–510, Cambridge: Cambridge University Press.
Sutter, H. (2013): *Bildungsprozesse des Subjekts*, Heidelberg: Westdeutscher Verlag.
Suzuki, S. (1969): *Nurtured by Love: The Classic Approach to Talent Education*, Los Angeles: Alfred Publishing.
Sweller, J., Ayres, P., Kalyuga, S. (2011): *Cognitive Load Theory*, New York: Springer.
Tajfel, H., Turner, J. C. (2004a): The social identity theory of intergroup behavior, in: *Political Psychology*, pp. 276–293, London: Psychology Press.

Tajfel, H., Turner, J. C. (2004b): An integrative theory of intergroup conflict, in: Hatch, M. J., Schultz, M. (eds.): *Organisational Identity: A Reader*, pp. 56–65, New York: Oxford University Press.

Tang, Y. Y., Hölzel, B. K., Posner, M. I. (2015): The neuroscience of mindfulness meditation, *Nature Reviews Neuroscience*, 16(4), S 213–225.

Tang, Y. Y., Posner, M. I. (2013): Tools of the trade: Theory and method in mindfulness neuroscience, *Social Cognitive and Affective Neuroscience*, 8(1), pp. 118–120.

Thaler, R. H. (2015): *Misbehaving: The Making of Behavioural Economics*, London: W.W. Norton & Company.

Thaler, R. H., Sunstein, C. R. (2008): *Nudge: Improving Decisions About Health, Wealth, and Happiness*, Yale: Yale University Press.

Thomä, D. (2004): *Vom Glück in der Moderne*, Frankfurt am Main: Suhrkamp.

Thomä, D. (2007): *Tell yourself: Lebensgeschichte als philosophisches Problem*, Frankfurt am Main: Suhrkamp.

Thomas, A., Utler, A. (2013): Culture, cultural dimensions, and cultural standards, in Genkova, P., Ringeisen, T., Leong, F. (eds.): *Handbuch Stress und Kultur*, pp. 41–58, Wiesbaden: Springer VS.

Thompson, E. (2007): *Mind in Life: Biology, Phenomenology, and the Sciences of Mind*, Cambridge: Harvard University Press.

Thompson, R. F. (2016): *Das Gehirn – von der Nervenzelle zur Verhaltenssteuerung*, Berlin: Springer.

Tillich, P., Siemsen, G. (1965): *Der Mut zum Sein*, Berlin: De Gruyer.

Traue, H. C., Kessler, H. (2003): Psychologische Emotionskonzepte, in: Stephan, A., Walter, H. (eds.): *Natur und Theorie der Emotion*, pp. 20–33, Paderborn: Mentis Verlag.

Triandis, H. C. (1994): *Culture and Social Behavior*, New York: McGraw-Hill.

Trigo, A. (2011): De memorias, desmemorias y antimemorias/On Memories, Unmemories and Anti-memories, *Taller de letras*, (49), pp. 17–28.

Tulving, E. (2002): Episodic memory: From mind to brain, *Annual Review of Psychology*, 53(1), pp. 1–25.

Tulving, E. (2011): Are there 256 different kinds of memory?, in: Nairne, J. S. (ed.): *The Foundations of Remembering*, pp. 39–52, New York: Psychology Press.

Urban, H. B. (2003): *Tantra: Sex, Secrecy, Politics, and Power in the Study of Religion*, Berkeley: University of California Press.

Vago, D. R., Silbersweig, D. A. (2012): Self-awareness, self-regulation, and self-transcendence (S-ART): a framework for understanding the neurobiological mechanisms of mindfulness, *Frontiers in Human Neuroscience*, 6, 296.

Van der Kolk, B. (2014): *The Body Keeps the Score: Brain, Mind, and Body in the Healing of Trauma*, London: Penguin Books.

Van Rullen, R., Koch, C. (2003): Is perception discrete or continuous? *Trends in cognitive sciences*, 7(5), pp. 207–213.

Varela, F. J., Thompson, E. T., Rosch, E. (1991): *The Embodied Mind: Cognitive Science and Human Experience*, Cambridge: MIT Press.

Varian, H. R. (2014): *Intermediate Microeconomics: A Modern Approach*, 9th edition, New York: W. W. Norton & Company.

Vessel, E. A., Starr, G. G., Rubin, N. (2012): Aesthetic experiences and the default mode network, *Psychology of Aesthetics, Creativity, and the Arts*, 6(3), pp. 255–260.

Viehöver, W. (2011): Diskurse als Narrationen, in: Keller, R., Hirseland, A., Schneider, W., Viehöver, W. (eds.): *Handbuch sozialwissenschaftliche Diskursanalyse, Band 1: Theorien und Methoden*, 3rd edition, pp. 193–224, Wiesbaden: Verlag für Sozialwissenschaften.

Von Contzen, E. (2018): Diachronic narratology and historical narrative research. A Stocktaking and a Plea. *Contributions to Narrative Research*, 1(2018), pp. 16–37.

von der Weth, R. (2019): Sinnmaschinen – Innovatives menschliches Handeln in soziotechnischen Systemen, *Journal der Psychologie des Alltagshandelns*, 12(1), pp. 5–22.

Von Franz, M. -L. (1971): *The Interpretation of Fairy Tales*, New York: Spring Publications.

von Kutschera, F. (2003): *Jenseits des Materialismus*, Leiden: Brill mentis.

Von Kutschera, F. (2014): *Three Forms of Consciousness – The Ontology of Intentional Thought*, Leiden: Brill mentis.

Vygotsky, L. S. (1978): *Mind in Society: The Development of Higher Psychological Processes*, Cambridge: Harvard University Press.

Wagoner, B. (2017): *The Constructive Mind: Bartlett's Psychology in Reconstruction*. Cambridge: Cambridge University Press.

Walsh, R., Shapiro, S. L. (2006): The meeting of meditative disciplines and Western psychology: A mutually enriching dialogue, *American Psychologist*, 61(3), pp. 227–239.

Walsh, R. (1998): States and stages of consciousness: Current research and understandings, in: Kaszniak, A. W., Hameroff, S. R., Scott, A. C. (eds.): *Toward a Science of Consciousness II: The Second Tucson Discussions and Debates*, pp. 678–686, Cambridge: MIT Press.

Walsh, R., Vaughan, F. (1993): *Paths Beyond Ego: The Transpersonal Vision*, New York: Penguin Publishing Group.

Watson, B. (1968): *The Complete Works of Chuang Tzu*, New York: Columbia University Press.

Weber, S. (2017): Wie Geschichten wirken – Grundzüge narrativer Psychologie, in Chlopczyk, J. (ed.): *Beyond Storytelling*, pp. 11–21, Berlin Heidelberg: Springer Gabler.

Wegmann, W. (1970): *Der ökonomische Gewinn*, Wiesbaden: Gabler.

Weil, A. P. (1976): Der psychische Urkern, *Psyche*, 30(5), pp. 385–404.

Wells, A. (2011): *Metacognitive Therapy for Anxiety and Depression*, New York: Guilford Press.

Wentura, D., Frings, C. (2013): *Cognitive Psychology*, Wiesbaden: Springer VS Verlag für Sozialwissenschaften.

Westerkamp, D. (2023): Semantic Holism and the Theory of Reflection Terms: Topik, Logik oder Synonymik?, in: Bondeli, M., Westerkamp, D. (eds.): *Vorstellung, Denken, Sprache: Philosophie zwischen rationalem Realismus und transzendentalem Idealismus*, pp. 175–196, Berlin, Boston: De Gruyter.

Westermann, R. (2013): *Strukturalistische Theorienkonzeption und empirische Forschung in der Psychologie*, Berlin Heidelberg: Springer.

White, D. G. (2000): *Tantra in Practice*, Princeton: Princeton University Press.

White, M., Epston, D. (1990): *Narrative Means to Therapeutic Ends*, New York: W. W. Norton & Company.

Wiest, G. (2010): *Hierarchies in Brain, Mind, and Behavior: A Principle of Neural and Mental Function*, Berlin: Springer.

Wilber, K. (1977): *The Spectrum of Consciousness*, Wheaton: Theosophical Publishing House.

Will, H. (2018): How unsaturated interpretations emerge – The work of figurability, *Psyche*, 72(5), pp. 374–396.

Wils, J. -P. (ed.) (2023): In Grenzenlosigkeit – Anmerkungen zu einer halbierten Anthropologie, in: *Die Illusion grenzenloser Verfügbarkeit*, pp. 19–28, Gießen: Psychosozial-Verlag.

Winogard, E. (1994): The authenticity and utility of memories, in Neisser, U., Fivush, R. (eds.): *The Remembering Self: Construction and Accuracy in the Self-Narrative*, No. 6, pp. 243–251, Cambridge: Cambridge University Press.

Winter, R. (2010): Symbolic Interactionism, in: Mey, G., Mruck, K. (eds.): *Handbuch Qualitative Forschung in der Psychologie*, pp. 79–93, Wiesbaden: Springer VS Verlag für Sozialwissenschaften.

Wittgenstein, L. (2019): *Tractatus logico-philosophicus, Werkausgabe Band 1*, 23rd edition, Frankfurt am Main: Suhrkamp.

Wundt, W. (1896): *Grundriß der Psychologie*. Leipzig: Engelmann.

Yates, C. J. (2015): *The Mind Illuminated*, Chicago: Dharma Treasure Press.

Yeats, W. B. (1916) [1914]: *Responsibilities and Other Poems*, Dublin: Cuala Press.

Zauner, C. (2018): Intuition in psychotherapy: Four perspectives on intuition. *Journal of Psychodrama and Sociometry*, 17, pp. 307–317.

Zeidan, F., Johnson, S. K., Diamond, B. J., David, Z., Goolkasian, P. (2010): Mindfulness meditation improves cognition: Evidence of brief mental training, *Consciousness, and Cognition*, 19(2), pp. 597–605.

INDEX

acceptance xxiin35, 106, 112, 113, 118, 132, 157, 160–62, 165, 168, 201–3, 208
accumulation process 34, 37
alienation 28, 203, 204
apperception 10
archetypes xiiin10, xvin22, 118, 208, 209
assumption xivn12, 101, 117, 133, 202, 203
awareness xi, xiii, xvi, 13, 24, 33n174, 35, 45n226, 50, 52n260, 53–60, 54n268, 55n270, 55n271, 56n276, 62, 63, 65–67, 69, 74, 75, 88, 96, 98–100, 103, 106, 108, 116, 124, 125, 129, 141, 141n540, 152, 162, 163, 165, 169–75, 169n613, 171n620, 180, 189, 197, 199, 203, 208, 210

complex 209
construct xxiv, 2, 5, 6, 25, 35, 48, 63, 130, 189, 195, 196, 203, 215
culture 1, 2, 5–9, 16, 69, 81n364, 82, 120, 121, 149, 150n553, 154, 154n568, 156–58, 161, 209, 210

doctrine of faith xix
dullness 55, 56n274, 210

economic system 24, 26, 84, 85, 100, 108
economics xi, xii, xiin4, xivn12, xv, xvii, xxiii, xxiv, 1, 9, 11, 16–19, 25, 32, 32n174, 33n174, 34–37, 42, 49, 50, 52, 64, 65, 88–90, 92, 93, 95, 100, 107, 107n455, 115, 118, 156–59, 161, 164n598, 165, 177–80, 180n643, 183–89, 193, 196–99, 201–3, 205, 206

economics and psyche xvii
energy allocation 44
experience xiiin8, xx, xxi, xvn20, 1, 3, 4, 7, 8, 8n66, 12, 19–21, 23, 27, 31, 34, 36n186, 38n194, 41, 48n242, 50, 53, 54, 54n268, 55n271, 57, 63, 69, 71, 72n312, 75, 77–80, 77n343, 82, 82n370, 83n375, 87, 91, 99, 101–3, 120, 123, 124, 127n507, 131, 134, 139, 140, 144, 145, 149, 152, 154–58, 163, 168–70, 178, 184, 186–89, 193, 195, 197, 200, 204, 205, 207–9, 211–15

forgotten 16, 27n148
gratitude 126, 205, 206

holism 34n179, 76, 77, 112, 117, 156n573, 190, 202–4

identity 1–9, 4n50, 16, 19, 20, 23, 41, 51, 52, 77–79, 78n346, 81, 81n364, 82, 82n370, 86, 88, 93, 99, 107, 131, 141–46, 154n568, 155, 157, 158, 160n584, 189, 195, 196, 200, 210, 214
imagination xvii, xxiii, xxv, 13n86, 20, 26, 27n149, 29–32, 34–37, 39, 40, 42, 43, 47–49, 47n235, 49n247, 51, 52, 70–77, 72n311, 74n318, 75n323, 75n329, 76n332, 83, 85, 86, 91, 94, 96, 100, 126, 128, 131–33, 136, 141, 149, 150, 153, 154, 158, 165
imagination reconstruction xxiii, xxiv, 71, 73, 75–78, 83, 91, 94, 100, 107, 110, 111, 128, 188

immersion xxv, 40, 80, 150, 153–58, 161, 211
individuation 4, 4n52, 118, 118n486, 119, 199, 212
internal economy xvii, 177

knowledge xv, xix, xx, xxii, 10, 16, 30, 33n174, 48n242, 104, 150–53, 155, 155n570, 156, 158, 178, 196, 210, 213–15

longing 34n179, 75n329, 76, 146, 147, 212

memories xii, xiii, xiiin8, xv, xvi, xvii, xxiii, xxiv, xvn20, xvin20, 2, 3, 6–9, 8n66, 12–14, 15n97, 16, 19–23, 26n146, 27–29, 27n148, 27n149, 28n151, 28n153, 31, 32, 34–41, 35n186, 36n186, 46, 48, 50n252, 51–53, 57, 63, 72n312, 76, 78, 79, 82n370, 83n375, 84–88, 85n382, 91–93, 96, 99, 100, 106–8, 110, 111, 119, 122, 123n496, 124–26, 130, 132–34, 136–38, 144n543, 149, 169, 177, 178, 184–87, 188n663, 189, 192–98, 200, 202, 204, 209
memory xi, xvii, xxi, xxiv, 1–3, 6, 8–12, 10n68, 15, 15n97, 16, 18, 22–24, 26–30, 27n146, 27n148, 34–40, 34n177, 34n179, 43, 45, 46, 48, 49, 71, 78, 79, 84, 89, 93, 125, 130n514, 137, 149, 177, 184, 188, 194–96, 205, 209, 211
memory xix, 10–13, 15, 16, 18, 20, 24, 26n146, 35n186, 36n186, 46, 65, 75, 86, 136, 151, 159, 177, 185, 186, 193, 209, 211–15
mindfulness xxiin35, 18, 44, 44n226, 45n226, 54n268, 61, 85, 86, 92, 92n417, 96, 97, 100–2, 104, 108, 112, 113, 118, 134, 153, 159, 162, 163, 167–72, 177, 197, 207, 208
moment xxiiin37, 45n226, 48, 53, 53n263, 54, 54n268, 96, 97, 101, 125, 168, 187, 196, 211

narration xxiii, xxiv, xxv, 13n85, 17, 20, 27–32, 27n149, 30n159, 34, 36, 37, 39, 42–52, 70–73, 72n311, 75, 77n339, 78–83, 78n351, 81n362, 82n370, 85, 86, 91, 94, 100, 102, 108, 120, 129, 130n515, 131, 133, 135, 136, 138, 139, 141, 146, 150, 153, 154, 158, 166, 188
narrative 72, 72n313, 73, 85, 90n408, 91, 93, 130, 131, 134, 136, 137, 181, 213

perception xix, xxi, 1, 14, 18, 19, 24, 35n186, 39, 40, 44, 48n242, 49, 50, 54n268, 55, 56, 58, 58n281, 64, 72n312, 81n364, 82, 102, 106, 121, 141, 151, 154n568, 156–59, 162, 163, 165, 170, 172, 173, 177, 178, 180, 184, 196, 199, 200, 206, 208–10, 212, 214
processes xiiin4, xivn14, xviii, xix, xxiii, xxv, 5, 15, 16, 18, 20, 21, 23, 24, 29, 31, 35, 36, 36n186, 38–40, 44, 50–52, 50n252, 56, 56n275, 56n276, 57, 61, 62, 65, 69–72, 69n305, 76n332, 81–83, 85n379, 88, 88n396, 89, 89n398, 89n403, 91, 92, 92n417, 94, 97, 103, 104, 106, 107, 112, 116–18, 118n486, 120, 121, 122n494, 123, 128, 129, 133, 136–38, 140, 144n544, 145–47, 149–52, 155–59, 155n570, 163, 167, 168, 171–75, 180, 183, 185–88, 193, 194, 197–200, 214
psychological dynamics 204
psychosynthesis 76, 77, 214

recognition xi, xiii, xiv, xv, xvi, xix, xx, xxi, xxii, xxiii, xxiiin37, 17, 18, 24, 26n146, 29, 35–39, 45, 46, 50, 52, 69, 71, 72n310, 76n332, 89, 91, 95, 98, 99, 104, 105, 131, 155, 155n570, 164, 166n601, 168n608, 174n628, 175, 184, 190, 197, 200, 201, 204, 205
reconstruction 6, 14, 19–23, 51, 52, 75, 76n331, 124
resource xiii, 9–11, 16, 24, 28, 29, 34–37, 40, 74, 77, 81, 82, 84, 106, 125, 130, 155n570, 156, 177, 189, 193, 205, 206
resource allocation 20, 24n140, 191n666

self xi, xiiin10, xvi, xvin22, xvii, xxi, xxv, 1–4, 4n52, 6, 21, 28, 28n153, 29–32, 31n165, 32n168, 32n172, 33n174, 34, 35, 37–39, 38n195, 43, 49, 49n249, 52, 59, 61, 64, 65, 70, 75–81, 76n332, 81n362, 85, 101, 104, 111–13, 116, 117, 118n486, 125, 127, 142, 144, 144n544, 145, 162, 163, 166, 168–70, 181, 186–90, 193, 194, 196, 197, 201–3, 204n682, 212, 214

self-actualisation xiii, xiiin10, xvi, xvin22, xxi, 49

self-perception xvii, xx, 7, 41, 43, 65, 70, 77, 101, 111, 113, 120–22, 129, 136, 142–44, 144n544, 146, 152, 187, 189

self-regulation xx, 31, 102, 103

spirit system xvii, xviii, xxiii, xxiv, 1–3, 9, 11, 16, 18–24, 21n127, 27–29, 27n148, 33n174, 34n179, 35n182, 36–41, 45, 49–52, 56, 57, 59, 61, 63–66, 69–72, 75, 82–85, 85n379, 89–91, 94, 99–104, 113, 116, 118–20, 124, 133, 136, 141, 142, 144–47, 144n543, 150, 152–54, 159–61, 165, 169, 178, 188n663, 189–91, 197–200, 199n675, 203, 204

suggestion xxiv, 37, 42, 42n215, 52, 71, 73, 77n339, 81–83, 83n375, 91, 94, 125, 141, 143, 150, 153, 154

suppleness 133, 177, 181, 207

theories of knowledge xxi

transaction processes 47, 50, 71, 73, 80, 81, 83, 85, 86, 90n408, 91, 94, 97, 98, 100, 101, 104, 106, 108, 112, 122, 132, 142, 143, 144n544, 145, 146, 153, 154, 159, 162, 178, 180, 181, 186, 189, 199

transactions 32, 34n179, 64, 65, 99, 197

transcendence xiv, xivn11, xvin23, 103n446, 166n601, 180, 180n643, 181, 183, 184, 201–3

transformation 70, 90, 91, 117, 119, 128, 140, 145, 152, 160n586, 163, 165, 178, 185, 186, 189, 197, 201–3, 210, 215

translation processes 51

unconscious 2, 8n66, 208

will 29, 31, 39, 49n247, 154, 168

wisdom xx, 151, 152, 215

www.ingramcontent.com/pod-product-compliance
Lightning Source LLC
Jackson TN
JSHW021707150925
91051JS00002B/3